Sarah,

ANGELS IN MY HAIR

Please Enjoy!!

Love

Cathy V.

April 2018

ANGELS

— IN MY —

HAIR

A MEMOIR

Lorna Byrne

DOUBLEDAY

NEW YORK LONDON TORONTO

SYDNEY AUCKLAND

DD

DOUBLEDAY

Copyright © 2008 by Lorna Byrne

All Rights Reserved

Originally published in a slightly different form as *Angels in My Hair* in Great Britain in 2008 by Century.

Published in the United States by Doubleday,
an imprint of The Crown Publishing Group,
a division of Random House, Inc., New York.
www.doubleday.com

DOUBLEDAY and the DD colophon are registered
trademarks of Random House, Inc.

LIBRARY OF CONGRESS CATALOGING-IN-PUBLICATION DATA
Byrne, Lorna.
Angles in my hair : a memoir / Lorna Byrne. — 1st ed.
p.   cm.
1. Byrne, Lorna.   2. Religious biography.   I. Title.
BL73.B97A3   2009
202'.15092—dc22
[B]
2008046552

ISBN 978-0-385-52896-2

PRINTED IN THE UNITED STATES OF AMERICA

1   3   5   7   9   10   8   6   4   2

FIRST EDITION

For my children

CONTENTS

Acknowledgments | ix

CHAPTER 1   *Through different eyes* | 1

CHAPTER 2   *The gatekeepers* | 10

CHAPTER 3   *Stairway to Heaven* | 22

CHAPTER 4   *Why do you hide from me?* | 35

CHAPTER 5   *Elijah* | 50

CHAPTER 6   *Absorbing the pain of others* | 60

CHAPTER 7   *A creature without a soul* | 70

CHAPTER 8   *The intermediary* | 79

CHAPTER 9   *The Angel of Death* | 85

CHAPTER 10   *The bombers* | 95

CHAPTER 11   *The Angel of Mother's Love* | 107

CHAPTER 12   *Country cottage* | 123

CHAPTER 13   *Telling Joe* | 135

CHAPTER 14 *I never knew I had a guardian angel* | 146

CHAPTER 15 *The power of prayer* | 153

CHAPTER 16 *The tunnel* | 162

CHAPTER 17 *Three knocks on the window* | 175

CHAPTER 18 *"Isn't Lorna lucky . . ."* | 188

CHAPTER 19 *"I'm here, I'm here ~ here I am!"* | 201

CHAPTER 20 *The golden chain* | 209

CHAPTER 21 *I need some miracles* | 221

CHAPTER 22 *Satan at the gate* | 229

CHAPTER 23 *Soulmates* | 242

CHAPTER 24 *Peace in Ireland and at Christmas* | 250

CHAPTER 25 *Michael tells me who he really is* | 267

CHAPTER 26 *An evil spirit shows himself* | 278

CHAPTER 27 *Joe* | 290

CHAPTER 28 *A feather from Heaven* | 300

ACKNOWLEDGMENTS

A heartfelt thank-you to Jean Callanan for her support, dedication, and courage. The first time I met her, the angels told me that she was going to play a fundamental role in helping me to write and publish this book. Little did she know how much time, effort, and hard work was going to be required. I thank her for her good humor, enthusiasm, patience, generosity, and friendship. I thank the angels for bringing me someone with a lot of business experience, which has proved to be invaluable.

I couldn't have asked for a better UK editor than Mark Booth. His trust, confidence, and belief in this book have made an enormous difference. He has gone way beyond what is normally expected of an editor. My profound thanks to a wonderful and special man who is becoming a good friend, and I thank the angels for sending him to me.

For the USA edition I've been blessed with another exceptional editor, Jason Kaufman. To have one brilliant editor is a privilege; to have two is proof of how the angels have been working miracles in relation to this book. I still think with astonishment about the spiritual depth of my first-ever conversation with Jason.

My thanks to the Doubleday team, particularly Trace Murphy, who has been passionate about this book from the beginning (without his passion, Doubleday would not have been my publisher), and Robert Bloom, who has been so helpful. No doubt, by the time these acknowledgments are being read, there will be a new list of people at Doubleday that I will wish I had thanked. Let me thank them now.

Teri Tobias of Sanford J. Greenburger Associates has been of considerable help. Thanks to her work, this book is on its way to being a global bestseller. Her contribution and support are very much appreciated.

Various people I am happy to call my friends have helped with this book. My thanks to Stephen Mallaghan for his generosity, enthusiasm, and kindness . . . and for being such a good friend; Daniel O'Donnell for his encouragement and for opening the first doors; Jim Corr for his support, generosity, and curiosity; Eoin MacHale for creating a wonderful Web site; Patricia Scanlan for her encouragement.

A thank-you to my friends Catherine and John Kerrigan, who have provided enormous support in good times and bad; Sally White for making me laugh; John Carty for being there; Brian Kelly for his support and generosity; the Quigley family for their support in the practical issues all mothers have to deal with.

Finally to my children who have made sure that I have always kept my feet on the ground! Many thanks to them for being there for me—particularly my youngest, whose life has been turned upside down by this book.

ANGELS IN MY HAIR

CHAPTER I

Through different eyes

When I was two years old the doctor told my mother I was "retarded."

When I was a baby, my mother noticed that I always seemed to be in a world of my own. I can even remember lying in a cot—a big basket—and seeing my mother bending over me. Surrounding my mother I saw wonderful bright, shiny beings in all the colors of the rainbow; they were much bigger than I was, but smaller than her— about the size of a three-year-old child. These beings floated in the air like feathers; and I remember reaching out to touch them, but I never succeeded. I was fascinated by these creatures with their beautiful lights. At that time I didn't understand that I was seeing anything different from what other people saw; it would be much later that I learned from them that they were called angels.

As the months passed, my mother noticed that I'd always be looking or staring somewhere else, no matter what she'd do to try to get my attention. In truth, I was somewhere else: I was away with the angels, watching what they were doing and talking and playing with them. I was enthralled.

I was a late talker, but I had been conversing with angels from very early on. Sometimes we used words as you and I understand them, but sometimes no words were needed—we would know each other's thoughts. I believed that everyone else could see what I saw, but then the angels told me that I was not to say anything to anyone about seeing them, that I should keep it a secret between us. In fact, for many years I listened to the angels and I didn't tell people what I saw. It is only now in writing this book that I am for the first time telling much of what I have seen.

The doctor's comment when I was just two was to have a profound effect on my life: I realized that people can be very cruel. At the time I was born, in 1953, my parents lived in Old Kilmainham, near the center of Dublin. My father rented a little bicycle repair shop there, which had a cottage attached. If you walked through the shop and around to the left you would come to a tiny and fairly dilapidated house. It was part of a row of old cottages and shops, but most of them were empty or abandoned because they were in such bad condition. For much of the time we lived in the one little room downstairs: here we cooked, ate, talked, played, and even washed in a big metal basin in front of the fire. Although the house had no bathroom, outside in the back garden, down a little path, was a shed with a loo. Upstairs there were two small bedrooms; at first I shared one of the bedrooms, and a bed, with my older sister Emer.

It wasn't just angels I was seeing (and I saw them constantly—from the moment I woke up until I went to sleep), but also the spirits of people who had died. My brother, Christopher, had been born a year before me but he had died when he was only about ten weeks old. Although I never saw him while he was alive, I could visualize him—he was dark haired, while my sister and I were fair—and I could also play with him in spirit.

At the time I thought there was nothing strange about this; it felt as if he was just another child, although he seemed a little brighter in appearance. One of the first things that made me realize that he was different, though, was that his age could change. Sometimes he appeared as a baby, but other times he looked about the same age as me, toddling across the floor. He wasn't there constantly, either, but seemed to come and go.

Late one cold winter afternoon, just as it was getting dark, I was alone in the little living room of the house in Old Kilmainham. There was fire in the open fireplace, which was the only light in the room. The firelight flickered across the floor where I was sitting playing with little wooden building blocks that my father had made. Christopher came to play with me. He sat nearer the fire—he said that it was too hot for me where he was, but it was okay for him as he didn't feel the heat. Together we built a tower. I would put one brick down and he would put another on top of it. The tower was getting very tall and then, suddenly, our hands touched. I was amazed—he felt so different from other people I touched. When I touched him he sparked; it was as if there were little stars flying. At that moment I went into him (or perhaps he went into me); it was as if we merged and became one. In my shock I knocked over our tower of blocks!

I burst out laughing, then I touched him again. I think that was the first time I fully realized that he wasn't flesh and blood.

I never confused Christopher with an angel; the angels I saw did sometimes have a human appearance, but when they did, most of them had wings and their feet did not touch the ground and they had a sort of bright light shining inside them. Some of the time the angels I saw would have no human aspect at all, but appeared as a sharp glowing light.

Christopher appeared around my mum a lot. Sometimes Mum would be sitting in the chair by the fire and would doze off, and I'd see him cradled in her arms. I didn't know whether my mother was aware of Christopher's presence so I asked him, "Will I tell Mum that you're here?"

"No, you can't tell her," he replied. "She won't understand. But sometimes she feels me."

One winter morning the angels came to my bed as the sun was coming up. I was curled up under the blankets; my sister Emer, with whom I shared the bed, was up and about and instead Christopher was curled up beside me. He tickled me and said, "Look, look, Lorna—over at the window."

As I have said, angels can appear in different forms and sizes; this morning they looked like snowflakes! The glass in the window seemed to become a vapor, and as each snowflake hit the window it was transformed into an angel about the size of a baby. The angels were then carried on a beam of sunlight through the window, and each one seemed to be covered in white and shiny snowflakes. As the angels touched me the snowflakes fell from them onto me; they tickled as they landed and, surprisingly, they felt warm, not cold.

"Wouldn't it be wonderful," Christopher said, "if everybody knew that they could fill their pockets with angels; that they could fit thousands of angels into one pocket, just like with snowflakes, and could carry them around with them and never be alone."

I turned and asked, "What if they melted in their pockets?"

Christopher giggled and said, "No! Angels never melt!"

I rather sadly replied, "Christopher, I wish that you could fit in my mum's pocket like a snowflake, and be there for her all the time."

He turned and looked at me, as we were cuddled up in bed, and said, "You know I'm there already."

When I was an adult my mother told me she had had a baby son called Christopher who had been born a year before me but had only lived ten weeks. I just smiled in response. I remember asking her where Christopher was buried, and she told me that it was in an unmarked grave (as was the custom in those days) in a baby's graveyard in Dublin.

It's sad that there is no grave with his name on it that I can go and visit, but he's not forgotten. Sometimes even now, all these years later, I feel Christopher's hand in my pocket pretending to make snowflakes, reminding me I am never alone.

I learned more about Christopher and my mother one day when I was about four or five years old. I was sitting at the table swinging my legs and eating breakfast when I caught a glimpse of Christopher looking as if he were about twelve years old, running across the room to the shop door just as my mother walked in with some toast. She had a big smile on her face as she said, "Lorna, there is a surprise for you in the back workroom under Da's workbench!"

I jumped up from the table, all excited, and followed Christopher. He went straight through the shop and into the dark workshop; I had to stop at the door because it was so dark in there that I couldn't see anything and I needed my eyes to adjust to the darkness. However, Christopher was just like a light, a soft shimmering glow that lit up a path for me through the cluttered workshop. He called out, "The cat has had kittens!" And there, thanks to Christopher's light, I could see four tiny little kittens—three were jet-black, and one was black and white. They were so beautiful, so soft and glossy. The mother cat, Blackie, got out of the box, stretched herself, then jumped out of the little window into the garden. I ran after her and called to Christopher to come too, but he would not come into the garden.

I walked back in and asked Christopher, "Why wouldn't you come outside?"

He took my hand, as if to comfort me—I loved the touch of his hand—and our hands merged again. It felt magical; it made me feel safe and happy.

"Lorna, when babies die their spirits stay with their mothers for as long as they are needed, so I stay here with Mum. If I went outside it would be like breaking those memories—and that I won't do!"

Even at that young age, I knew what he meant. My mother had

poured so much love into him: all the memories she had of being pregnant and carrying him inside her, the birth, the joy and the happiness she had holding him in her arms and bringing him home—when even then she had a feeling that something was wrong, despite what the doctors told her. Mum had a precious few weeks at home with Christopher before he died, and Christopher told me of all the love that she had poured on him, and he now poured that love on her.

So my spirit brother would remain in the house, never going out, until the day came when it seemed that my mum felt strong enough to move on and was ready to let my little brother go. That day was the day when we had to leave that little shop in Old Kilmainham for good.

When I see an angel I want to stop and stare; I feel like I am in the presence of a tremendous power. When I was younger the angels generally adopted a human form—to make it easier for me to accept them—but now that's no longer necessary. The angels I see don't always have wings, but when they do I am sometimes amazed by their form; occasionally they are like flames of fire, and yet they have shape and solidity. Some of the angels' wings have feathers; one angel had wings that were so slender, tall, and pointed that I found it hard to believe that they were wings. I wanted to ask the angel to open them up.

When angels have a human appearance—with or without wings—their eyes are one of their most fascinating features. Angel eyes are not like human eyes; they are so alive, so full of life and light and love. It's as if they contain the essence of life itself—their radiance fills you completely.

I have never seen an angel's feet actually touch the ground; when I see one walking toward me I see what looks like a cushion of energy between the ground and their feet. Sometimes it looks like a thin thread, but other times this cushion grows between the earth and the angel, and even sinks into the earth itself.

Ever since I was very young there was one particular angel who used to appear to me often. The first time I saw him he was in the corner of the bedroom and he just said, "Lorna." In some ways he looked like other angels, but there was something different about him, too; he shone more strongly than the others and he had a commanding presence, a powerful force of male strength. From that first time I saw him I always felt he was ready to protect me, like a shield, and from then on he kept appearing and gradually I befriended him. He told me his name was Michael.

School was difficult for me; most of the teachers treated me as if I were slow. My First Holy Communion was at school when I was six, and it was horrible. It should have been a very special day—as it is for most Irish children. When we were preparing for First Holy Communion in the classroom the teachers would ask the children questions, checking that they had learned their catechism, but they wouldn't bother with me; they'd say, "There is no point asking you!" And when all the other children had to stand in line and say something about the Communion, I would stand in line, too, but then I'd be dragged out and told to go and sit down. As a young child this really hurt. So while I sat down at the back of the class or on one of the benches in the corner I'd ask my angels, "Don't they know that I know my catechism, too? They aren't even giving me a chance."

Then in church on my First Communion day, as I finally made my way up to the altar I was grabbed by the arm and pulled out of the queue again because the teacher decided that the better girls should go ahead of me.

There were some kind people, though; when I was about four

there was a nun called (I think) Mother Moderini. She had been told that I was slow and "retarded," but I felt she knew better. When I was in her class she would come down and ask me little questions to which I always knew the answer, so then she'd smile and rub my head.

But despite these occasional acts of kindness from a few people, I grew up an outsider. People could see that I was different and they just couldn't understand it. That aspect of my life has been very, very hard—and it still is today. People say I'm too trusting, too truthful for this world, but I cannot be any other way! The strange thing is, that to be truthful in every way—in how you think and in how you speak—and to be truthful to those around you is hard and it does tend to isolate you.

The way people think about or look at me does affect me greatly even now. Even though they may not know me, or know what I do, they know that on some level I am different. If I go out with friends and meet someone new who knows nothing about me, they will often report back to my friends that there is something unusual about me, something that they can't quite put their finger on. This can be difficult to live with.

My life at school was made much more bearable by one particular angel called Hosus. One morning I was running to school, trying to keep up with the older girl who was with me, when suddenly I saw a beautiful angel hiding behind a lamppost. He made a face at me, and from that day on Hosus used to appear most mornings on my way to school. I still see him regularly today.

Hosus looked—and looks—like an old-fashioned schoolteacher. He wears a swirling robe that is blue most of the time (but can change color), and a funny-shaped hat, and he carries a scroll in his hand. His eyes are radiant and sparkle like stars, and he looks like a young professor: a man full of energy and with great authority and wisdom. Hosus always looks the same, unlike some of the other angels who surround me. Michael, for example, adopts a human appearance most of the time—something I asked him to do, because I find it easier—but he changes his appearance frequently, depending on where we are or the message he has to give me.

To me, Hosus represents knowledge. He looks very serious, and he can be, but he is also wonderful at cheering me up when I feel a little down. It was Hosus who would comfort me and tell me to ignore the other children when I felt ridiculed at school, or when I saw adults talking in a huddle and then turning and looking at me. Hosus would say to me, "They know nothing."

At the beginning I didn't know this angel's name, and he didn't actually talk to me. Hosus would appear in the classroom, mimicking the teacher or another child or playing games in the classroom, or doing something else to make me smile. Sometimes, on the way home he would be waiting at the school gate or on the far side of the road. I remember the first time I spoke to him: I had no one to walk home with that particular day, as my sister was going dancing and had left early, so I took my time coming out of school and wandered slowly through the playground. I made my way toward the big gates at the entrance to the school in the hope that I would see Hosus and be able to talk to him, so I was thrilled to see him peeping around the pillars. He shouted to me to hurry up: "You've got to get home before it starts to rain."

I stopped at the gate and looked around. There was no one nearby so I asked him his name.

"Hosus," he said. I just giggled in response. I skipped home from school and he skipped along with me, and all I can remember is laughing most of the way.

CHAPTER 2

The gatekeepers

Da didn't make much money out of mending bikes—in fact, no one had much money to spend in that area, so they were always asking him for help and promising to pay "next time." Da was a good-hearted man, so we frequently went hungry. The meals we had were often bread and margarine, or bread and jam, but I never complained of pains in my tummy because I knew that Mum and Da were stressed enough. Eventually, though, I started breaking out in sores so I was taken to the doctor. He told my parents that I was vitamin deficient and they needed to give me fresh fruit and vegetables every day. But with all the pressures on money I rarely did get fruit and vegetables, other than when our neighbor—who had a big garden—gave us some. For clothes we depended a lot on parcels coming from relatives in the United States, and whenever one arrived we thought it was marvelous. Things were tough for us, as they were for many others.

Da's shop was a dark little place and behind it was a lean-to with a tin roof, which was his workshop. It was full of benches and tools—all kinds of things—and it smelled of oil and grease. Sometimes before Da came in to the house for his tea he would call me into the workshop and get me to help him by holding the tin of grease he used to clean his hands. It was black and sticky and smelled horrible, but it did the job. After rubbing the grease into his hands for a few minutes he would wipe them with a dirty old cloth and rub them hard. Then he would go into the kitchen and wash them with cold water (the only way to have hot water was to boil a kettle on the fire); after all this his hands would be all clean again. I loved helping my da—even just to hold the tin for him—and sometimes he would ask me to stay in the shop while he was having tea with Mum, in case someone came in.

At school, Hosus would sometimes sit in the teacher's desk when the teacher wasn't there. The first day I saw Hosus in the classroom my eyes nearly popped out of my head. I asked aloud, "What are you doing here?" The teacher heard something and turned and glared in my direction. I had to put my hand to my mouth to stop myself from laughing.

The reason I was surprised was that while there were always guardian angels in the classroom, Hosus was different. He was not a guardian angel. The guardian angels of the children were extremely luminous, like bright lights. Hosus looked completely different, much more human: his robe would brush against the desk. Hosus showed me the difference between the guardian angels and the special angels who were given to me to be a part of my life. As a child I had to learn how to differentiate between different types of angels.

Different types of angels have different skills. Just as I and every child had to learn to differentiate between a teacher and a doctor, I had to learn to recognize a variety of angels so that I had some idea of how they could help me and others.

Frequently Hosus made me laugh, and I once asked him, "Do you think they think I am simple, or that word I've heard them use, 'retarded,' because they see me smiling and laughing so much and don't see what I am laughing at? What do you think they would think if they knew you were sitting there on the teacher's desk dressed like a teacher?"

Hosus laughed. "They would run out screaming that the place was haunted."

"Wouldn't they know that you were an angel?"

"No. They don't see us the way that you do."

As I say, I had always thought other children could see and talk to angels as I could, and it was only then when I was about six that I started to notice that this was not always the case.

"You know, Hosus, I know some children can see angels."

He replied, "Yes, of course they can, but only when they are very little and then they grow up. By the time they are your age most children don't see us anymore; some stop seeing us when they are as young as three years old."

In fact, all babies see angels and spirits, but at about the time children start to talk they begin to be told what's real and what's not real, and so if things are not solid like their toys, then they are told that they are only pretend. Young children are conditioned and lose the ability to see and experience spiritual things. Because education starts earlier nowadays, fewer people are talking to angels, and this is one of the reasons the angels gave me when they told me I had to write this book. This is something I am scared about doing because I don't want to be ridiculed, but I know I have to do it; I always do what the angels want eventually . . .

There are millions of angels out there—they are impossible to count, like snowflakes—but many are unemployed. They are doing their best to help, but they can't always get through to people. Imagine millions of unemployed angels hovering about! They have nothing to do because most people are working hard at getting through their lives and are not aware that these angels are there to help them, and that they are everywhere.

God wants us to be happy and enjoy our lives, and so he sends angels to help us. We have so much spiritual help waiting for us, and while some of us do reach for help, many of us don't. Angels walk beside us telling us they are there, but we are not listening: we don't want to listen. We believe that we can do everything ourselves. We have forgotten that we have a soul, and we believe that we are simply flesh and blood. We believe that there is nothing more—no afterlife, no God, no angels. It is no wonder that we have become materialistic and self-obsessed. Human beings are much more than flesh and blood, and as you become aware of this and start to believe that you have a soul, your connection with the angels will blossom.

As you sit there reading this—whether you believe it or not—there is an angel by your side: it is your guardian angel, and it never leaves you. Each one of us has been given a gift, a shield made from the energy of light. It is a part of the guardian angel's task to put this shield around us. To God and the angels we are all equal; we all deserve to be protected, to be cared for and to be loved, regardless of what others might think of us—good or bad. When I look at someone I can physically see this shield around them; it's as if it's alive.

Your guardian angel is the gatekeeper of your body and your soul. He was assigned to you before you were even conceived; as you grew in your mother's womb he was there with you at every moment, protecting you. Once you were born and as you grow up your guardian angel never leaves your side for an instant; he is with you when you sleep, when you are in the bathroom, all the time—you are never alone. Then, when you die, your guardian angel is there beside you, helping you to pass over. Your guardian angel also allows other angels into your life to help you with different things; they come and go. I call these angels teachers.

You may find all this hard to believe; if you don't believe, you should question your skepticism. If you are cynical, question your cynicism. What do you have to lose by opening up to the possibility of angels, by opening up to your spiritual self and learning about your soul? Ask the angels to start to help you now. Angels are wonderful teachers.

As a child I had the angels with me so much of the time, teaching me and showing me things, that I was very happy to be on my own for hours on end. One of my favorite places was the cozy little bedroom I shared with my sister, Emer. The ceiling was low and sloped and the window was low down so I could kneel or crouch on my hunkers and watch all the comings and goings on the street. I would watch neighbors passing in the street below, and sometimes I would see beside them what I now know was their guardian angel—it was as if there was a beautiful, bright person with them. Sometimes the guardian angel seemed to be floating, but at other times he looked as if he was walking. Sometimes he even seemed to have become a part of the person, or was behind them with his wings wrapped around them, as if in a protective embrace.

These angels also came in all kinds of sizes; sometimes they would appear as a spark that would then grow and open up to full size; sometimes they would be massive, much bigger than the person they were minding. The guardian angels were radiant and were often dressed in all gold or silver or blue, or wore a variety of colors.

At other times I would see a spirit—just as I saw my brother Christopher. One neighbor who lived at the top of the hill used to pass the window sometimes with her children hanging on to her— a baby and young child in a big old stroller and two older children who were hardly more than babies themselves—and I would see an old man walking alongside them. One day this neighbor was with my mum in the shop and I heard her saying that she missed her father, who had died recently. I knew then that the old man I had seen was her father and the children's grandfather. I smiled because even though she was missing her father, he was still there with her—she just couldn't see him. He loved her so much that his spirit had stayed with her to offer her help and consolation, and he would be with her until she was ready to let him go.

At first it was easy to confuse the appearance of these spirits with humans—I had done it myself with Christopher—but over time the angels taught me how to recognize the difference between a spirit and a real person. It's a little difficult to explain. A spirit looks just like one of us, but more luminous—as if they have a light inside of them. They can turn this light up and down; the higher the level of the light the more translucent and transparent they are. If the spirits have their lights turned down (which they do occasionally to make themselves less obtrusive), it's possible to mistake them for real flesh and blood people. In simple terms, it's as if you said hello when you walked past a neighbor on the other side of the road, then a few minutes later it dawns on you that it was Johnny you had greeted, but that he had died six months ago. It might only be then that you realize that Johnny looked brighter than normal people.

One of the other things I loved about watching from the windows was seeing the energy flowing around people. Once I saw one of my friends' mothers, and I saw swirling rays of light coming from her—shiny, sparkly mauve, purple, red, green, or turquoise—which derived from a central point, like a whirlwind. It was an energy that was different from the woman's energy, and it fascinated me. Later, I heard my mother say that this woman was going to have a baby and I smiled to myself.

In the same way I also could see if people were ill, even if I didn't understand what I was seeing. A flowing dark shadow would move around the person's body, showing me that something was wrong with their blood. Sometimes a bone would flash and I could see that the bone was damaged or not forming properly. I would know instinctively that something was not right with a person even though I had no words to explain it.

One day I was sitting crouched at the window and I saw a man cycling down the road on a big black bicycle with his little daughter on the back carrier. The angels told me to keep watching them and not to take my eyes off them as they passed the window. I didn't ask them why; as a child I would do what the angels told me to without questioning them. I knew I was being asked to help this father and daughter, so even when they were passing my window I was praying for them. I didn't know what was going to happen, but I asked that it mightn't be too bad.

As the man and his daughter cycled past the front of the house everything seemed to slow down, like a film in slow motion. A big doubledecker bus began to overtake them, and the next moment the little girl let out a scream and the man started to fall. Somehow, though, the child didn't fall off the bike. She had caught her foot in the spokes. I watched the father carefully disentangle her little foot and leg from the buckled and bent wheel with his shaking hands. He carried the crying child—she was gently sobbing rather than screaming—to the footpath just below the window where I was watching. Adults ran to help, including my mother. I dashed down the stairs and out the door to see if she was okay. As usual no one took any notice of me. The little girl's shoe had come off and her foot was all raw and bloody; the spokes had taken the skin off the sole of her foot, but there was nothing broken. I asked God and the angels to help her still.

Even then, at five or six years old, I felt that I had a role to play in helping people. I believed that because of my watching and praying as the father and daughter passed, something worse hadn't happened. Maybe she would have fallen under the bus, or fallen off and hit her head, but in the end she had only hurt her foot and, thanks be to God, she was all right. From then on there have been many occasions when I have felt I was put in a place to help, to prevent something from happening or, if I couldn't stop it happening completely, to make the situation a little better. This was part of the training that my angels were giving me; I may have had problems learning in school, but I had no problems learning from the angels.

One day I was able to use this gift to help a friend's da. Josie was my best friend. She lived up the road from me and I liked her because she was different too—she had a stammer. In fact, she stammered quite badly, but when she was playing with me her problem practically disappeared, and then it would come back if anyone else joined us. She had long, straight reddish hair and green eyes and she was taller than me and very skinny. Her da had a garage down the road—it wasn't like a gas station, or the garages we have nowadays; it was an enormous yard full of wrecked cars and car parts. Her da was always telling us not to play there, but there was a little space to the right as you went in the gate that hadn't much in it, and eventually he said we could play in there on the condition that we never went anywhere else in the yard.

One lovely sunny day, a Sunday, we had our clean clothes on and were trying not to get them too dirty. We were playing with our dolls in this little place in the yard and we were laughing and joking. I remember feeling the angels talking to me all the time and telling me to listen. I thought they meant that I should listen to them, but that wasn't what they meant this time. Finally, they touched me to get my attention. I remember I stopped playing and listened. I thought I heard something, but I wasn't sure. When I asked Josie, she couldn't hear anything. So we went on playing, and the angels again said, "Listen!" I listened again and got a strange feeling—I can't describe it; it was as if I went into another time and space. I felt disoriented. As I listened I could hear Josie's father calling for help very faintly in the distance. Josie couldn't hear anything.

We were afraid to go down among the wrecked cars, which were stacked high, because we knew that we were strictly forbidden from going there, but I decided to go anyway, and Josie followed me. As I followed an angel down through the wrecked cars,

I remember repeatedly saying, "Please God, please angels, please let her da be all right!"

We found Josie's father; a car had fallen on him and there was blood everywhere, but he was alive. I remember running off to get help and I think Josie stayed there. I'm not sure where I ran to—their house or my own. Everyone came running. They sent us away because we weren't allowed to be there when they were lifting the car off him, but I remember the ambulance coming. The hospital, St. James's, was only up the road. Afterward he was all right. He got better. I thanked God and the angels that he was all right. Again, my angels had helped me to help someone.

As I have said before, your angels are there to help you, and as you start to acknowledge that they exist, you will start to feel their touch in your life. Angels have been touching you all along, willing you to realize that they are there. They want you to know that there is much more to life than there might seem to be. We do not live our lives on our own; we may be in a human body, but each of us has a soul that is connected to God. Angels are connected to God, too; as soon as we call God's name we empower the angels.

In other words, we empower them to empower us. God has given us free will, and the angels will not overstep that. If we tell them to go away, if we say we don't want help, then God and his angels will step to one side. But they will not go away completely; they will wait somewhere nearby.

Have you ever had an experience when you were heading off somewhere and you went right instead of left? Deep inside you knew that you should have gone left, and later you kick yourself for it. That would have been your angel whispering in your ear, telling you that you should go left. Angels are all around us, unseen and waiting to help. But they need to be asked for help. By asking we allow them to help us and we make the connection stronger between us and our angel.

I realize now, after all these years, that I am an interpreter between angels and people, and as such I am frequently called on to intercede. While I have a particular role, all of us have the power to ask the angels to help at any time.

I have often asked the angels for help for my family. Things weren't easy when I was growing up; by the time I was six, Mum had had three more babies—two girls, Helen and Aoife, and a boy, Barry—so there were five children. On top of this, Mum was often unwell and was frequently in the hospital. When she went into the hospital, the family was divided up and sent away to her relatives.

I was four when my older sister, Emer, and I first went to stay with my aunty Mary. She lived with her husband and three children not too far away. Although it may not have been many miles away from where we lived, to me it was a world apart. When I first saw their house I thought it was a palace; it seemed enormous compared to our home. Everything in it was so luxurious and beautiful and it was warm, whereas our house felt damp and cold much of the time; here I could run around in my bare feet on the soft carpets. Mealtimes were incredible—loads of food served on a beautiful table laid with matching cups and plates that seemed to be so delicate I was afraid I would break them. Every meal was like a feast—there was so much food to choose from. One day I was asked if I would like a fry-up for breakfast, and I couldn't believe what I was given: sausages, fried egg, rashers, black pudding, tomatoes, and toast—all for me! Nothing was halved or shared like at home. The best thing of all was the bathroom. I had a bath filled with hot water right up to the top of the bathtub: I felt like a princess.

This visit was the first time I realized how poor we were.

While we were staying at Aunt Mary's, Mum's parents came to visit and I was made to put on my good dress—a greyish blue one with smocking across the front. I always loved wearing dresses and this was one of my favorites, so I was happy to put it on. I had only met my grandparents on a few previous occasions and I was very shy of them. They were both tall and looked like giants to me. Although they were both big, Granny was fat, too, and she walked with a walking stick because she had had a stroke some years before.

Sometimes when Mum was well, if the weather was good, we would go off and have a picnic in the Phoenix Park—an enormous wide-open space on the outskirts of Dublin, with deer and all kinds of wonderful things. It was about two miles from home so we could walk there without too much problem. One Sunday when I was seven we all set off. Da pushed a bike with the picnic on the back carrier and Mum pushed my little baby brother, Barry, in a big old-fashioned stroller. Emer and I walked, and my two younger sisters, Helen and Aoife, alternated between walking and sitting up on the stroller with their legs dangling.

We had a great picnic of tomato and jam sandwiches and apples from the next-door neighbor's garden, and Da boiled up a billy can and made hot sweet tea for us all. After lunch I played football with my sisters, and then I wandered off on my own among the big old trees. I loved playing among the trees there; the energy of certain trees—not all trees—would pull me toward them. It felt wonderful, a tingling, magic feeling that drew me toward a tree as if it were a magnet. I used to play a game with the trees, running around until the energy of a particular tree grabbed me, and then I would escape from it. I could play like this for hours. On this afternoon my sisters came over and asked me what I was doing. I just said I was playing; I didn't bother to explain—they wouldn't have understood.

At the end of the afternoon we were exhausted from all the running about and were looking forward to getting home and having supper. Even before we turned the corner into the Old Kilmainham road, where our house was, I knew something was wrong. Two very big angels were walking up the road toward me, and I knew from the way they approached that something terrible had happened. When they reached me they each put an arm around me, and as we walked up the road they told me that the roof of our house had fallen in. I was shocked.

When we got to the house I was horrified by what I saw: a large part of the roof had collapsed. My da tried to open the door but he couldn't get it open, and when he forced it with his shoulder a cloud of dust came out. Inside nothing was recognizable—it was just rubble. When the roof collapsed it had brought the ceilings crashing down. To my child's eyes the house was all broken. I remember thinking, *Where are we going to sleep now?* We climbed in over the rubble, and to my little child's legs each bit of concrete or stone seemed enormous. There was dust everywhere and everything was broken into smithereens—all the furniture, all our toys, all Mum's precious things. I saw her crying as she picked up things from the ground, and I stood in shock just watching Mum and Da try to salvage things. I remember Mum picking up a little dark brown milk jug with a cream stripe and saying, "This is all that's left in one piece."

That jug was all that was left of her wedding presents—she had so little, and now all she had was gone. I still remember seeing the tears in her eyes. It made me cry, too; in fact, all of us cried, except my da. He told us not to cry, that he would make things all right. Somehow Mum and Da cleaned things up a little and Da propped the roof up a bit so we could sleep there that night, but it was very dangerous. I slept thinking about the fact that our house had fallen in and I wondered, *What will we do now? Where will we go?*

We were homeless, now, and Da had also lost his livelihood.

CHAPTER 3

Stairway to Heaven

Thankfully, my cousin Nettie came to our rescue. She lived in a big house on her own even though she was hardly more than a child herself. A year or two earlier, at sixteen, she had inherited the family house when both her parents died. I don't know quite how it was agreed, and if we paid rent, but we went to live with her in her house in Ballymun in the suburbs, on the north side of Dublin City—miles from Old Kilmainham.

At first I felt miserable about moving—I loved Old Kilmainham—but when I got to Ballymun and saw the big garden and the big rooms I was happy. Most important, this house was solid and I knew it would never fall down. It had three bedrooms upstairs and, a real luxury, an indoor loo and a bath. Downstairs there was a lovely long kitchen at the back overlooking the garden, a front room, and Nettie's bedroom, which had probably originally been a dining room.

The house had a magical garden; no garden since has ever seemed as big to me. We had so many adventures there. There was even a haystack, and when there was a birthday party sweets would be hidden in it. When he had time Da grew vegetables—rows and rows of vegetables—everything you could think of, including peas, which we loved to pop, and he built huge strawberry beds.

At that time there were five children in the family. My brother,

Barry, was only a baby, and between him and me there were two girls, Helen and Aoife, and then, of course, Emer, my older sister. I didn't play much with my brother and sisters; I only played with them when there was a birthday party or something like that. I suppose I had different interests. I saw the world with different eyes.

At first my new life was a little lonely, but I soon made new friends. I got to know a little girl, Rosaleen, who lived on the other side of the wall along the back of all the gardens. It was a wonderful big wall that ran the length of the road, and Da built a ladder for us so we could get up on it without destroying our shoes. It was a great wall for walking—good and wide so we could move along it safely— and this was how we traveled from one house to another, or to the fields down the way. I loved that wall, and all I could see from standing on top of it.

Rosaleen became my best friend. She lived in a big posh house at the other side of the wall, about six houses away, and most of the time we visited each other via the wall, rather than going the long way around. She came from a large family, too, but some of her siblings were already grown up and had left home. I knew her little sister, Caroline, and her brother, Michael, who was eight years older than her. Rosaleen was tall and skinny with long, dark, straight hair and she was full of fun and laughed a lot. I loved spending time with her and her family, and, in fact, I spent more time with them than with my own family.

Rosaleen's father was German, I think, and a big strong man with dark hair that was starting to go grey. He was away on business a lot of the time, but when he was home he was very good to Rosaleen and her brother and sister—and to me. On a Sunday he would buy a little bag of sweets for each of the children and I was very pleased and proud that he always included me—he included me in everything. There might only be six or eight sweets in the bag, but they were gorgeous and I'd try to make them last as long as possible.

There was another Sunday ritual in Rosaleen's house that I loved: her mother would read us a story. We'd all go to her bedroom and sit on the bed, and sometimes it would just be Rosaleen, Caroline, and I, and sometimes Michael or one of my sisters joined us, too. Rosaleen's mother was wonderful at reading stories, and we would all sit and listen enraptured for an hour or so before she would send us away. Sometimes the book was very long and it would take weeks for her to finish reading it. One of my favorites was *The Secret Garden* by Frances Hodgson Burnett.

There was a big wooden swing in our garden, which Da repaired so it went really high. I played on that swing for hours on end, and while I sat on it the angels taught me a lot of simple lessons about life and living. In fact, often while I was there in body I was in another world, where the angels showed me some wonderful and very magical things.

Sometimes when I was alone on the swing one of the angels would say, "Lorna, stretch out your hand. We have something to show you." Then the angel would put something tiny in my hand, and as the little thing touched my palm the angel would take away her hand and a light would start to materialize there. Sometimes this light looked like a little star or a daisy, then this light would start to grow, almost as if it were coming alive. As it grew and grew it started to glow and a bright yellow light came from it. The light rose up from my hand and went upward, getting bigger and brighter all the time until it partially obscured the sun. Then I would see a most wonderful sight reflected back, as if through a mirror—a beautiful face, like a human face, smiling down at me.

The first time this happened the angels told me that this was the Queen of the Angels. They liked to use terms that made sense to me as a child; they reminded me of the fairy tales I knew and that the Queen was like a mother, just as my mother was like the queen of my family. The angels explained that this person was the Queen of the Angels, the mother of the universe, the mother of creation, the mother of all the angels. All of a sudden the yellow orb in which I had seen the face exploded into millions of little pieces and fell like golden streamers coming from the sun.

Over the years the angels have regularly given me this gift, even as an adult, particularly when I've been in need of some reassurance.

The move to Ballymun, of course, also meant attending a new school. My three sisters and I went to a small national school for boys and girls, more than half an hour's walk from home. My sisters took the bus, but I preferred to walk most of the time. On my way to school I had to walk fast and keep hurrying, otherwise I'd be late and get into trouble, but coming home I could take my time.

Located on the same piece of ground was the school, which was on one side, the church, which was in the middle, and the parish hall, which was on the other side. There were only three classrooms, and that wasn't enough, so the parish hall next door was used for two classes. For my first year there I was in the hall; the two classes were held at either end of the hall, with no wall between them. Mr. Jones was my teacher and he treated me very badly; as far as he was concerned I was a dummy and it really irritated him that he had to have a child like me in his class.

One morning the angels told me that something special would happen at school that day that would make me feel happy. The angels were right, as always; what happened did make me happy at the time, and it still does when I think about it! We were studying the Irish language and Mr. Jones announced a one-question quiz with a prize of half a crown for the child who got the right answer. He wanted to know what the Irish word "crann" meant in English. He asked each child in turn, starting over on the right—he sat me on my own across to the left. He went through the whole class, one by one, and no child knew the answer. As usual, he didn't ask me. Sitting in my desk all on my own, I knew that I knew the answer. I was all excited. I couldn't stop fidgeting in my seat. I wanted to jump up and shout the answer at him. The angels had a hard time holding me still. "Angels, tell him to look my way, please. Tell him to ask me." I was nearly crying with excitement.

"Don't worry, Lorna," they said, "he will ask you."

Mr. Jones was shocked at his class and kept saying, "Come on! What's wrong with you? This is easy!" I laugh when I remember the expression on his face—his eyes were getting bigger, his face redder. He was dumbfounded. He asked the last child but me and then announced, "Well! It looks like no one has won the half crown."

Hosus was standing right beside Mr. Jones the whole time, pointing in my direction, but of course the teacher couldn't see him. I wanted to shout at Hosus to grab the teacher by the hand and bring him over to me. The whole class stayed silent, not a child made a sound. Despite the angels' assurances it looked as if Mr. Jones wasn't going to ask me after all. He walked toward his desk. Still there was complete silence in the room. Suddenly Hosus and Mr. Jones's guardian angel took him gently by the arm, turned him around, and led him over in my direction, all the time whispering in his ear. "I know there is no point," Mr. Jones said, "but I'll ask anyway!"

So he did ask, and in a confident and happy voice I said, "It means 'tree.' "

His face dropped. It was the right answer. The whole class laughed and clapped; they were delighted. He had to give me that half crown, and I'll always remember him putting it into my hand as I said thank you.

I had never had so much money of my own before—a whole half crown.

Most children hurried home after school, but I preferred to take it slowly and spend time on my own playing with the angels. Walking home from school could take me hours; I would walk along the big bank at the side of the lane so I could look over the hedge on the far side into the fields and the grounds of the big house that was there. Sometimes I would skip along the bank with the angels and we would laugh and joke with each other. Sometimes they would show me things. One time they pulled back the overgrowth and let me see a hole in the bank with a wasps' nest in it, and because it was the angels who were pulling back the camouflage, they were able to do so without disturbing the wasps. I could stand there for ages watching the wasps without fear of being stung. I remember going back to look for that wasps' nest later, only to discover that adults had found it and poisoned the wasps. That made me sad.

The angels also often used to show me the cattle in the field beyond the bank. They taught me to look at things differently from the way others do. I wouldn't just glance at a cow; I would really look to see everything about it: every line, every little bump. The angels would make each detail glow or stand out more than normal, so that I could really notice it. They would also allow me to see into the animals' eyes; even if they were a long way away I could still see deep into those eyes. I was being allowed to see things that most people never see. It was fascinating. I could see all the light and energy and things that were going on in and around the animal. Sometimes it looked as if there were balls of light dancing round the animals; other times the energy would be flashing on and off. I would see a calf in a cow's belly; sometimes I could hardly make it out, and then the angels would tell me to look more carefully and I'd see it. Sometimes, being honest, the calf looked like something all gooey and moving—a bit like the jam my mother used to make.

I was so fascinated by everything the angels showed me outside school, it's no wonder I had little time for what was going on in the classroom. When the angels explained something to me when I was a child I would think I understood their answer fully, but as I grew older I began to get a deeper understanding of what they meant.

One of my friends at school was Marian, although I never saw her outside of school. Whenever we left the hall to go to the school building or to the church she would insist on walking beside me. Even if the teachers paired her with another girl she would find a way of walking beside me, and she always wanted to ask questions. She used to wonder how I knew so much, but I couldn't tell her about my angelic teachers. One day as we were walking through the playground toward the church she asked me to tell her about God. I was so surprised I could hardly breathe. I looked at her and didn't know what to say. Eventually I said, "The teachers and priest tell us about God, so why are you asking me?" I was trying to get out of giving an answer, but she insisted, "I want you to tell me."

So I started to tell her about God. "Do you see the finch, that beautiful finch with all those golden colors and yellows and blues? That bird is like God. Really look at that bird and see its beauty and perfection. You are like the bird; you are beautiful, because you are like God. If that bird falls and hurts itself it won't feel all the pain of that fall, because God will feel ninety-nine percent of it. God feels everything that happens to each and every bird and it is the same with us—when something happens that would hurt us, we feel only a fraction of it. God feels the rest and takes it away."

I know these weren't my words—I was too young for words of wisdom like this—they were words I was given by God or the angels.

I loved the church on the school grounds; sometimes I'd be a bit late for school because I would slip into the church before I would go into class. I love churches—they are full of angels. There might only be a few people in the church, but there is always a great hustle and bustle among the angels there. People don't realize how many angels there are in a church; the angels are there praising God and waiting for God's people to come and join them, but frequently no one does. At Mass on a Sunday the place is packed: there are guardian angels with every person, angels standing around the priest at the altar, and lots more angels that God sends down. Churches are very powerful places; when I see someone at church surrounded by angels and light, I pray for them: "Please let that person hear their angel today and in some way come into contact with their angel, and through him with God."

Angels are not just found in Christian churches; they are in the synagogues, in mosques, and in all the holy places. Your religion makes no difference to the angels; they have told me that all churches should be under one roof. Muslims, Jews, Protestants, Hindus, Catholics, and all the other different religions should be together under one umbrella. We may look different, we may have different beliefs, but we all have souls. There is no difference between a Muslim soul and a Christian soul. If we could see one another's souls we would not be killing each other over different interpretations of God.

One day I was walking with my aunt Nellie near her house and we passed a church. Standing at the door of the church were two beautiful angels. My aunt turned to me and said, "Don't be looking across at that church." I looked at her in amazement. She continued, "That's a Protestant church. You are forbidden ever to go inside the gate or the door of any Protestant church!" I glanced back and watched the people going into the church; they looked no different from us. The next time I passed that church I smiled to the angels at the door. I wasn't allowed to go in, but I knew the church was full of angels.

Our next-door neighbor, Mrs. Murtagh, was a beautiful woman with a fabulous figure—but she always used to shout at my friend and me for walking along the wall. One particular afternoon when I was about eight she asked me to keep an eye on her children while she went to see my mum and have a cup of tea. Just as I was going into her house an angel stood in front of me and said, "When you are in there, be very careful."

I was immediately scared, but I reluctantly went into her kitchen. Mrs. Murtagh was getting ready and had a pot boiling on the stove. I said to her, "Are you leaving that on?"

She replied, "Yes, it will be grand."

"Won't you turn it off?" I asked.

She wouldn't listen to me, and she was the sort of woman who would get very angry at you if you didn't do exactly as she said. There were two children in the kitchen—a toddler and a baby in a huge stroller. As soon as she left I found myself looking around the kitchen. The back door was locked and there was no key in it.

All of a sudden, with a whoosh the cooker blew up. I don't know what happened but there were smoke and flames everywhere. I grabbed the toddler then the stroller and tried to maneuver it out the door into the hall. The cooker and the table were between the stroller and the door to the hall, so I had to pass the burning cooker to get out. The stroller was very heavy and I couldn't move it easily. I grabbed the toddler and got her out into the front garden and screamed at a passing neighbor that the house was on fire.

I ran back in; the house was full of black smoke, and I was terrified the baby would suffocate before we could get her out. The neighbor followed me and, thank God, he was able to maneuver the stroller out.

The children were safe. I ran crying and shaking into my house. Mum and Mrs. Murtagh were sitting in the kitchen having tea— they had heard nothing. I sobbed that the house was on fire and they ran into the garden next door. I remember Mrs. Murtagh throwing her arms around her children, shaking and crying. She looked at me and thanked me. The whole downstairs of the house was black, but the fire was out; the neighbor had managed to put it out.

The fifties and sixties in Ireland were a very difficult time economically; there was little employment and a lot of people had to emigrate. Things were very hard for my family with my mum often sick and in and out of the hospital. When she was away the garden would become overgrown as Da would have no time for it, with work and minding us. Even with our help, he still had an awful lot to do, and I would worry a lot. I would talk to the angels on the way to school about all that was happening at home. They would tell me not to worry, that Mum would get better.

Da would get us up early in the morning and get us ready for school; we would help make our breakfast and sandwiches for lunch. My sister and I would help to look after my younger brother and sisters, and we would clean the house and set the table for dinner. There was very little money, and Da had the additional expense of the bus to and from the hospital, so a lot of the time when Mum was sick we didn't eat dinner—we lived on crackers and cheese.

During the seven years we were in Ballymun, Mum had two more children, both boys, named Cormac and Dillon. Now there were seven of us children—all under the age of twelve. Things were tough. At one stage Da went to England to work and he seemed to be gone for months. So, again, there were no vegetables grown and the garden went wild. I used to talk to the angels about how I missed Da and how sad it was that he had to go away.

I always remember the day Da arrived back home unexpectedly. The angels told me to look out the window and I could see him walking down the road toward the house, wearing an overcoat and hat and carrying his case. I noticed how handsome my da looked; it was as if I expected him to look old, much older than he had looked when he went away, but he actually looked so young—which he was; he was only in his early thirties. I was so happy; I ran down the stairs as fast as I could and told Mum. I hid behind her as she opened the door to welcome him home. We were all so happy that day.

Da had to go out and start to look for work again immediately, but he did start working on the garden and we all helped. I always loved helping my da and I loved growing vegetables; pulling the weeds away from around them and asking the angels to help them to grow. I desperately wanted to help more, but when you are so small how much can you do on your own? Often I would cry with frustration at not being able to do more, but I would try to make sure that no one saw me by going around the back of the garden shed.

I used to play a lot with the family across the road from us in the cul-de-sac; they were a big family like ours and I was very friendly with the middle child, Alice, who was about the same age as me. Their da was away a lot working in England and their mum worked very hard, both outside and inside the home. Their father came home every few months, but one day the angels told me that his next trip home would be his last, because he was going to Heaven.

I felt so sad. Things changed; I no longer wanted to go over to my friend's house to play in her garden. I distanced myself, but I did my best to make sure that no one would notice, especially Alice. Then one day the angels said, "In a few days we will tell you to go over to Alice's house, and you will need to go over."

Three days later the angels told me to go over to Alice's house. I took a big, deep breath and went out the hall door, walked straight across the road through the side gate of Alice's house, around the back and knocked on the kitchen door. Alice's mother opened the door. I looked straight into the kitchen; it seemed darker than usual. Alice and one of her brothers were there, and my friend turned and gave me a big smile. I took a few steps inside the door; I didn't want to go any further. Alice told me excitedly that her dad was coming home, and coming home for good, that he had finally found a job in Ireland. She was so excited. I felt so confused—happy for her, and yet inside my heart was crying. I knew that her mother and father had been hoping for a long time that he would get a job in Ireland, so he could come home. Now he had one, but he wasn't going to live to enjoy it. I asked Alice to come and play with me in my house because I didn't want to stay in hers.

Later that day I remember going down to the church and sitting in front of the altar and talking to God, asking him if there was any way he could let Alice's dad come home and stay.

There was great excitement in Alice's house the day her father came home—and I felt happy for the family. However, a few days later I was sitting on the swing in their back garden while the other children were playing in the front, when the sky suddenly changed and an angel said, "Turn around and open your eyes."

When I turned around and looked at the house there was an incredibly bright beam of light coming down through the sky—a beam of light full of angels. I called that beautiful light "the Stairway to Heaven." This beautiful sight, and the wonderful singing and music that accompanied it, took my breath away. I wanted to go toward it, but I stayed sitting on the swing, gently moving back and forth.

The light went straight through the roof and seemed to engulf the house. Then it was as if the outer walls of the house disappeared and I could see Alice's dad lying there on his bed. His wife was trying to wake him. His body lay there, but his spirit was elsewhere— it was standing at the end of the bed with two spirits by its side. His spirit seemed to know the other spirits—I didn't recognize them, but they looked like him so I guess they were family who had come to help him on his journey. There were also a lot of angels there. Alice's dad went up into the light with the spirits and the angels, who held him ever so gently. I saw them going up among all the angels along that beautiful beam of light while the singing and heavenly music continued. Her father and the two spirits seemed to stop for a moment, then he looked back down.

Time stood still for me; suddenly the house came back into view and the stairway was gone. Alice's mother stood at the door, calling out to her children. They were playing in the front garden and I was alone in the back, sitting on the swing. She looked straight through me as if she did not see me. Then she turned and walked out the side gate into the front garden. I sat there, knowing the bad news that was awaiting Alice and her brothers and sisters. I felt so lonely and sad and asked the angels who were with me, "Will he be able to come back to comfort them—even for a while? Particularly to comfort Alice who loved him so much and missed him so much when he was away."

The angels replied, "Yes, he'll be back shortly. He will be there with them for a little while." That made me feel a little better, and I took a deep breath, got down off the swing, and said to the angels, "I think I'll go home now."

I could hear crying coming through the windows of Alice's house as I left. I walked out through the side gate across to my own home. No one was home—my mother was already across the road comforting Alice's mother.

That was one of the saddest days in my very young life; I always thought mums and dads would live forever.

CHAPTER 4

Why do you hide from me?

One day Da brought home a beautiful, shiny red car. It looked enormous, but perhaps that was just because I was so small. He had borrowed it from a friend because we were going on a holiday—my first ever! The car was piled up with luggage, and my parents and all seven of us children climbed in. We were heading down to my grandmother's place in Mountshannon, County Clare; it was in the country, 120 miles away. The journey seemed to take all day, but I loved every minute of it; I loved looking out the window. Every so often Da would stop the car and we'd all get out for a little break, and once we were lucky enough to get an ice cream.

This was the first time I met my da's parents. They lived in a youth hostel and Granny was its caretaker. I remember arriving that first day. Da drove in through a big, grand gate, into a yard through an old arch, then under another smaller arch into another yard. There, in front of us, was an enormous old house surrounded by big stone sheds that were like houses themselves—Granny told me later that these were coach houses, where the horses and carriages had been kept long ago.

Da stopped the car and we all tumbled out. I looked in wonder at the house. We went in and I was introduced to Granny and my grandfather. My grandfather had a wooden leg; I was always told that he had lost it as a young man while fighting for Irish freedom. My grandparents had very little money, but Grandda had a wonderful old-fashioned car that was designed so that he could get around with his crutches. That first evening he showed me a baby swallow that had fallen from its nest; he was feeding it with a dropper and keeping it in a shoebox. He also had found birds' eggs and was trying to keep them warm in the hope that they would hatch. Grandda looked very feeble and he stooped, and that first evening I also noticed that the light surrounding him was much weaker than that around other people; it was very dim, almost invisible, but at the time I didn't think too much about it.

My grandmother was a small, good-looking, elegant woman with short grey hair. She worked very hard, making sure that the hostel was clean. She was also a great cook and spent hours in the kitchen baking brown bread, apple tarts, and all kinds of delicious things. In fact, Granny and Grandda spent most of their time in the kitchen, which always smelled of fresh baking. I loved to sit there at the table with them enjoying a cup of tea and a slice of hot brown bread.

The big house was wonderful. Beyond the kitchen was a long, long corridor with lots of flowerpots. In summer, when I was there, this corridor was always full of flowers of all colors. At the end of the corridor was a glass room, and there was nothing much in it except more of Granny's flowers, but it was a place I loved. I used to spend a lot of time there, talking to the angels.

The garden was fantastic, too. There were the yards with the coach houses where the swallows nested, and beyond the yards was a little gate—which I always climbed over instead of opening. This gate led into a garden with big trees and lovely flowers that always smelled wonderful. There were rabbits and birds there, and sometimes, if I sat under one of the big trees with sloping branches, I could look into a blackbird's nest and see her chicks. Beyond the garden were fields and open countryside. I felt very safe there.

From the first day in Mountshannon I went for long walks on my own; I could slip out and nobody seemed to notice, or care, where I had gone. I was very good at not being noticed. Most of the time, with adults, it was as if I didn't exist. Sometimes I felt they might be happier if I didn't really exist; I've never been quite sure whether this was because I could feel what they were thinking or because of the things I had heard said about me over the years. Once when I was a young child I heard my neighbor telling my mother I was lucky I hadn't been locked up and the key thrown away. When she said this my mother didn't reply or defend me.

I would walk for miles—across bogs, through woods, across hayfields, along the banks of the River Shannon—but I never felt alone. I was always talking to the angels who were with me, and watching and listening to the birds and animals. Occasionally the angels would say, "Go quietly now, very gentle steps." Then up ahead there would be something for me to see. I remember being enchanted when I was shown a family of little rabbits playing. They didn't run away, so I sat down very close to them and watched them for hours. I know some days I must have walked for miles, but I never got lost and I never had an accident. When I think now of the things I did—crossing roads, rivers, bogs, and fields full of cattle—I have to wonder how it was that I never came to any harm. But the answer is clear: God and the angels had me in the palms of their hands. The angels made me laugh and cry and were the best friends I could possibly have; they are everything to me.

One day after I had slipped out and gone through the little gate, one of the angels appeared out of nowhere and caught me by the arm. "Come on, Lorna, we have something to show you, something we know you would like to see."

As we walked across the field I turned to them and laughingly said, "Bet I can race you!"

So off we ran at full speed and I fell. I cut my knee and cried.

"It doesn't hurt that much—it's only a little scratch," said my angels.

"Hmmm," I said, "it's only a little scratch to you, but a big scratch to me. I can feel it stinging. It does sting, you know!"

They just laughed at me and said, "Come on, up you get and let us show you something."

So up I got and, sure enough, I soon forgot my sore knee. As we walked through the field to the woods beyond they told me to listen. I listened and I could hear lots of animals in the distance.

"What am I to listen for?" I asked.

"Listen for one animal. Separate out all the sounds until you hear only one," the angels said. "This way we can teach you to hear us more clearly when you grow older."

So I separated out all the sounds I was hearing as I walked through the woods, and with every step I took I could hear the ground crackle under my feet. After a little while I was able to distinguish all the various birds, the different songs of the sparrow, the wren, the finch, the blackbird, and many others. I could hear and identify what birds they were and exactly where they were, just as I could with any animals that were around. I seemed to learn things very quickly when the angels taught me.

Then I stopped and said, "I hear a cry—that's the sound you want me to hear, isn't it? It's like someone crying."

I walked on through the woods; the trees seemed to get taller and it got darker. I said, "Oh, angels, it's too dark in here. Can you not lighten it up for me?"

"Don't be afraid," they said. "Follow the cry; follow the sound you hear."

So I did, and the cry brought me out into a clearing. I stood there listening and I could hear the cry again. I knew it was so, so close. It was to the right of me, so I walked back into the trees to the right, where there were thorny bushes. I got thorn scrapes on my legs and on my hands. There was no sound of crying now, so it was really difficult to find the source of the sound. The light was behind me and it was dark among the brambles and the bushes.

"Angels, I can't see anything," I said. With that a light appeared at the bottom of a tree.

One of the angels said, "Look at the light over there by the tree, just where the little gorse bush is. That's where you will find it."

And that's where I found a bird, not an ordinary bird but a bird of prey. I later learned it was a sparrow hawk. It was maybe the scrawniest, most horrible looking thing, but to me it was beautiful. I picked it up and looked up into the tall tree from which it had apparently fallen; I could never climb that high to put the bird back. As it moved in my hand I saw that it was hurt—its two legs were deformed and crooked and its neck was cut, probably from the fall. The angels told me that its parents didn't want it, that they had thrown it out of the nest.

"It's a gift from God to you," the angels said, "for you to look after this summer holiday and the next summer, but it won't go home with you after that."

Sometimes the angels would say things to me that I didn't understand; I would just take it that what they said was true. So I took the bird and walked back home through the woods and the fields and found an old hat and put it inside a box to make a home for the bird to live in.

My bird slowly grew stronger but it still couldn't walk properly, so I carried it everywhere. It couldn't fly well either, because it couldn't land on its legs. Da and I taught it to stretch its wings and fly briefly when we tossed it between us.

Feeding it was a problem, too, because it needed bloody raw meat, but I wasn't going to go out and kill something to feed it. I knew the meat had to be fresh, and what made it more difficult was that the bird would only eat such a tiny amount at a time. My parents couldn't give me a penny or a halfpenny to buy a bit of raw meat for the bird, so I'd say to the angels, "You really make it hard." I remember going into Killaloe, some miles away, with the family. I went into a butcher's shop with my bird and told the butcher I needed raw meat from him, but that I didn't have any money. I hated having to beg, but he was very nice and told me to come in anytime during the holiday and he would give me the raw meat. It sounds simple, but it wasn't—my parents hadn't the money for gas to go up and down from Mountshannon to Killaloe.

I didn't, and still don't, understand why my parents wouldn't provide more for the little bird. People who didn't really know me helped to feed the bird, but my parents didn't. When my mum was cooking I might look for a little raw meat—just a teaspoonful—but the response would be hems and haws. I was willing to go without my share and give it for the bird, but she wouldn't let me, so I was put into a situation where I had to beg. I always felt that if one of my brothers or sisters had had the bird, it would have been provided for. It was very hard. But the bird got fed somehow, and it grew strong.

One day when I was feeling sad Hosus said, "We know your heart is sometimes heavy and you are such a little thing, but you have to remember that God made you different and this will always be your life. You will have special work to do."

I replied, "But I really don't want to. Why couldn't God pick someone else?"

Hosus just laughed at me and said, "One day you will know why for yourself."

"I'm afraid!" I replied. "It makes me want to cry."

"You will have to cry," Hosus said, "because it is *your* tears that souls need to set them free."

I didn't understand what he meant at the time.

My grandmother, like many others, thought I was mentally deficient in some way, so it was rare that she talked to me. But one day when she did I learned a lot about her and my family. She invited me to help her clean and dust her bedroom—and that was something she had never asked me to do before. I had only been in her bedroom once or twice before, and even then it was just to look and not touch. This time she was inviting me to help her dust!

Granny gave me a cloth and asked me to dust a table while she cleaned a cabinet, carefully picking up all the precious things and dusting them. I watched as she picked up a photograph in a big oval frame, and I could feel a great sadness within her. She must have felt me looking because she turned and brought the photograph over to me, sat down on the big old high bed, and patted the space beside her. I pulled myself up onto the bed and sat with my legs swinging. She showed me a beautiful old photograph of a little girl about the same age as me, in a ragged dress with bare feet and tossed hair. Beside her was a little boy who was down on his hunkers and playing with a stick in the mud and the puddles. "These are my two little children that God has taken and who are now in Heaven with him." As she said this her eyes filled with tears.

I said to her, "You will see them again; you know that, don't you, Granny?"

"Yes Lorna," she replied, "I hope I see them again someday soon."

She told me the family had been extremely poor and her little boy—Tommy was his name—had gotten sick, probably because he didn't get enough of the right food. I could feel this great sadness, this great heaviness when she was telling the story. Her little daughter, Marie, had had a growth on her throat. My grandfather had carried her on his bike for miles and miles—from where they lived in Wicklow to a hospital in Dublin. His enormous effort wasn't enough, though; she died before the doctors could operate. Granny told me that when she looked at my da, with his dark good looks, she always wondered what Tommy would have looked like had he grown up. She said she looked at me and my sisters and wondered what her daughter Marie would have looked like. "I know that someday I will hold them again in my arms, and I can't wait for that day," she said. I could feel the terrible hurt that she felt.

She then said, out of the blue, "You know, Lorna, don't be afraid. Spirits cannot harm you or hurt you in any way. Even when you are afraid you just have to say one little prayer, just say, 'Jesus and Mary, I love you. Save the souls.' " She smiled at me and didn't say another word on the subject, then or ever. I would have loved to tell her all that I saw, to share with her the pain and the joy I felt, to ask her about what *she* saw and felt, but the angels had told me I wasn't allowed. I always felt that Granny understood that I saw more of the world than most people—but she never said anything more to me about it. She got up off the bed and continued dusting and then, when she was finished, she walked out of the room. I followed her and closed the door.

My grandmother went back to the kitchen and I went into the bathroom and prayed. "Thank you, God and the angels. Please will you help my grandmother—she is sad and hurting."

Later that summer I got a further insight into what had happened with little Marie. It was a bright sunny afternoon and my grandda was polishing his car in one of the coach houses. I peeked in at him and he sent me off to get him a cup of tea. When I came back he asked me to sit down beside him in the yard. We sat there watching the swallows flying to and from their nests with food for their chicks. It was very unusual for me to be sitting beside Grandda like this. The only other time I had spoken to him was that first day when I had helped him feed the baby swallows. This time it was different. I asked the angels, "What's happening?"

"Just listen," the angels said. "He needs to tell you about Marie and bringing her to the hospital."

Grandda described that day for me. "It was a chilly day but the sun was shining; your gran got Marie ready for the journey. She wasn't well, and we knew that she needed to go to the hospital urgently. I was shaking as I got the bike ready, knowing the bike would not last the whole journey of more than twenty miles, but there was no other way to get her there—there was no one around to help, no one with a horse and cart, no one to share the journey with me."

At that he smiled down at me, "Only you, Lorna, you are the first person I've ever told about it.

"I tied a bag with sandwiches, an apple, and a canister of water to the back carrier," he continued. "I was scared that Marie would die on the journey. I hugged your gran; she was in tears because she couldn't come with me as she had to mind your father and your uncle, who were little more than babies. I took Marie from her arms and carried her over to the bike. I balanced her on the crossbar and held her close to my chest and cycled off. I could not even turn around to your gran to say good-bye. It was very difficult cycling along with Marie in my arms and with my wooden leg—I was scooting along, really, rather than cycling. I cycled a long way. Many times I stopped and gave Marie some water on my fingers—she could not eat or even drink properly because if she tried, she might die, because the lump might move and block her windpipe. After some hours—it must have been about lunchtime—I was feeling hungry so I stopped and ate the sandwich and drank a little water. I cycled a bit more, but then the bicycle got a flat tire and that was the end of the bike. I abandoned it there and I walked on, carrying Marie in my arms. I held her close; I could feel her heart beating and her breath so shallow. It was dark when I eventually got to the hospital. Somehow they knew we were coming; I walked up the steps of the hospital, exhausted, hardly able to take another step. A nurse came toward me and took Marie from my arms. I didn't want to let her go. I sat down on a chair and waited, and a doctor came out and told me they would take her into surgery first thing the following morning."

He looked at me with tears in his eyes. "It was too late!"

The little lump in her throat had moved and blocked her windpipe as they were bringing Marie down to surgery, and she suffocated. Grandda turned around and said to me, "I became very bitter after that—having lost Tommy and then Marie. I just didn't believe in God anymore. I have made life very hard for your granny."

As I looked at my grandda, with tears coming down his cheeks, I saw Marie and Tommy standing in front of him, reaching out to him and touching his tears. I told him what I saw. "Grandda, Marie and Tommy are with you right now, don't cry."

He gave me a big hug, and in a choking voice said, "You'd better not tell anyone your grandda was crying."

"Don't worry," I said, and smiled at him.

At the same time the angels whispered in my ears, "It's a secret."

I told Grandda, "I will never tell anyone," and I never have, until now.

While he was talking to me the light around Grandda became much brighter, like the light around other people. I realized then that his hurt and anger at the death of his two young children had made him so bitter that it had killed his joy for life. Grandda got up and went back into the coach house to work on his car. It was as if he had never spoken to me. He changed back to his normal self, the light around him became very faint, and I never again saw him with that brilliant light around him.

I was very little to be told this story, but I knew that I was working for the angels again, this time helping them to help my grandfather.

I very much enjoyed my summer in Mountshannon and hoped that the following year we could holiday there as well. The year passed quickly, and when the days got longer again I couldn't wait for the holidays, to go back down to Mountshannon.

This time we didn't stay in my grandmother's house, though. We drove past her house and down through the village of Mountshannon and stopped on the outskirts, outside a big house with a wild garden. The house was almost completely empty—I think there was a table, a couple of chairs, and a cooker, but no beds or anything else in any other room. That didn't matter to us; we thought it was a great adventure and we slept in sleeping bags on the floor.

That summer, while we were staying in the empty old house, a lovely old lady called Sally gave my da a small piece of land near Mountshannon. It was high up in the mountains and a hard climb up a mountain road to get there, but I loved it. The piece of land was next door to the little cottage where Sally herself lived. The cottage had a traditional-style door and the top half of it was always open. She would hear us coming and would be standing there with a big smile; sometimes she would have a cat in her arms. She made us feel so welcome, giving us tea and biscuits or apple tart. She loved having company. I loved sitting at the table with her, drinking tea and listening to her stories of growing up in County Clare. After hours of listening to her I would eventually get up to leave. She would ask me to come again tomorrow, or encourage me to get Mum and Da to come and visit her.

Sally was very lonely there, up in the mountains on her own, and this was why she gave my da a small piece of land a short distance from her cottage—she hoped that he would build a little house there and then she would have company. She used to say to me that maybe in the future I would come and live there with my children. At eight, children were very far from my thoughts and I would giggle when she said this.

Sally had lots of cats and there were always kittens everywhere as well. They kept her company, she said. The cottage may have been full of cats, but it was spotless. The little house was packed full with furniture, but there was never any dust, no piles of papers, and it always smelled clean and homey.

I loved Sally very much, and I enjoyed all those childhood summer visits to her and her little cottage; I loved that mountain and the nights we spent out in a tent with a campfire and owls hooting nearby. Of course, my bird enjoyed these nights up the mountain very much, too. He was getting bigger and stronger now, but it was strange that he never once pecked my fingers with his big dark beak or scraped me with his long claws. One afternoon I picked him up, as I often did, and took him for a walk with me. I brought him down the mile or so to my grandmother's house and showed him all around the gardens.

As we were walking, the Angel Michael appeared beside me, and he walked all around the garden with me and the bird. We walked through my grandmother's kitchen and dining room without my being seen (sometimes the angels do things so that people won't notice me) and into the beautiful bright corridor with the wonderful flowers and the big windows.

"Your little bird is growing so big and so strong. You never named it?" asked Michael.

"No, it didn't need a name," I said. "My bird is just 'Love,' that's all."

Michael looked at me and said, "One day you will understand why you called it 'Love.' "

Michael's eyes were so bright it was as if you could see for miles and miles inside of them; as if you were going down a long, long road; as if you were passing through time itself.

I always had my bird with me. Don't think I ever forgot him, even for one minute. On the last day of the holiday I was up on the mountain with my da. We had the tent and we had lit a fire, even though it was a great sunny day. I looked at my bird sadly. The angels had told me when I found him that he would not be going home with me at the end of this holiday.

I stood behind the tent holding my bird and talking to him gently.

"How am I going to live without you? I'll miss you so much."

Da called me over and said, "Come on, Lorna, that bird needs to exercise his wings more."

I picked him up sadly. He was so cheerful and flapped his wings and let out a loud squawk.

My father called and I whooshed the bird out of my hands up into the air. Da caught him and he flapped his wings in Da's hands. Da whooshed him up into the air back to me. But three-quarters of the way across his body fell to the ground. My bird was gone! His spirit flew away; his wings seemed enormous and he seemed to turn golden. He turned his head to me; his eyes were so bright they smiled at me. He wasn't an ordinary bird; he was a gift from God and the angels.

I felt happy and sad in the same moment. I was happy for my bird—he was perfect now and he was soaring like an eagle—but I knew I would miss him terribly.

My father rushed over, he was so upset. "Oh Lorna, I'm sorry, I know you didn't want the bird to fly further. You didn't really think he should."

"It's all right, it's okay," I said. Da felt so sad, so hurt and so guilty, and I couldn't comfort him because I couldn't tell him what had happened, that it wasn't his fault.

Michael had been very clear: "You can never tell him. You are different, Lorna. He can only see its body there on the ground. He wouldn't understand. Don't you know how hard it is for man to understand God as it is?"

I begged, "But my da is so hurt, Michael."

"No, you can't tell him," he said. "One day you will tell him some of what you know about God and His angels, but not now. Don't worry, little one." Michael would always call me "little one" when he was trying to comfort me.

Da and I never discussed the loss of the bird again, but I think that for a long time after he felt guilty about it.

One sunny day I was walking up the lane to Granny's from the empty house and smiling to myself; I felt enormous strength and confidence because I knew that someone very special was close by.

My angels told me not to continue up the lane but to go through the fields instead. I climbed a gate and as I was walking through the long grass toward the woods He ruffled my hair.

He has an extraordinary presence, too powerful to manifest in physical form. Instead, when He's present it feels like a powerful force swirling around me. He has a habit of ruffling my hair, which makes it feel all tingly. I feel so special and so good when He is near me.

As a child I didn't know who or what He was; I just knew that He was a completely different order of being.

"You're here!" I laughed with delight.

"I never leave you," He said. "I'm always with you. Don't you know that? Don't you feel me? I ruffle your hair a lot. Why do you hide from me?"

He was right: I did hide from Him sometimes—even to this day I try at times because He is so big and so powerful. I remember turning and feeling His powerful force on my left side, moving alongside me. I replied, "Because You are so much bigger than me and I am so small."

He laughed and said, "Lorna. Don't hide anymore. Come, let's go for a walk now and I will take away your fear of what you have to do for me in this life."

We continued until we reached the woods. In a gap between the trees, overlooking the lake, there was an old wooden chalet and we sat down there in the sun to talk.

"You know I'm afraid," I said to Him.

"There is no need for you to be afraid, Lorna. I will not let any harm come to you," He said. "People need you, just as I need them."

"Why me?" I asked tearfully.

"Why not you?" He replied. "You may be a child, but you know more than most people out there in the world. You are my human angel, here to help people and their souls. Shed your tears freely my little one, my bird of love."

I looked at Him. "Why do You call me Your 'bird of love'?" I asked.

"Because you carry love like your little bird did. You are pure in your soul; you are my little bird of love and I need you, and so do others."

"You know I don't like being different from other children," I replied tearfully.

He wiped away my tears. "Lorna, you know I am always beside you," and He put His arm around my shoulder and held me tight.

The two of us walked back through the forest and cut through the fields and back toward my grandmother's house. All of a sudden He had gone. I continued up to my grandmother's house and my mum was there, helping Granny bake apple tarts and make the dinner. I just watched them and listened—that's something I did an awful lot of. I always let others talk, but I would listen and I would hear the words they were not saying, the words that they wanted to say, the words they kept in their heart—their joy and the happiness, and also their pain.

We had four or five very enjoyable summers in Mountshannon, but when I was about eleven or twelve Granny had a heart attack and was unable to continue in her job, so she left the house and we never went back to Mountshannon on holidays again.

I never saw Sally again, either. Years later I was told that she had died all on her own, up there in that cottage on the mountains, but I know she wasn't on her own; the angels were with her. After my father died no one was able to find any proof of my father's ownership of the land, so none of us ever fulfilled Da's dream and built a house there.

CHAPTER 5

Elijah

I have been given visions on many occasions throughout my life. When I was about ten I was out in the fields walking along the river and the angels said, "Just up here we are going to meet Elijah."

"Who's Elijah?" I asked. I laughed at the name "Elijah"; I had never heard it before and I thought it sounded lovely.

The angels weren't laughing, though.

"Elijah is going to show you something, Lorna. You must try to remember, because this is part of your future."

An angel walked toward me across the river from the far bank. It's hard to describe him; he was a rusty color—that rusty, amber color that has a little red in it—and absolutely beautiful. He seemed to shine, and his clothes were long, draping over him as his sleeves did over his hands. Yet, when he raised his arms, the long sleeves seemed to roll back so gracefully, as if they were a part of him. Elijah's face even seemed to be that same rusty amber color.

I was fascinated to see Elijah walking on the river; he was coming toward me, but his feet were not touching the water.

"Can I do that, too?" I asked. He just laughed at me.

The ground was uneven on the river bank, with big tufts of grass. Elijah invited me to sit down beside him and smiled. "I'm glad to see you are not nervous with me."

"No, they told me you were coming," I replied.

As I looked around I realized that all the angels who were usually with me had disappeared except my guardian angel.

"Where have they all gone?" I said.

"They have gone away for a while," he said. "Now, I'm going to hold your hand, Lorna." He held out his hand to me and I put my hand in his. All I can say is, it was as if my hand got lost in his, as if my hand became part of his hand. "I don't want you to feel afraid," he said, "because there is nothing to be afraid of. This is something that you can look forward to when you grow up, something that will happen to you."

"Why do I need to know it now?" I asked.

He didn't answer my question and instead said, "You will see someone and we will tell you about this person you are seeing."

Then it was as if a curtain had been pulled back and I was watching this big huge screen in the middle of the river in front of me. In the vision I could see a pathway surrounded by trees. I seemed to be sitting at the far end of the pathway, and I could see a figure in the distance starting to walk through the trees along the path. I looked at Elijah beside me and said, "I can't see very well."

"Keep watching!" he replied.

As the figure got closer I could see it was an extremely tall young man with red hair. He was very, very handsome, as far as I could make out. Then Elijah started talking again. "You can see him quite clearly now."

I turned to the angel sitting beside me and nodded.

"Keep looking," he said. "We want you to remember what he looks like. We won't show you any more, but what I need to tell you is that this will be the young man you will marry. You will recognize him from this vision the first time you see him, many years from now. But you have to grow up first!"

I smiled and giggled at the idea of being in love, or married, and asked Elijah, "Is he big like that now?"

"No," Elijah replied, "he is only a young boy, too, a few years older than you are." Elijah continued talking. "You will be very happy with him—he will love you and you will love him. You will have ups and downs, good times and not so good times. You will have healthy children and they will all be very special, too. But you will end up looking after him, and God won't leave him with you forever. You won't grow old together."

I turned and looked at him and said, "What do you mean, Elijah, 'looking after him'?"

"His health won't be the best," Elijah replied. "God will take him one day, when he is still quite young."

"I really don't want to know that," I said.

But Elijah continued, "Lorna, don't get cross. We just want you to remember. We're preparing you for the future, preparing you to be strong. Think of all the love and happiness that you'll have. Just look at how handsome he is. You said so yourself."

I looked again and I could see him, and I said, "Yes, he's nice."

Then the vision was gone and Elijah asked, "Will you remember that?"

"Yes," I replied, "I will remember, and I understand that he won't be staying with me forever, and that I will have to look after him."

I turned around to Elijah and, despite my young age, I said, "I will be strong."

Elijah took my hand again; we got up and he walked with me. After a little while he stopped and said, "Don't think too much about this now. Just put it at the back of your mind. You will recognize it the day it happens."

Then Elijah was gone and, of course, the vision did happen one day, some years later. In the process of writing this book I asked my angels for more information about Elijah, and I was told that Elijah was an Old Testament prophet—a man with the soul of an angel.

⁓

My family was on the housing list with Dublin Council to get a house. It was a real fight but eventually, after five years, we were given a rented council house in Edenmore. It was a lovely house in a brand-new estate of several hundred houses. All the homes were more or less the same: three bedrooms, semidetached, with small front and back gardens. There was another estate next to ours, but the area wasn't completely built up and there were fields and open spaces around us. Everyone there was new; most people were in their own house for the first time—having perhaps lived with their parents or in old tenements in Dublin city center. It was a friendly place, and I liked it immediately.

So at last we had a house—even if we didn't own it. Things were improving, but it was still tough for my parents. Da was working as a delivery man for a big gas company; it was hard physical work and long hours, and Mum went out to work the night shift in the local chocolate factory. Every evening after school Mum would give us our dinner and then leave myself and Emer to mind the younger ones until Da came home—which was often quite late.

Edenmore was a long way from Ballymun, so the change meant new schools and new friends for all of us. There was no school nearby so we had a long walk every morning—through the housing estate, down into the old village, then past the church to the main road. The school was directly across this busy road. My class was in a prefab that was very crowded, with the desks packed tightly together. In the morning it was a hard squeeze to get to your desk— you practically had to crawl over your classmates.

I was very happy in Edenmore; I didn't have any particular close friends, but there was one family of neighbors, the O'Briens, with whom I spent a lot of time. My real favorite in the O'Brien family was their wonderful Alsatian dog, Shane. I used to take Shane for a walk three times a week, and it was on one of these walks that I met another special angel.

I call this angel "the tree angel" because she always appears in a tree. I have seen her many times since and still do to this day. She's all the shades of emerald green, emerald gold, and emerald orange that you could imagine—the colors are magnificent. She seems to be alive in every part of the tree, yet I can see her so clearly. Her hair is curly and full of waves, and when she moves every part of her moves and her eyes sparkle like gold dust. She stretches out her arms and holds her hand out toward me and as she does so the tree moves with her. I have often spoken to her, and her voice when she speaks back to me is like a whistle; it is as if her voice rustles among the leaves of the trees.

One day while I was out walking Shane, we had crossed the field and were about to go back in toward the estate when Shane stopped and started to bark at this big tree on the left. I looked at the tree and saw nothing; I laughed at Shane, asking, "What are you barking about?"

Then I saw her. There was the tree angel—Shane had seen her before me. I laugh at that when I think of it. It amazes me that animals see angels so easily.

Sometimes on the way home from school I played in the quarry with the other children. One day instead of playing with them I tried the gate of the monastery next to the quarry. It was a place we weren't allowed to go into, but I lifted the latch and peeped in. I saw gardens full of vegetables and fruit; it felt so peaceful that I wasn't afraid. I walked round watching the monks in their brown robes busy in the gardens. They took no notice of me; it was as if they didn't see me. I sat down on an old tree trunk and watched.

It definitely was a holy place, a place where lots of prayers had been said. All of the monks shone so brightly—they were so clean, and not just in their bodies, but in their souls, too. They prayed as they worked, and I noticed the angels were praying with them. I felt very much at peace there; I wanted to stay, but eventually my angels dragged me out of there. They kept telling me to go home, that my mother would be worried. I did as they told me. Although it was getting dark, the angels lit the way for me. Mum had already gone to work when I got home, so I didn't get into trouble.

During that year I must have gone to the monastery at least twelve times or more. Only once, the last time I visited, did a monk speak to me. He was picking gooseberries off a bush and I walked right up and stood beside him. He glowed so brightly, and his angel standing beside him was also dressed like him. He looked up at me— he was very young—and said, "Hello."

I asked him his name. He told me it was Paul. He spoke very softly and asked me mine. I told him.

He offered me some gooseberries, asking me why I came to the monastery so often. I answered him, "Just to watch you all pray. I need your prayers."

"I will always pray for you, Lorna," he replied.

I said good-bye, knowing that I would never go back to the monastery again.

One of my favorite outings on a Saturday morning was shopping with my mother. This involved a trip to Moore Street, a busy street market in the center of Dublin with stalls down both sides of the street and women with broad Dublin accents crying out their wares. I would pull the shopping cart along behind me while Mum chose the best fruits and vegetables.

One Saturday as we turned into Moore Street an angel pulled at my shoulder and whispered in my ear, "Let your Mum walk ahead of you—she won't notice." I took two steps back and my mum walked on, looking at the fruits and vegetables on sale. As I stood and looked down Moore Street the view changed. Suddenly Moore Street was like a golden palace: everything was a golden color, even the people. Then the colors changed and other colors appeared—vibrant brighter colors, much brighter and more vibrant than normal. These colors started to flow from the fruits, vegetables, and flowers, like waves full of energy. Then these waves became balls of color that bounced around the street, from one side of the street to the other, bouncing off the stalls and even off people; but no one seemed to notice.

The street was not just full of people; it was full of angels—many more than usual. Some of the angels were dressed like the women selling fruits and vegetables and were busying themselves helping. I thought it was very funny to watch the angels imitate every move that the women made—angels are such wonderful mimics. They were singing too—it was as if they were humming in time to the street life going on around them.

I had been in Moore Street many times before, but I had never seen anything like this; perhaps it was especially for me, to make me laugh, or perhaps it happens every day there but this was the first time I was allowed to see it. I found all the hustle and bustle so exciting.

Suddenly my mother, who was about three stalls ahead, noticed I was not standing by her side.

"Lorna, wake up. Come here with the shopping cart."

I thought everything would change back to normal, but it didn't. I stood beside my mum and my angels whispered in my ear, "Watch the lady selling fruit."

I did as I was told and I saw the lady's guardian angel standing right behind her. Her guardian angel looked like her and was dressed like her; she was full of light and had a wonderful smile and she winked at me. Mum asked the woman for some apples, pears, and bananas. As the woman put the fruit in the brown paper bag her angel attracted my attention, shaking her finger.

I realized that the woman had put bad apples among those Mum was buying and her angel was talking to her, but she was not listening. Her angel continued wagging her finger. I couldn't keep a straight face and I giggled out loud. The woman glanced sharply at me. I could see from her eyes that she knew I had seen what she was doing. Suddenly the bag broke and the fruit went everywhere. The woman tried to catch it and she did grab an apple—it was rotten! I know this wasn't by chance; her angel and my angel allowed it to happen, and that made me laugh even more.

Mum noticed the rotten apple and said, "I hope you're not giving me bad fruit."

The woman denied it as she filled a new bag and glanced guiltily at me. Mum paid her and I put the bag of fruit into the cart. As we walked away the woman called out in her broad Dublin accent, "Hey, Missus!"

Mum turned around and the woman was holding out a bag. "Here, Missus! Some extra fruit for your kids!" Her angel was standing behind her, smiling—finally she was being listened to.

I have been down Moore Street many times since, both as a child and as an adult, but it has never again come alive to that extent. I know that just because I don't see something, it doesn't mean it's not happening. The angels cannot allow me to see everything that is going on all the time; if they did it would be too much for me and it would make it impossible for me to live my daily life—I would be too distracted.

The angels taught me a lot about the idea of choice, too, and one afternoon they helped me to understand that it is never too late for us to change our minds and make the right choice, and also that angels can help us to make the right choice—if we choose to listen.

I enjoyed running errands for Mum as I could be alone and free to talk to the angels. I enjoyed skipping with them and watching the birds and trees. On this particular afternoon I was about halfway to the shops when the angels told me, "Stop, Lorna! We want you to have a look at something that is going on in another street, so we can explain some things to you. When you get to the main street, instead of going left for the shops and crossing the road, we want you to go right and just keep walking straight on."

So that was exactly what I did. Soon I saw loads of furniture out on the footpath and a police car and people gathered around. There was an old man coming out of his hall door and walking with the help of a walking stick, and all his furniture and belongings were there on the street. I was very shocked; the sight has stayed with me all my life.

"Angels," I said, "what is happening to this poor man?"

As I stood there on the footpath looking the angels started to talk.

"Lorna, the old man has lived in that house all his life. It's his house, but as he got older he became stubborn and refused to pay his taxes. He had a choice: he could have paid—he has the money—and none of this would have happened. If he was still talking to his family they might have helped him to make the right choice, but because of his stubbornness he is not speaking to them. He is on his own, for now."

I asked the angels who the woman was who was trying to talk to him—was it his daughter, and might he listen to her? They replied, "Lorna, can't you see his angels whispering in his ear. He does hear them, you know! See, he is crying now. He is letting his daughter take his arm. Now he is starting to make the right choices. It is never too late to make the right choice, if we are prepared to listen."

"I understand," I said. "Will you angels always help me to make the right choices?"

"Yes, Lorna, we will," they replied.

Sometimes things only seem like tragedies. That's the way it was with Da's accident.

He was working for a big gas company, delivering paraffin, and there was an accident. The company offered compensation, but Da said he didn't want money, he wanted a permanent job. Eventually, the company offered him a contract as manager of a gas station in the center of Dublin. Da was presented with a choice, and undoubtedly the angels helped him to choose the right thing. This permanent job gave my parents some financial stability, and, finally, they were able to afford a deposit on a home of their own.

My father's accident was a blessing in disguise. Sometimes tough things have to happen in order for people to change, and for things to change in their lives. Miracles happen all the time. People just fail to notice them.

CHAPTER 6

Absorbing the pain of others

I had learning difficulties that no one understood fully, so my parents decided I shouldn't go back to school when we moved to the new house in Leixlip, despite the fact that I was only fourteen. I was hurt that they didn't consult me about this; their taking me out of school was another example of their treating me differently. They never sent me away, as had once been suggested to them, but they did treat me differently.

I saw things getting easier financially, but none of this seemed to make a difference in relation to me. We now had a telephone. My brothers and sisters used the phone all the time and nothing was ever said to them, but when I asked to use it I would be told how much it cost and wouldn't be allowed. When I wanted to have a bath, I'd be told "No" or "Only a little one." This happened so often that I was afraid to ask if I could have a bath, so I used to just fill the basin with water to wash myself so that I wouldn't have to ask only to be refused. I never really understood; I still don't now, it was as if I was worth less than the others.

I helped Mum around the house and garden, watching as my brothers and sisters went off to their new schools. One evening while I was sitting at the table having dinner with my mum and brothers and sisters Mum announced that she wanted me to go with her to a funeral the following day. A relative had died and she didn't want to go on her own. My brothers and sisters were very interested in who the relative was; my brother, Dillon, wanted to know the dead woman's name. Mum said, "Theresa," and she showed us a photo.

"We'll have to get an early bus," Mum said, "as we have to travel to the far side of the city, and at the other end we have to walk to the church, which will take us about ten minutes."

The next day was very cold. As soon as my brothers and sisters had gone to school, Mum told me to dress up warmly, and I put on my coat, hat, scarf, and gloves. Mum took an umbrella as well, just in case it rained. We headed down to the bus stop. On the bus I sat looking out the window, thoughts going through my mind, wondering what a funeral would be like. This was a first for me.

A while later Mum turned to me and said, "We are nearly there. Now remember, Lorna, you are to stand beside me all the time and not wander off. You could get lost."

The bus came to a stop and we got off. There was a good walk to the church, and it was crowded inside. Everyone was so sad. The priest said the Mass and I watched everything with my eyes open wide.

After the service we went to the graveyard, which was quite close to the church—just a short walk away. There, in the graveyard, I was amazed to see how many angels were standing crowded among my relatives—most of whom were strangers to me. I moved a little away from the crowd of people to have a better look. Mum was busy talking and did not notice. There was an angel standing at a bush beside a grave, a beautiful angel dressed in a human way, but she was a vibrant, sky blue.

I asked her, "Why are all the angels here?" I'd often seen angels in graveyards before, but there were so many here.

She smiled at me and said, "Lorna, we know you still have lots to learn. This is one place where angels are called on, one place where people are in pain and grief and are crying out, 'Oh God, help me! I can't cope with this alone,' so this is a place we gather."

This beautiful blue angel took me by the hand and guided me through the large crowd. We weaved our way through the throng; it was as if the crowd parted to let us pass, and, although people must have noticed me moving, no one tried to stop me. We kept walking until we were at the very far side of the mourners gathered around the grave.

There at the edge of the group, by a headstone, was the spirit of Theresa, my relative who was being buried that day—I recognized her from the photo Mum had shown us the night before. Theresa was surrounded by some ten angels, maybe more; she was so beauti-, ful, much more so than in her photograph—like a beautiful daffodil, just glowing, with the light shining out of her. This beautiful spirit was being allowed to watch her own funeral. As I joined her she turned around and asked the angels who were with her to send more angels to comfort her grieving relatives. (The spirit of some-one who has just passed over can ask for the angels to console and help those who are left behind.)

As Theresa made this request, angels instantly flew to the side of everyone who was there in the graveyard—friends and acquain-tances as well as relatives. Each and every one was surrounded by an-gels. The angels were so gentle and kind, putting their hands on people's shoulders, whispering in their ears, rubbing them gently on the head. In one case I watched the angels embrace a person as if with human arms; I was told that this person had lost someone at an-other time and was secretly grieving for that loss, too.

I will always remember the beauty of what that blue angel showed me. She radiated such compassion and understanding; I have to laugh when I think how absurd it is that someone has to die in order for us to ask angels for help. We need not wait until we are desperate and in great pain to ask for this assistance; we should be asking every day, or every month, or once a year: "I want my angels with me through everything I do." This simple request will empower the angels to help us.

Ever since that day, whenever I am going past a graveyard, I glance in. I always see angels there. If there is a funeral going on the place will be full of angels, but even if there is just a single person there, they will be surrounded by angels giving them the comfort they require.

Some months after we moved into the new house Da came home from work with good news for me. It was autumn and still bright outside; it was probably around seven o'clock, or maybe later, because Da worked long hours. He followed his normal routine of going into the big, long sitting room, settling onto the couch, and turning on the TV to watch the news, and just relaxing after his long day. Sometimes I would watch him; I never told him I could see his angel there with him, or the energy field around him. At times I would see his energy take a sigh and droop down—that's the only way I can explain it. As he sat there, Mum would bring in his dinner from the kitchen and put it on a small wooden table so he could eat and watch the TV at the same time. This evening, though, he asked me, "Would you like to come and work with me in the gas station? You can see how you like it—it would be a start for you."

I was so delighted I could have kissed my da, but, as always, I held back. Da was a very good man and accepted me in a lot of ways; I always felt he *knew* something but he couldn't quite put his finger on it. But the angels had been telling me since I was a young child that there was a very real possibility that I would be locked up: I was continually warned by them that if I gave either of my parents any cause, I would be sent to a mental institution. Because of this I was never overemotional with Da, and I was very careful about how I behaved around him.

A few days later I started work. On that first day I had breakfast, said good-bye to Mum, and went off with Da in the car to the garage—The Grosvenor, as it was called. It was in Rathmines, a suburb of Dublin. It was a very good location for a garage: on a corner in the middle of a busy junction, with main roads to the right and left of it. The garage was a big old house, with a large forecourt and four gas pumps, a diesel pump, an air hose, and a water tap. The building was smelly and damp, literally falling down—reminding me of our house in Old Kilmainham. Part of it was used for offices, part for selling things like tires, tire repair kits, batteries, and other basic essentials for cars, and there was also a big room for tire repairs.

I was very excited on my first day, but also very nervous: I was scared that I might let Da down by doing something stupid or silly. I didn't want to disappoint him. But I needn't have worried; everyone was very nice and helpful, and the angels, of course, also helped. I learned how to do all kinds of different jobs: to pump gas, to sell things, and I also started to learn some of the office work. There were nine or ten people working there—all men except for a lovely lady called Anne, who took me under her wing from that first day. I got on very well with her and she taught me an awful lot.

My first day at work was great, and at the end of it I went home with Da quite happy with myself. I did wonder that day, and at other times, how it was that Da didn't notice that I had no problem pumping gas or giving back the right change, and yet he continued to think I was mentally deficient.

Shortly after I started work it was decided that the old garage would be demolished and a new one built. Early one Saturday or Sunday morning I sat in the car with Da and watched with fascination as they hit the old building with a big demolition ball until it tumbled down. Eventually, a wonderful new modern garage was built; there was a new shop, new gas pumps, and a very bright and nice new office with big windows out of which I could see into the shops and out onto the forecourt where the gas pumps were.

As always the angels showed me lots of things. One day they told me to watch a regular customer, a man called John, whom I knew well. "Watch him; he's going to steal from your da."

Da considered John a very wealthy man and an important customer, so I was shocked when the angels said this. I said, "Go away, he's not going to steal!"

"He is," they insisted. "You can watch—he won't see you."

I still didn't believe them. I watched John talk to Da and I heard him complimenting him on the new shop and all the different things he was selling. Da invited him to have a good look around, then went off to do something else. I was in the shop alone with John, but the angels told me he couldn't see me. I said, "Listen, angels, of course he can see me; I'm flesh and blood."

But they laughed at me and said, "No, he can't see you!"

Sometimes the angels tell me something but I don't understand it fully. But suddenly I understood: he couldn't see me because they had made me invisible to his eyes.

I watched as John walked around and looked at everything, including the new music cassette tapes that Da had got in (cassettes were expensive then). John picked up a cassette and put it in his pocket. I couldn't believe it.

"Why?" I asked the angels.

"It's something he does all the time," they replied. "He steals; stealing makes him feel as if he's got one up on someone else."

The angels explained that when John saw someone being successful or doing well, it made him envious and his response was to take something from them that he thought was of value.

"Should I tell my da?" I asked the angels.

Do you know what they replied? It might be hard to believe, but they told me, "No! Someday this man's conscience will get at him for all the things he has stolen in the past; but this is not the moment. This is not the right time. Just leave it."

I felt very sad; John had been coming into the garage for years. After that whenever he came into the shop I would follow him around, pretending to be cleaning.

One day I was in the office sitting at the desk with Anne and double-checking the figures in the ledger. Anne was a great secretary and she taught me a lot. Sometimes I was amazed with myself that I found the work so easy. The shop door opened and a man walked in. While I was serving him I noticed a quietness about him and a stillness in the air; I noticed, too, that he didn't talk much either. I gave him what he was looking for, said good-bye to him, and he left the shop.

As I walked into the office and back up to the desk there was not a sound to be heard; Anne did not move. I stood behind her to the left, looking out the window, and an angel put its hand on my shoulder. The forecourt looked empty; there was just one parked car beside one of the gas pumps. I looked down the street as far as I could see. I could not see around the corner, but then, all of a sudden, I was allowed to see: I saw young boys on bicycles cycling up the road toward the garage.

These boys were happy, laughing and joking with each other, reaching out and touching each other, having a good time. I could hear them talking to each other, but I could not hear clearly what they were saying. I stayed focused on them. A car passed them; as if in slow motion, everything else was completely still; it was as if I was right there with the boys on a bicycle myself. Then I saw a tractor trailor truck, coming up the road behind the boys. I held my breath. In that moment I knew what was going to happen next. The car was gone now and the truck and the boys were the only things moving.

The boys continued to enjoy their cycle, racing each other up the road, reaching out to each other and laughing. Everything was in slow motion again: the truck passed and as it did both the boys and the truck became luminous. They passed through each other like ghosts. The truck went around the corner and on up the road, the driver completely unaware of what had happened. There was no loss of continuity; everything flowed on. The boys were oblivious to what had just happened; it was as if they had never fallen. They had never noticed; they just carried on following the truck, enjoying their cycle. Then as the truck drove on an enormous circle of light appeared—it was as if it came from the back of the truck.

Suddenly the road was thronged with angels. The boys and their bikes were luminous and they were heading toward the light. As I watched, the bikes started to slowly rise above the ground, and the road became a beam of light, full of angels. It was a gentle crossover from one life, to be born into another life—they went straight to Heaven. Then the boys disappeared from my sight and everything returned to normal.

Suddenly a car drove into the garage and a man got out shouting, "Did you see in which direction the tractor trailor truck went?"

The man in the kiosk, Steven, shouted, "What's wrong?"

The man said there had been an accident: someone told him that the truck had gone off to the right. The man took off in his car again. Just then, another car passed the garage, moving very fast up the road. I just stood there, kind of dazed.

The shop door opened and I turned around. It was Da, saying there had been a terrible accident and asking me to make some tea. I was relieved to get out of the office and have a little bit of space. As I walked round to the canteen to make tea, I scolded the angels, saying, "Why did that have to happen?"

The answer I got was "Lorna, that is the way. Death for most humans is a continuous flow from one life to another, in perfect harmony. Remember, at the moment of death the boys felt nothing. It's the same even if someone has been sick and suffering; at the moment of death they don't feel any pain."

The angels comforted me while I made tea and continued working, but I was glad when the day was over and I could go home to Mum's baking. When I got home, I gave my mum a big hug. From that day on I was conscious of the importance of giving my mother a hug each day.

I knew I would have to pass the spot where the accident had happened. So one morning about a week later I got up the courage to walk down to the shops. I did not go there alone, as Angel Michael held my hand. As I walked across the forecourt of the garage he whispered in my ear, "Walk down to the hardware store; that will help you to focus; you will have somewhere to go to."

As I approached the spot where the accident had happened I could see bloodstains on the road. I was amazed and shocked. The accident had happened maybe a week before, and I never thought I would see bloodstains on the road; it was like a bolt of lightning hitting me. It may have been that the bloodstains were not there for everyone else to see; maybe only I could see them.

At the exact spot where the accident had happened I could hear the wailing cries of the mothers, fathers, and families of those boys. The emotion filled my body—tears ran from my eyes; it was overpowering. I asked God, "Please help the families. Let me take as much of their pain and grief as possible. Somehow let the parents know that their children are in Heaven with you. Please, God."

I was in a state of oblivion, completely unconscious of everything going on around me. Somehow the angels carry me through space and time; sometimes I wonder how I get from one spot to another. It is a mystery. Suddenly I was standing in front of the door of the hardware store. I felt the angels lift me out of spiritual space and put my feet back on firm ground. "It's done now, Lorna," Michael said. "God heard your prayer."

I walked through the doors into the hardware store and wandered around the shop, just to get myself grounded and back to normal. Then I walked back toward the garage again, past the accident spot. I knew I had taken away some of the families' pain and grief. I can't tell you which is worse: the pain within the physical body, or the pain within the emotional body. I will always do what God and the angels ask of me: if I can take pain away from another human being, I will do it. This is my life. It is part of the healing gift God has given me—to take on the suffering and pain of others. Some people might call it a curse, not a gift, that by taking on pain I can ease the pain of others. I'm like an intermediary, taking the pain and passing it on to God. At times the pain I feel might be overpowering, I may even think I am dying, but it won't kill me because God takes the pain from me. I don't know what God does with the pain; it is a mystery to me.

CHAPTER 7

A creature without a soul

One day when I was sixteen and had been working in the garage for about eighteen months, Elijah's vision came true.

I was in the office with Anne and my father, and from where I was sitting I could see straight out the big windows and over to the far side of the road, where there were some trees. I saw a young man in the distance, walking along that side of the road, and all of a sudden I recognized him.

I knew straightaway—even though he was a distance away—that this was the young man I was going to marry. I could hardly breathe. I knew he was going to cross the road and come into the garage, looking for a job.

I felt my hair being ruffled and I turned around to see my guardian angel standing there. I looked back out the window, and as I watched the man walking across the forecourt I could see his guardian angel faintly within the energy around him. The young man looked extremely handsome, with reddish fair hair. He was very tall, and I like tall men. I was extremely excited watching him; I knew what the outcome was going to be.

Despite this I turned and said to Anne, "Here's someone looking for a job. I hope he doesn't get it!" I have to laugh at that. I was fearful of this great change in my life—and also very shy. Deep down, though, I knew that he would get the job because it was what was meant to be.

The young man walked straight into the shop. Da looked up from the desk, saw him, and signaled that he would be with him in a moment. When Da went out to him I sat where I was, almost paralyzed. I just didn't want to be there, and I was trembling and shaking. All that Elijah had said flooded into my mind: this was the man I would marry, I would love him and he would love me, we would be happy together most of the time, but in the end I would take care of him and we wouldn't grow old together.

My father and the young man stood talking in the shop for some time. Eventually I started gathering up dirty cups and took them to the canteen to wash them. I walked past him as he was talking to my da. I secretly took a look at him. Oh, I did like what I saw! I took a long time washing the cups and making fresh tea. When I brought the tea back he was still talking to Da. I didn't know what to do. A customer came into the shop and I went and served him. I felt really nervous and just ignored the young man.

Of course, my father gave him a job and the next day he started work. I was introduced to him and I learned his name was Joe. I watched from a distance as he learned how everything worked, how to pump gas and mend flat tires. On the way home, at the end of Joe's first day, Da told me that he thought Joe was a very bright young man—a quick learner.

I tried to avoid Joe, but I couldn't help watching him surreptitiously, because I felt so attracted to him. I wondered if he noticed me, if he could feel the connection. The angels seemed to make sure that every time I went into the canteen to make tea or wash cups he was there. He would give me a radiant smile, and then my heart would know that he felt something too. I would smile back, but I wouldn't say much and would rush back out of the canteen as quickly as I could.

One day, about six months after he had come to work in the garage, Joe asked me out. As I was filling the kettle and rinsing out the cups in the canteen, Joe walked in and offered to help me wash up. I laughed at him and said there was no need—there were only three cups! Just as I was about to leave with the teapot and cups on a tray, Joe said, "Lorna, what would you think if I asked you for a date?"

I smiled at Joe. "Of course, I'd love to go out with you."

Joe suggested we go out that night, but I said no, I couldn't; it would have to be Friday after work.

"Okay, that'll be great," Joe said, as he held the door open for me.

"We'll talk about what we'll do on Friday night later," I said, as I walked through the open door.

I was so happy I was floating on air. The week seemed to pass very quickly and before I knew it, it was Friday. When I walked into the canteen that morning Joe was already there waiting for me. He gave me a big smile and asked, "Lorna, what would you like to do tonight?"

"I'd like to go to the pictures," I replied. "Let's meet at about half past six on O'Connell Bridge."

Joe suggested that I choose the film, but just then one of the other staff walked in, so we did not speak again that day. I asked Da could I finish work early that day—instead of staying until six, I wanted to leave about four. Da said okay and never asked me why. The angels had already told me that I would have to keep my date with Joe a secret.

At four o'clock I headed home on the bus. As I walked up the road to the house I was talking to my angels. "It's so exciting. I know nothing about any pictures that might be on in Dublin. It has been so long since I've been to the pictures—maybe two years. I don't care what film we see. I just want to be with Joe." The angels laughed. As I talked to them I was remembering all that the angel Elijah had told me.

When I arrived home I told Mum I was meeting a friend in Dublin and I was going to go to the pictures. Mum said, "Just make sure you're on the last bus home."

She didn't ask any questions, either, so I guess the angels were helping.

There was a newspaper on the table in the dining room, so I opened it and went straight to the film section. There were so many pictures on, I just picked one. I knew nothing about it, but I didn't care, and the angels didn't say anything either, so I assumed everything was okay. I have to laugh at that now.

It was a beautiful summer evening and O'Connell Bridge looked wonderful in the evening light, with its lamps and big flowerpots. Joe was a few minutes late, and as I stood there I watched what was going on around me. There was a woman and child begging from the many passersby rushing home after their day's work. There was a woman selling roses, but no one seemed to have the time to stop and buy. I could tell from the colors of the energy around the people what kind of humor they were in: whether they were in a hurry or full of excitement. Joe came from the opposite direction and tapped me on the shoulder. I jumped and he laughed as I turned around. I was so happy to see him. He took my hand and we went straight to the cinema.

The film I had chosen was called *The Virgin and the Gypsy*. The cinema was packed: lots of people were going to see this film, so we had no choice but to sit quite near the front. About ten minutes into the film I started squirming in my seat; this was not a film I wanted to see, certainly not with Joe on our first date. The sex scenes were very explicit. I was shocked. This kind of film was not common in Ireland at that time, back in the 1970s. Perhaps that's why there were so many people there!

After a few more minutes I told Joe I wanted to leave. We did, and Joe didn't mind at all; I think he felt as uncomfortable as I did.

We walked away from the cinema up O'Connell Street. It was such a beautiful evening that I was glad to be out of the cinema. Strolling hand in hand with Joe was a much nicer way of spending our first date. We talked as we went. One of the first things Joe said was that he was glad he hadn't chosen the picture! We both laughed.

We walked in front of the General Post Office—a beautiful grey-stone building I always loved. We nodded hello to the policeman standing guard outside. I noticed a couple kissing and cuddling, their angels tall and standing very close to them, as if they were helping them to join together. I smiled. Joe put his arm around me; it felt good. I felt safe in his company.

We crossed over the road at the traffic lights and went into a restaurant. I had never been in a restaurant at night before; this one was long and narrow with a tiled marble floor and the tables were enameled and screwed to the floor with high wooden benches on each side. The backs of the benches were about four feet high, so when you sat down you couldn't see who was at any other table. Joe must have known by the look on my face that I had never been in a restaurant like this before, and he told me that the tables were called booths. Just then the waitress came over with her pencil and paper and we ordered tea and sandwiches.

We talked about our parents—his father was dead. We talked about brothers and sisters—Joe was the youngest of his family and I was the second eldest of mine. Joe asked, "What do you think your da would say if he knew we were on a date together?"

"I am not sure about my da," I replied, "but I know Mum would more than likely object."

So we both agreed we would keep it secret.

We left the restaurant and walked the streets for a while, looking at the shop windows; then we walked down along the quays to the bus terminal. Joe lived in a different direction from me and would need to take a different bus; my bus had just pulled in but wasn't due to go for a few minutes, so we were happy to sit on the bus together for a while.

"You'd better go for your bus," I told Joe.

He got up and said he would be back in a minute. He talked to the bus conductor and then he came and sat back down beside me and said, "I'm going home with you on the bus. I'll walk you right up to your house."

The bus conductor had told him about an unofficial bus that was not on the timetable; it was known as "the ghost bus." It was a scheduled bus on its way out from Dublin to near my home, but on its return to the garage in the center of Dublin it was not meant to pick up any passengers. It did take passengers, though, and, from then on, whenever we went out Joe always brought me home and then got the ghost bus back into town and walked to his own house.

Joe and I didn't tell anyone we were going out with each other. Other girls my age might have shared the secret with a girlfriend, but I had no friends I confided in like that. Anyway, the angels told me that it was important it was kept a secret, and whenever they tell me this, even now I do as they say. I don't know if Joe told anyone; I never asked, but I don't think so.

While we were keeping our dating secret, Joe's sense of mischief meant he couldn't resist teasing me whenever the opportunity arose. He used to call me "Hercules" when I tried to lift a repaired tire into a customer's trunk (I'm five-foot-nothing tall) and he would tease me that the miniskirt of my uniform was way too short (he was proba- ·
bly right!).

Whenever I could I loved to go fishing with my father. It was something we had done every so often when I was a child, and it continued when I was working in the garage and going out with Joe. I didn't always bring my fishing rod, but I loved the opportunity to be in the quiet by a river, and I liked spending time with my da. One day we went fishing in the Wicklow Mountains. We set off early in Da's car and, as always, we brought a picnic with us. We also had a billy can, so that Da could light a fire and make tea.

It was a chilly day; we had been fishing for an hour or two and Da had caught a trout, when it started to rain. Nearby, on the river-bank, there was a cluster of trees with an old dilapidated house. Da suggested it would be a nice place to shelter, light a fire, and have our tea—we would be out of the cold. Da walked ahead of me, and as we got closer to the trees I noticed there was no light of energy around them and that the place looked very dull.

Angel Michael tapped me on the shoulder. "This place may frighten you," he said. "We're going to show you something that is bad. It won't harm you, but it will be aware of you as soon as you walk into that little house. It will respond to you angrily, but it won't touch you."

Until then I had been protected from seeing anything evil.

"Is it a ghost?" I asked.

"No, Lorna, this is a different sort of creature," Michael replied.

Da called out to hurry and I looked up. He was some distance ahead and had climbed up onto a bank in front of the house. When I turned around to talk to Michael again he had disappeared.

I ran and caught up with Da. We walked among the trees sur-rounding the house. Everything around the house seemed dead to me—there were no leaves on the trees, and no grass or flowers growing nearby. The door to the little house was ajar, hanging off its hinges with pieces of board missing. Part of the roof and some of the windows were also gone. Da went in; there an old broken wooden table and chairs there. To me it felt as cold as ice inside, but Da didn't seem to notice; he went straight to the fireplace.

I stood there, just inside the door. I could not move. I just kept saying to myself, "Oh, my God, oh, my angels." I could see a creature near the fireplace, to the right. It was unlike anything I have seen before or since: it looked like melted wax, about three feet long and about as thick as a large man's chest. It was horrible and horrific looking. I couldn't say that it had a mouth or eyes.

I knew Da couldn't see or feel anything. He gathered pieces of debris from the floor and piled them into the fireplace and struck a match. The fire exploded immediately—it was a big and noisy explosion and came out into the room. The creature had massive energy. It was just throwing off evil! It was very angry; it had been keeping that place for itself and it didn't want us there. As far as it was concerned, we were trespassing.

Just after the fire exploded, one of the chairs moved and went flying across the room, hit the far wall, and broke.

Da jumped and ran for me and the door, grabbing his bag as he went. He pulled me out the door and we ran as fast as we could through the trees, back down along the banks of the river. We were both scared out of our wits and ran faster than we had ever run before in our lives. Da was faster and dragged me behind him. Eventually, out of breath, we slowed down. The rain had stopped and the sun had come out; I felt its warmth on my face.

Silently Da tried to light a campfire. His hands were shaking and he was having difficulty lighting it. I was watching Da, waiting for him to say something. I spoke to the angels without words and asked them to calm Da down. After some minutes Da got the fire going, and when the billy can boiled he made tea. We ate our sandwiches in silence.

Eventually Da said, in a trembling voice, "I'm sorry for frightening you like that, Lorna. I got a big fright myself. I don't really know what it was, but the only thing I've ever heard of that moves chairs around is a poltergeist, and I've never heard of anything making a fire explode like that."

Da knew a lot about fires and he was very careful about how he handled them. I think the fire exploding had scared him more than the chair moving.

I never said a word; I just continued drinking my tea. I didn't want my da to know how frightened I had been. I had been terrified—even though deep down I knew we would be safe because the angels were minding us.

As I sat by the fire Michael touched my shoulder, although he didn't appear to me. Michael said Da was right. The creature I had seen was a poltergeist. He explained to me that poltergeists are creatures without souls that belong to Satan. Sometimes people invite them in. They can do this by experimenting with black magic or Ouija boards, or other things like that. Poltergeists, Michael told me, are sly creatures. They creep in wherever they are given an opportunity, and they can cause enormous destruction.

Da and I finished lunch in silence. Da suggested we continue fishing on another stretch of river. Being honest, we both wanted to get out of there! Fishing calmed us down, and later on we even caught fish for dinner.

As we enjoyed eating the fish at home that night we didn't make any mention of what had happened during the day. Da and I never spoke of it again.

CHAPTER 8

The intermediary

One afternoon while I was washing my hands at the sink in the garage toilets I looked in the mirror and an angel appeared—just her face at first. She startled me and I jumped. As I stepped back the mirror on the wall seemed to disappear and the angel came into full view. Her radiant light filled the place.

The angel spoke before I did; she called my name.

"Lorna, call me Angel Elisha."

As she said this she reached out and took my hands in hers. Her hands felt like feathers, and when I looked down at them they resembled feathers, too, but they had a completely human shape.

I'm referring to Elisha as a she because she appeared to me as a female, but angels are in fact neither male nor female as we are; they are sexless beings. They only appear in a human form to help us to accept them and so that we will be less afraid. They change their appearance to be female or male so as to make us feel more at ease, or to help us to understand more clearly the message they are bringing.

I said earlier that the angels told me a little about Elijah while I was writing this book, and at the same time they told me that Elisha is the prophet to whom the prophet Elijah gave his mantle shortly before he ascended to heaven in a chariot. Elisha is a man in the Old Testament.

"Angel Elisha, why are you here? Is something going to change in my life?" I asked.

"Yes, Lorna," she said. "You are going to get a new job. I'm going to help your mum meet an old acquaintance of hers, and you'll get a new job in a department store in Dublin."

I was about to ask Angel Elisha when this was going to happen when someone knocked on the toilet door. I shouted, "I'll be out in a minute."

Angel Elisha put her feathered finger to her mouth and disappeared.

I was very excited at the idea of getting a new job, even if it meant that I wasn't going to be able to see Joe every day. I felt that working somewhere other than the garage would give me a lot more independence from my parents, and it would help them to see that I was capable of doing things on my own. While I was in the garage under my father's protection, they couldn't see this.

Some weeks later I was out in the back garden feeding my rabbit when Mum suggested I ask Da for a day off.

"It has been a long time since we've been shopping together," she said. "We can browse around the shops and then maybe have lunch in Arnotts department store."

"I would love that," I said.

The next day I asked Da about having that Thursday off and he told me that Mum had already asked him, so it was all settled.

The angels make me laugh and smile a lot. I knew all of this had to do with Angel Elisha: she had manipulated the situation, putting thoughts into Mum's head. I could see the plot unfolding and I had no doubts in my mind that it would all come about; it made me feel good to know that my mum was listening to her angels.

The anticipation was almost too much to bear—knowing what the outcome of the shopping trip with Mum in Dublin would be. That Thursday we went into the city by bus. The city was quite busy, with all the usual hustle and bustle. Mum and I visited many department stores along O'Connell Street, Henry Street, and Mary Street and we browsed through many beautiful things. Mum always loved looking at the china section, so I managed to escape for a while, pretending to look at other things.

Then I heard Elisha say, "Look at your mum, Lorna."

I looked down along the aisle to where Mum was standing, looking at china. I saw two shining beings; one was Mum's guardian angel, but the biggest surprise was seeing my spirit brother, Christopher. It had been so long since I had seen my spirit brother—many years. I was thrilled to see him; I wanted to run down and take his hand like we did when I was a child in Old Kilmainham, but my guardian angel held my feet fast to the ground. (He does that when he knows I am overwhelmed and he doesn't want me to move.)

Christopher turned to me and smiled; then he turned back to my mother and started to whisper in her ear. Now I knew how my mother was able to hear the angels—it was because Christopher was acting as an intermediary.

"Angel Elisha," I said, "I would love to tell Mum that Christopher is standing there with her."

"You can't, Lorna," she replied.

"But he is so magnificent, so beautiful," I said, pleading with her. Just then light engulfed my spirit brother, Christopher. He was enveloped in a light emanating from my mother's guardian angel. It touched me very deeply; it was one of the most magnificent sights I had ever seen.

Mum turned around and called me, and as I walked toward her the light around her became brighter and brighter. Then the angels disappeared, but I knew they were still there.

"Let's go and have lunch over in Arnotts department store," Mum said. We went in and, as usual, there was a big queue in the restaurant. We got our lunch and found a table to sit down. Mum talked about all the lovely things she had seen. She had bought some spoons and a plate that had a little flaw. While we were having lunch Mum said, "We will get the two o'clock bus home; we will have just enough time to go to one more department store on Mary Street."

As soon as we were finished lunch we walked down to Mary Street. As I pushed open the doors Angel Elisha was standing just inside. The whole place felt vibrant to me. I could feel the energy; something good was going to happen for me, and there would also be a surprise for my mum.

Mum had turned to go to the sweater department when a man approached her. He was small and skinny and was wearing a suit. Mum didn't seem to recognize him, but he recognized her and called her by name. He introduced himself and there was a look of surprise on my mum's face.

"Surely," he said to her, "you must remember me. I lived a few doors up the road from you. We even went out together on a few occasions."

All of a sudden Mum's face lit up as she recognized him. They talked and laughed. Mum seemed to forget all about me standing there beside her. Then the man asked Mum, "Who is this young lady with you, Rose? Is this your daughter?"

"Yes," my mum replied, "this is Lorna."

Just then my spirit brother, Christopher, whispered in Mum's ear and without hesitation these words came out of Mum's mouth: "Lorna is looking for work; she's been working with her Da for the last two years and could do with a change."

The man turned to me and said, "Lorna, see where the stairs are? Go up the stairs to reception and ask for an application form. Fill it in and take it to the office. Ask to speak to Phyllis."

I did as he said. I knocked on the office door and asked to speak to Phyllis; I was feeling nervous and asked the angels to stay close to me. The lady in the office asked to see my application form. She told me the manager was not in the office and sent me back down the stairs to find her. She told me to turn left, go down the little corridor, and then I'd see a door on the left. I thanked her and went back down the stairs, took a left turn down a little corridor, and knocked on the office door, which was slightly ajar. I called out, "Hello?"

"Come in, the door is open," a woman's voice replied.

I opened the door fully and looked into the office. It was quite dark, and inside, sitting at a desk, was a small, middle-aged lady. I noticed you could see right across the shop floor because the front of the office was made of glass. Angel Elisha was standing there with the lady, so that made me feel more at ease. The lady introduced herself and said she was the manager of the store.

"What can I do for you?" she asked.

I told her that the manager on the shop floor had sent me to see her. She asked to look at my application form and asked if I had ever worked for anyone other than my da.

"No, this would be my first job outside of the garage," I replied.

She told me that I was lucky; there were a few vacancies and I could start the following Monday. She told me to come straight to her office at nine o'clock on Monday morning and if she was not there she would be on the shop floor. She would show me to the department I was to work in and have one of the girls show me the ropes. We shook hands and I said good-bye.

I was so delighted I nearly danced down the stairs. A new job—and in a fashion store—I was thrilled. I was singing praise and thanks to all my angels. When I got back to where Mum was I found her still in conversation with her friend. I noticed then that he looked a lot older than my mum. He turned to me and asked how I had got on with Phyllis.

"I start work on Monday," I replied.

"Great," he said. He and Mum spoke for another couple of minutes and then he said he had to go.

I met Joe the next evening and told him about my new job. He was delighted for me, even though he said he would miss seeing me at work every day. He told me "absence makes the heart grow fonder," and he agreed that not working for Da would make me a lot more independent. Joe and I were so close by now that working in the same place or not made little difference. We were spending an awful lot of time together, but we were still keeping our relationship secret from everyone.

On Monday morning I walked into the store. It looked so empty, although there were a lot of staff on the floor. The store manager was there, so I walked up to her. She told me to follow her down to the cloakrooms, which I did, even though I was extremely nervous and afraid. This was my first job away from family, completely on my own. She introduced me to Frances, who was in charge of one of the ladies fashion sections—skirts—and I was to be her new assistant.

I was very apprehensive that first day, and I was particularly concerned about the lunch break, but I needn't have worried: a girl called Pauline, who was much the same age as me and worked in the same department, came over to me during the morning and told me that we were both on the same lunch break and invited me to join her. She showed me the ropes and we became good friends.

From the beginning I very much enjoyed working there. I liked dealing with people and I loved the atmosphere of the shop. The management was decent, and quite caring. I was in my element working in the fashion department; I soon learned everything there was to know about skirts and, sometimes, when the skirt department was not too busy, I would help out in other ladies sections.

CHAPTER 9

The Angel of Death

After only a few weeks in my new job, the angels brought my attention to a young man called Mark who worked in the handbag department. He was tall and thin with wavy brown hair and brown
eyes and he always seemed to wear a brown suit. At times when I
looked over at him I would see a soft, subtle light around him.

One afternoon when the shop was quiet I stood watching Mark
from across the floor and I saw an angel appear behind him. This was
not a guardian angel I was seeing—the vibrancy and light surrounding him was completely different from that of a guardian angel. This
angel was elegant, slender, and extremely tall.

I knew there was something very different about what I was seeing. The angel turned and looked at me with compassion on his face.
Then he stood behind Mark and leaned forward over the young
man's shoulders and reached into his body and touched his soul. I
saw him lift Mark's soul very gently, like a newborn baby, and rock
it forward and backward through his body with gentleness and compassion. The young man seemed to stand there, very still, as if in a
trance, totally unaware of what was going on.

I started to cry, but I didn't know why. I was full of emotion, but
I didn't know what it was about. I felt a tap on my shoulder. It was
Angel Hosus. I turned and looked at him. He put his hands up to my

face to wipe away the tears that were filling my eyes. He told me to find an excuse to go to the storeroom and he would meet me there.

I looked around to see where the manager was; to my relief he was standing at the back entrance of the store, talking to a security guard. I told him I was going to the stock-room.

I went into the storerooms through the two heavy doors that, when pushed swung open and then closed behind you as you walked through. The rooms were packed with boxes everywhere. I made my way through them then up the big stone spiral staircase. The fashion department storeroom was three flights up on the top floor. I ran up the stairs as fast as I could and pushed a small door open. The room was poorly lit and was full of racks and boxes of clothes.

I looked down along the racks; they were as high as the ceilings. But I couldn't see Hosus. Knowing no one else was there, I called out his name. I walked down the last aisle of racks and there he was, sitting on a box in the corner, waiting for me. My heart lifted when I saw him.

"Angel Hosus," I said as I sat down, "I need to know about the angel I saw. What is going to happen to that young man?"

Hosus reached out and took my hand. "I can only tell you a little. The angel you saw was different; he is the Angel of Death. This angel does not appear unless someone is going to die in extraordinary circumstances. The Angel of Death does everything in his power to try to prevent it from happening, and he has many angels working with him. You can be sure, for instance, that when an agency is planning an atrocity that will destroy innocent life, the Angel of Death will have been trying for a long time to convince the people involved that God does not want this to happen. There should not be war, but peace, and only peace. The Angel of Death works everywhere— even among the very highest level of government—to prevent the taking of innocent life, especially in times of war. The Angel of Death works extremely hard trying to convince people, but do they listen to the angels? Sometimes, maybe, but not always!"

Before this if I had thought of an angel called the Angel of Death I would have envisioned an angel carrying nothing but disaster, pain, and anguish; yet this angel was full of love and compassion.

I thanked Hosus and went back to work. I had learned when not to ask more.

We are all brought up to fear the Angel of Death, but the Angel of Death is for life. The Angel of Death is a good angel who fights on behalf of the living and for what is right and good.

From that point onward I became much more aware of Mark; every time I looked at him I also saw the Angel of Death. I know he had a guardian angel with him, too, but I was never shown it. Every day my attention was being drawn to him; it was as if I was watching over him, trying to intercede for him so that maybe, somehow, things would change and the angels would be listened to.

Normally two other girls worked with Mark in the handbag department, but one day, to my surprise, I discovered he was aware of me watching him. Sometime later he came to my department and asked the floor manager if he could borrow me for a while, to work on the handbag counter. I knew this was not Mark's doing; it was the angels; they had whispered in Mark's ear and he had listened to them. They wanted Mark and me to spend some time together.

As the months passed my heart was really heavy. I learned more about him from the other girls. He had a girlfriend in Northern Ireland and he traveled by bus and train to visit her every weekend. I kept hoping that everything would be okay, but my angels were still asking me to help him, so in my heart and soul I knew he was not safe.

The shop was always very busy, especially at the weekends, and several times a year there were sales. These sales were always packed—mostly with women, and some of them would bring young children and babies in strollers. During the sales the staff spent most of their day picking up clothes from the floor, where they had been dropped by women in their frantic efforts to find bargains. It was difficult to keep the clothes off the floor. It was chaotic and there was a constant queue at the cash register, but I quite enjoyed the sales, because I was always busy and the day passed very quickly. I also liked helping people.

One particular Saturday during a sale I was squeezing in between customers, trying to hang skirts back on the rails, when I felt a pull on my uniform. I looked down and to my amazement I saw two little angels. They were childlike in appearance, about two feet tall with wings. They were bathed in a beautiful bright light and joy poured from them; they were so bubbly they sparkled. I had seen angels like this before, and every time I see them they make me feel like a child myself; these little angels touch the child within me; they fill me with joy, happiness, and laughter.

As I looked down, one of the little angels said, "Come quickly, Lorna! You must follow us."

They guided me through the crowd to the other end of the fashion department. The little angels disappeared into the crowd but I could still hear them calling to me.

"Underneath the blouse rack, Lorna, look underneath the blouse rack," they said.

When I reached the blouse rack I stood there looking at all these women searching through the blouses, frantic to find what they wanted and practically fighting over things. I was shocked that they were so aggressive. The little angels had said "underneath the rack," so I knew where to look. I knew there had to be a young child under there.

I was pushing my way in between the women, excusing myself and pretending to tidy the blouses, when I felt a little hand touch my ankle. I bent down, pushing some women away, and picked up a little child. I walked away from the crowd, and within no time at all a mother came over and told me it was her child I was holding. I said that this was a very dangerous place to leave a young child unattended, but she ignored me, took the child from my arms, and walked away.

The two little angels looked very sad. I said to them, "That mother just isn't listening."

The two little angels asked me to follow this mother and child and keep an eye on her. The little angels also followed them, and I could see the mother's guardian angel whispering in her ear.

I tried to look out for them, but it was very difficult as customers were constantly asking me for help. There was pandemonium everywhere. Every chance I got I would look for the mother and her child, and the little angels helped me by sending up a beam of light. Whenever I saw this beam of light I felt relieved. Suddenly the little angels were pulling at my clothes again.

"Come quickly! Something is about to happen and we may not be able to stop it if the mother doesn't listen to us," they said.

I followed the little angels as quickly as I could. To my amazement, they left a trail of sparkling light behind them as they disappeared into the crowd. I could actually see through the crowd because, from the waist down, they had become transparent to me. In among this crowd of women I could see where the little child was standing. As I approached I called out, "Be careful of that child!"

The women around the rack were so engrossed in their search for a bargain that they did not hear me; they were not listening. I could see what was about to happen, but I could not prevent it. I wanted to reach out, I wanted to stop it. Many hands were pulling garments from hangers—this way and that—and, in doing so, one of the women accidentally pulled a hanger across the child's face, catching the corner of the child's eye and pulling it from its socket.

I saw one of the little angels put a hand up to the child's eye; even though the eye was out of the socket the angel's touch prevented the hanger from ripping the eye away altogether. The child started to scream, and when the mother saw what had happened she screamed too, grabbed her child, and held her in her arms. I reached the mother and child and stretched out and touched her, asking God to intercede and save her eye.

A voice cried out, "Somebody call for an ambulance!"

It was very hard to look at the child, with her eye hanging out of its socket and the little angels holding the eye to prevent the threads from breaking. To see such caring and tenderness is to know that we are loved; even at difficult times when we think nobody cares, that nobody loves us, the angels are there. Always remember: angels' love is unconditional.

The child continued to scream, and the manager rushed over and took the mother and child up to the office.

I heard later from the floor manager that they had been able to save the little girl's eye.

Joe and I were falling in love and we continued to grow closer. I started to go to Joe's mother's house most evenings after work. She always gave me a great welcome and made me feel part of the family. She was a tall, well-built woman with curly hair and she always had a smile on her face. I talked with her a lot; I would sit at her kitchen table while she was cooking and she would never let me lift a hand. I loved talking with her. One particular conversation made me feel very happy: she told me she was glad that Joe had met such a nice young woman, that this was something she had always prayed for and that she would love to see the two of us get married and have children. She told me that seeing her younger son settled with a wife would leave her with no worries. She told me not to tell him this, though, that it was only between her and me.

Joe would come home to his mother's about an hour after me and we would all have dinner together. Joe's mother was a great cook, and I loved her bacon and cabbage and apple tarts. After dinner Joe and I would go to the bus stop, hoping to catch the ten o'clock bus into the city and then another bus to Leixlip, where I lived. When I think of it now, we spent an awful lot of time traveling on buses.

I still hadn't told my parents about Joe, although we had now been going out together for more than a year. Strange as it may seem, my mother never asked where I was in the evenings—perhaps she presumed I was working late all the time. I was a little apprehensive of what Da might think, whether he would approve or not, but I did know that Da really liked Joe. My big fear was what my mother would say when she found out.

It was normal practice to work late restocking the racks one or two nights a week. We worked out a roster for a two-week period and I usually worked Thursday and Friday evenings; some of the girls didn't want to work Fridays, but I didn't mind because I saw Joe most evenings, and he often had to work late on a Friday, too. Sometimes I would also work on Wednesday evenings, depending on how busy the store was. Often I would find Mark working late on the same evenings as me. The Angel of Death was always visible to me, constantly holding on to Mark's soul. Mark was so happy he just beamed with life, but in my conversation with the angels they told me they had lost the battle.

One day I was working at the cash register with Valerie, one of the girls I was friendly with, folding clothes and putting them into bags and Mark did something he had never done before. He came over to talk to us. He told us all about his girlfriend, how she was from Northern Ireland and he was going to see her at the weekend. He told us that he was crazy about her, that she was the best thing that had ever happened to him and that in the future he hoped to marry her.

I saw his beautiful angel holding him as if he were the most precious human being in the world and I started to tremble. The Angel of Death did not want to take Mark, but he would be left with no choice because people were not listening to their angels. I could hear the angel clearly speaking to me; I could have reached out and touched the Angel of Death as well as Mark, but I was told not to. Then Mark said he had to go.

I turned to Valerie and told her I had to go to the loo. I ran out of the shop, out the back door, and into the loo. I sat there and cried. Eventually, I plucked up the courage to go back to work, all the while scolding the angels and demanding to know why they could not stop this from happening. I felt devastated that nothing was changing and people were not listening.

After I'd been working in the store about a year I was asked to work late one day, and I agreed. I knew I had to be there: Mark was working late as well. As I worked I watched Mark and his angel and I prayed. I could feel Mark's great joy and happiness, the great love he had for his girlfriend. I felt so sure that he was now engaged, that he was imagining his future with his girlfriend; that's what he was living for.

Everyone else had gone home, only the floor manager, Mark, and I were left. The manager came up to me and asked if I was finished. I told him I needed about five minutes. When I finished stocking the racks I started to walk toward the cloakroom. I looked back to see Mark at the handbag counter. I hurried down the stairs to the cloakroom to get my coat, and then went back up the stairs quickly in the hope of getting another glimpse of Mark. I did—he was talking to the manager. I knew that would be the last time I would ever see him.

The shop door closed behind me. As I walked out through the car park and through the lanes at the back of the department store I was still scolding the angels. I felt so helpless. All of a sudden angels appeared in a brilliant light, surrounded me, and reached in and took my soul from my body. From that moment on I remember nothing.

I don't remember my journey home or anything else that evening. Upon waking up the next morning, I knew that the angels had transported my soul so that I could be with Mark spiritually, leaving my body and soul connected by a thread.

As I got out of the bed my body felt so light that I could hardly feel the floor beneath my feet. I felt very still and quiet in myself. I got dressed slowly and went downstairs. I was very weak and unwell. In the kitchen Mum asked if I was okay and told me that I looked very pale.

I poured myself a cup of tea, took a slice of toast, and went out into the back garden, tea and toast in hand, to check on my pet rabbit. This was only an excuse; I did not want to worry Mum. I said good-bye to her and headed down the road to the bus, and then I noticed two angels, one at either side of me—they were carrying me.

I smiled and said, "Thank you, angels. Please help me to feel a little bit better, physically, or I won't make it through the day."

I could hear the angels whispering in my ear, "Don't worry, Lorna. We're taking care of you."

There were a dozen or more people waiting for the bus as I walked across the road to the bus stop. As I approached I was saying to the angels, "Please let me get a seat. I won't be able to stand."

Within minutes the bus arrived; it was crowded but I got a seat at the very back. I fell asleep and was awoken by rustling—the man sitting directly in front of me was reading the morning paper. The headline read: "Young man gunned down in Dublin City." I closed my eyes; I was devastated.

When the bus reached the terminal, I got off with a crowd and walked across the bridge toward Mary Street. I kept walking, and as I was passing a shop called Hector Greys, there was a radio blaring. I heard the newscaster saying, "A young man has been gunned down."

I started to run, and as I entered the lane alongside the department store the tears were running down my cheeks. There was no one else around. To my horror, I saw chalk marks on the ground and torn yellow tape—this is where Mark had been murdered, where he had been gunned down. There was no one there; no police, nobody! I felt as if nobody cared. I felt so cold and completely overwhelmed.

Everyone at work was talking about it. I kept myself away from all of them so I wouldn't have to listen. I couldn't avoid it, though. People thought it was a sectarian murder. This was the early 1970s, when there was awful violence in Northern Ireland, with Catholics killing Protestants and Protestants killing Catholics, simply because of religion. Mark was a Catholic, and his girlfriend in Northern Ireland was a Protestant. Sometimes this violence spilled over into the Republic of Ireland. The angels told me that this was why he was killed—the Angel of Death worked hard to get those involved to listen, but he didn't succeed.

One thing I do know about Mark, though, is that he went straight to Heaven. Remember, I had seen his soul when the angel stooped over and touched it; his soul was beautiful, blue and crystal clear without a stain. When he died the angels were there with him and especially the Angel of Death—as were some members of his family who had gone before him—and they all gently took Mark straight to Heaven.

When lunchtime came that day I called Joe and asked him to meet me after work at the back entrance to the store. I told him that I was off work the next day and we could go out that night. I still felt terrible and I needed his arm around me, to make me feel a little better. I was also very weak and felt unable to walk as far as the bus stop. I've never forgotten Mark.

CHAPTER 10

The bombers

Joe and I loved the weekends. Every four weeks I would have a long weekend off work, and Joe arranged with Da to have those weekends off, too, whenever he could. I teased him that he was lucky to work for my father. We always planned the weekends ahead of time; some of our favorite places to go were the Dublin Mountains, the Wicklow Mountains, and Brittas Bay, a beautiful beach along the coast, south of Dublin.

Traveling on the bus home with Joe one evening he said, "How about going to the Sally Gap in the Wicklow Mountains this weekend?" So when Sunday morning came around Joe arrived at my house at nine o'clock sharp. I met him across the road, around the corner, where my family couldn't see us. I had packed a picnic of ham and cheese sandwiches, apples, and a bar of chocolate. He gave me a big kiss and said, "Let's go," and we headed straight down to the bus stop—just in time, too, as the bus was coming.

When the bus reached the Wicklow Mountains everyone got off and seemed to be walking in the same direction we were. I was surprised to see so many couples and families with children. I said to Joe that I didn't realize this area was so popular. That day we walked about a mile to a place high up and full of enormous rocks. It was fabulous: mountains all around us, the fresh air so clear and crisp. We clambered over the big rocks, something I loved doing, but Joe had to help me frequently as they were gigantic and I am tiny, but they were no problem for Joe. We had a lot of fun.

We sat down on one of the big rocks and had our picnic and we talked for hours, sitting there, soaking up the sun, admiring the beauty of the mountains. Eventually we packed what was left of our picnic into the bag; Joe took the bag from me and put his arms around me. As we were about to climb down off the rock, something happened that was a great surprise to me. Joe's angel appeared behind him, at his right and about one step behind him. I smiled at the angel and it said, "Lorna, see where the sun is shining on that little lake. Go there."

Joe asked, "What is that great smile for?"

I couldn't tell him that I was smiling at his angel; I still hadn't gotten up the courage to tell him that I could see angels and other things. I was afraid of his reaction.

"Look over there," I said, "where the light from the sun is shining on that small group of trees and rocks. Is that a tiny little lake I see?"

"How come we didn't see that before now?" asked Joe.

We walked in the direction of the little lake, and when we reached it we met a couple who were having a picnic and they invited us to share a cup of tea with them. We all sat together and talked and laughed on the shore of the little lake.

The angels allowed me to see beautiful things that day. It would have been wonderful if I had been allowed to share my secret with Joe then, and if the angels had allowed him to see what followed, but it was not to be.

The lake was like a sheet of glass; the reflections of the trees bounced off the water, as did the reflection of a kingfisher who flew across the lake. I could see another kingfisher moving under the water, then its reflection as it rose out of the water, showing an iridescent flash of the colors of the rainbow. It bounced up, breaking through the surface of the lake, causing a ripple and almost touching the end of the other bird's tail. It looked like there was more than one bird; it was as if there were a multitude of birds flying behind.

Then the angels said, "Lorna, it's time to go."

I told Joe it was starting to get dark and that we had better head back. The couple with us said that they had a compass and knew a different way back and they suggested we should walk together.

We did. I don't know how long it took us to get back to the bus stop, but I was exhausted when we got there. Joe, gentleman as ever, came all the way to my front door, gave me a good-night kiss on the cheek, and ran down to catch the "ghost bus" back into Dublin. I asked the angels to protect Joe so he would get home safely. I also asked the angels to keep Joe well: Joe appeared to be full of beans, full of energy, but I could see the organs of his body had shriveled slightly in size and seemed to have a grey look about them. The change was slight, but it was clear to me. I feared this was the beginning of the ill health that Elijah had spoken about.

The day came when my mother finally found out that I was going out with Joe. I was off work, and I was doing a few jobs around the house for Mum and spending some time with my rabbit, Isabel. My sister Emer was there that afternoon too, and, as usual, Mum more or less ignored me. All of my life I have noticed that if I walked into the room when one of my sisters or brothers was talking with my mum, they would stop talking. If I stayed in the room or sat down and joined them, the conversation would stop altogether. Sometimes I felt sad that my family did not want to share with me.

Joe and I had a date at six-thirty, so later that afternoon I came in from the garden to get ready. Mum was in the kitchen and she asked me where I was going. I told her I was going to catch the five o'clock bus and continued on through the hall and up the stairs.

When I was in the bedroom I heard Mum and my sister coming up the stairs. I shared the bedroom with my sister, so I thought she was going to come in, but she didn't. They went into Mum's bedroom. I could hear them talking, but I was too excited about meeting Joe to take any notice. Now I realize that Mum must have been quizzing Emer. As I came out of the bedroom they were both standing on the landing. Emer looked at me guiltily.

"What's wrong?" I asked.

Mum screamed at me, "Where do you think you're going?"

I was shocked! I had never seen Mum this way before. I told her I was going to Dublin. Mum shouted back at me, demanding to know was it true that I was going out with one of the gas station attendants in my da's garage? She was going ballistic. "You're going out with that Joe! How long has this been going on for? I want to know! It ends right now!"

Mum was extremely upset. I looked at Mum and said in a very clear voice, "I have been going out with Joe for months now, and I'm going to continue to go out with him. Now I'm going to meet him."

As I turned to go down the stairs Mum grabbed my arm firmly and started to pull at me.

"How dare you shame us by going out with someone lower-class!" she shouted.

I was really shocked at how upset she was—this was a part of my mother I had never seen before. To her mind, Joe was beneath us. I looked at Mum for a moment and then continued down the stairs. She grabbed my arm and pulled hard. "You are not going for that bus to meet that young man Joe."

I could see Mum's guardian angel standing behind her in tears; some of the teardrops fell on Mum's head. Now that Da was doing well and we had a house of our own, Mum had forgotten that we as a family had once been homeless, that we had once considered ourselves lucky to be given a council house. We had been poor, like so many other families in Ireland at that time. Perhaps what made it worse for Mum was that she came from a well-off family, and then felt she had married beneath her.

She held on to me so tightly. "Let go of my arm, you're hurting me," I cried. "I don't want to miss the bus. You'll have to accept the fact that Joe and I are going out together."

Mum's beautiful angel bent over her and embraced her whole body, and just then Mum let go of my arm.

"Mum, I love you."

I continued down the stairs, out the hall door, and ran down the road to the bus. As I sat on the bus, I thought about my mum and her guardian angel.

Joe was standing at the bus stop in Dublin, waiting for me. I was so happy to see him that I gave him a big hug, but I never told him how upset I was. I never—then or ever—told Joe what Mum had said, because I knew it would hurt him.

We strolled in the direction of a nearby pub, Maguire's, which had a music night—I always loved hearing music. Joe had a pint of Guinness; I seldom drank alcohol and had a 7Up. Slowly the music and having Joe's arm around me calmed me down, but I didn't forget about my mother, and her guardian angel.

A few days later Da spoke to me. "I hear from your mum that you and Joe are a couple."

He had noticed something between us, but had no idea. "God! You kept that a big secret."

Da said that all that mattered was that I was happy. Da did a lot for Joe: he helped him to learn the business and encouraged him to move on in life, which was great for us. Mum never spoke to me again about what had happened that day—it was as if it had never happened.

Sometimes the angels give me visions to prepare me for things that are going to happen, and then everything around me just vanishes.

It's like being transported to another time and place. Sometimes it is like having a flickering television screen in front of me; other times it's like a film going very fast. Sometimes this is very difficult for me because I am unable to understand what is happening. The "film" might stop for a brief second, then I might see a person or a place.

One spring morning when the weather should have been getting brighter and sunnier I got out of bed and dressed for work. I drew back the curtains of my bedroom window and looked out. Everything seemed to have a touch of grey about it: It was as if grey paint was being sprayed into the atmosphere and was covering everybody and everything. I stood there for a moment, looking out the window. A neighbor came out of his house, said good-bye to his wife at the door, and walked toward his car and was driving away. He, his car, and everything around him had a touch of grey. Another car came down the road and it too was covered in the same grey-ness. A young man ran past the house, and although the atmosphere around him danced, it was also grey.

I went downstairs, made myself some tea, and gave Tiger, the cat, some milk. As I left for work I shouted good-bye up the stairs. Walking down to the bus stop I called my angels but they did not appear to me physically. I asked them, "Why does everything look so strange?"

"Don't worry, we are protecting you," they whispered.

As I approached the main road I saw the bus and I ran to catch it. It was crowded but I managed to get a seat. I felt very strange: I was starting to feel stillness and silence creeping up on me. The people on the bus, also, had that touch of grey about them. Even the bus itself did not feel right; nothing looked real. When the bus pulled into the bus stop on the quays by the River Liffey, I called my angels again. They didn't answer me.

As I walked through the doors at the back entrance to work I felt so light—it was like everything was happening in slow motion. I saw some staff and managers already working. Only then did I notice that nobody had an angel with them, not even on the bus! I was shocked, and I felt myself tremble.

The department store also looked grey. I went down to the cloakroom, hoping I would see guardian angels with some of the girls I worked with, but the cloakroom looked the same as in the store— the girls there had no angels with them either, even though I knew they must be there.

I kept calling on my angels, but they didn't seem to be answering me. I left the cloakroom and went upstairs to the shop floor. I stood in the fashion department, at one of the racks, looking toward the main entrance. I watched the manager of the store and a security guard open the doors and saw the customers start to walk into the store. Slowly I started to see guardian angels with people, but the angels did not look their usual selves; their "radiance" had disappeared and they were dull—they seemed to be covered in that same grey that filled the atmosphere.

I felt a tap on my shoulder; Angel Michael was standing there beside me, smiling. He was looking as radiant as ever. I asked Michael what was wrong.

"This is frightening me!" I told him. "I never saw this happen to angels before. What is that greyness? It's literally in everything and everywhere."

"Lorna, it is going to be like this for a while," Angel Michael replied. "We are going to keep you in a spiritual state to protect you. You will still go to work, go home, and do all the usual activities, but things won't feel quite real to you. It will be like we've put you in a bubble to keep you safe."

"Michael," I said, "nothing looks real, even now. I can feel the changes physically—I feel so light, still, and quiet within myself. The feeling has been getting stronger as the day has gone on. That greyness is literally in everything. It's horrible outside on the street." I turned and looked at him.

"Michael, can you and the angels not protect everyone out there, the same way you are protecting me?"

"No, Lorna," Michael replied. "Sometimes you are protected differently. That will have to remain a mystery until it's time for us to take your soul. No more questions now, Lorna. Just listen to what I have to say. When you get into work every morning you must not leave the store. Only do so when it's time to go home, and then you must head straight for the bus. Understand?"

Just then, my workmate Valerie called me and Michael disappeared. I walked up toward the cash register where she was standing with Pauline and two other girls. We were chatting about what needed to be done when the floor manager came over to us.

"Good morning, girls," he said. "I don't want to frighten you, but the management has informed me that we must be on the lookout for suspicious packages, like a paper bag or a packet of cigarettes. Last night one of the cleaners in another store found a packet that looked like cigarettes, but it was actually a firebomb. When we close this evening I want you girls to search the racks of garments and check the changing rooms for anything suspicious. If you find anything you should call me straightaway. Don't forget to check in the pockets of garments. We don't want the store to burn down and for all of us to lose our jobs."

As the floor manager walked away I said to myself, "So that is what is wrong." I walked into one of the customers' changing rooms where I called Michael, and he appeared.

"Why didn't you tell me about the firebombs?" I asked.

Angel Michael never answered my question; instead he reached out and put his hand on my head and all the concern and worry was taken away from me. I really don't remember much about the next few weeks; it was as if I was in a dream, in another time and place.

Joe was very concerned. He would say, "You are not yourself.

You are not talking. You seem to be somewhere else." He would ask, "Have I done something wrong? Don't you love me anymore?"

"I'm just tired," I would reply. "I'll be okay in a little while. Don't worry."

It was very hard for both of us that I couldn't share what I knew with him; but then the bombs went off. I was not conscious of the day of the week: time was of no consequence; I was oblivious to it. Standing at the racks in the department store late one afternoon I was startled by muffled sounds nearby.

As I write this I find myself reliving the experience of what happened that day.

I am beside a bus, holding a man in my arms as he dies. I am watching angels gathering souls that are leaving human bodies; seeing some little souls and talking with them as if nothing has happened.

I am watching angels kneeling beside people, holding them in their arms, being with them, whispering in their ears that they will be all right.

I can see people running out of shops, angels shouting for help and trying to get the attention of people passing by.

It is horrific.

I cannot feel my human body; it's as if I am in two places at the same time—out on the streets of Dublin, where it is all happening, and at the same time in the department store standing at a rack of garments. I am moving along the streets without my feet seeming to touch the ground. Debris is flying everywhere, broken glass, people screaming and crying, souls leaving their bodies. I am laying my hand on people as I move along, reaching out and touching them.

That day my soul left my body and I was in a different world— out on the street with those who were suffering. Slowly I came back to myself in the store. I realized I was clinging onto the bar of a clothes rack so tightly that my hands had gone very red. The shop was so silent.

The next moment a young girl burst through the shop doors screaming and shouting in a terrified state. She ran about the shop screaming that bombs had gone off, that there were bodies everywhere. She was looking for her sister who worked with me in the department store. Somehow the two sisters found each other and the young woman started to calm down.

Then one of the management staff went to the office and, using the microphone, announced that all staff were to meet at the back entrance of the store in five minutes to be taken home.

I knew it was all over! There would be no more bombs going off in Dublin that day. As I went down the stairs to the cloakroom, an angel whispered in my ear to go back to the telephone at the staff entrance and ring my mum. So I turned around and walked back toward the phone, made my call, spoke to Mum and told her I was okay. I hung up, ran downstairs, and grabbed my coat. All the other staff were already coming up the stairs, heading for the back entrance of the store.

The delivery trucks were lined up and each of the drivers called out the different destinations they would be driving to. I climbed into the van that was going in the direction of Joe's mother's house. I was dropped at the door. Inside, Joe's mum and his sister Barbara were watching the TV news. Joe's mum hugged me and said she had been worried about me. We had a lovely cup of tea and I started to feel better. Then dinner was put in front of me; I was so hungry I felt I had not eaten for weeks. Then Joe arrived home and threw his arms around me. We were all in tears, feeling the pain of all the families who had lost loved ones and all of those who had been hurt. As a result of the bombs in Dublin that day, May 17, 1974, twenty-six people and an unborn baby died and hundreds more were injured.

Living in the Republic of Ireland, we had had little experience of the horrors of war, up to that day, but in Northern Ireland, less than two hundred miles away, more than three thousand people were killed over the period from 1969 to 2000. Until that day we had little idea what it was like for the people of Northern Ireland, or in any other part of the world, to live with bombs going off without warning.

Angel Elijah once said to me, "It is easy to make war; peace is the hardest thing to keep. You think that going to war puts you in control. You forget who gave you the power in the first place, and that He can take control at any time."

For a long time after the bombs went off my body and soul were hit by shockwaves, spiritually, physically, and emotionally. I could feel the terror of those who were hurt and those who had died, and the shock of the families and friends. I could hear their voices, their crying. For months faces would appear in front of me, not only the faces of those who had died, but also of those who were seriously injured and were trying to stay alive and the faces of their heartbroken families. I was tormented by the horror of that day.

When the shockwaves blasted me, the angels did what they could to protect me. They wrapped me in what felt like a huge blanket; it felt like feathers, and it was snow white with what I would call an electrical charge running through it, sparking all the time.

Angel Elijah held my head in his hands, saying, "Lorna, we know this is hurting you. We have wrapped a blanket around you to help make it more bearable. It helps to keep your body and soul together."

Then Elijah blew on my face and disappeared, and I felt a little stronger.

The days and weeks passed; I still needed to find places to hide where I could cry. Sometimes during my lunch hour I would go to the car park. When I knew there was no one in the loo at work I would hide there. On other occasions I walked through the back streets to find a corner or an old wall where I could sit. Many times I told the angels I wanted to be alone.

On one of these occasions Angel Elijah appeared; he would not leave me alone. Again, he took my face in his hands. Then Angel Elijah and I seemed to become one. It was as if I was seeing through his eyes. I was seeing all the horror of the world: the wars, the hunger, the mistreatment of human beings by other human beings. My soul screamed in pain.

Then Angel Elijah showed me the other side: the wonderful love, laughter, and joy and all that is good in humanity. I laughed and tears of joy rolled down my cheeks. When Angel Elijah disappeared I continued crying tears of joy.

I walked back to work that day knowing that every man, woman, and child has that good, that love, that joy inside of them. I believe one day all that goodness will overcome all the bad and the human race will evolve triumphantly, body and soul united.

CHAPTER 11

The Angel of Mother's Love

I used to babysit every couple of weeks for my uncle Paddy and his wife, Sara. They had three little girls and lived in Walkinstown, in the suburbs of Dublin. I would take the bus directly from work to their house, stay overnight, and go straight to work the following morning. The kiddies were lovely, gorgeous little girls, so I never minded looking after them. It gave my uncle and aunt an opportunity to get some time away—even if they only went to the pictures.

This particular evening I was on my way to babysit, sitting on the bus, lost in my thoughts, when an old lady tapped me on the knee.

"Young lady," she said, "your smile is filling me with happiness."

Just then everybody started to stand up. I said good-bye to her as the bus pulled into Walkinstown.

While I was babysitting that evening the doorbell rang. I wasn't expecting anyone and I hoped the doorbell would not wake the children. When I opened the door I was surprised to see Joe standing in front of me.

"Close your eyes, no peeping!" Joe said as he led me down the garden path to the gate. "Now, open your eyes. Surprise!"

Parked in front of us was a beautiful dark green Ford Escort. Joe was so happy. His first car!

"Joe, where did you buy the car from?" I asked.

"One of the car dealers that comes into your da's garage," Joe replied. "I told him two weeks ago that I was thinking of buying a car, and then this morning he arrived with this. Your da and the mechanic checked out the car with me and said it was a bargain."

I gave Joe a big hug; I was so excited about it. He opened the car door and I sat inside. It was fabulous. I said to Joe, "You'd better go now. Pick me up after work tomorrow in your new car."

I waved good-bye to Joe as I closed the door.

Having the car gave us great freedom, and I always loved the long evenings in the summertime. One of the places Joe and I often visited on those long evenings was Castletown House; we would walk along the banks of the river and watch men fishing, children swimming, and parents holding the hands of toddlers as they paddled in the shallow water.

I would also watch angels rising out of the water—seeing the water clinging to them as they soared high into the air before descending back into the water next to a child. Some angels had wings, some didn't, but the angels seemed to spin around the children having just as much fun.

I loved to see a child splashing water in the direction of an angel—the splashes of water hitting the angel and the angel splashing back—and hear the laughter of the angels mingling with the children's laughter. To see a child dive under the water and an angel do the same thing at the same time was wonderful! One time the angels formed a circle around a group of children; beams of light, full of colors—gold, silver, and white—reflected from the angels. Then the beams of light turned into balls of all sizes, dancing on and under the water and through the air. On one of the balls an angel was riding. It was astonishing to see this angel's wings—feathers dripping with water, the golden hair wet. Another time, the angels swung their heads from side to side, moving their wings simultaneously, splashing sparkling raindrops of silver and gold.

One day while we were sitting there by the river I saw a wonderful example of the way angels care for us. I watched a mother and a little child, maybe about eighteen months old, at the edge of the river. The little child was full of excitement at the water running over his feet, and the mother had her hands around his waist, trying to teach him to get his balance and to stand on his own. Sometimes she took her hand away, to see how long he could keep his balance and not fall. I watched the child's guardian angel sitting in the water under him. The child's legs became a little wobbly and he went down. The mother couldn't catch the child in time, but the angel did! As the child went splashing into the water he landed right in his angel's lap in a sitting position. Instead of crying, he started to splash the water and laugh. I smiled at this. Joe asked me, "What are you smiling so happily about?"

I smiled at him and said nothing; yet again I passed up the opportunity to let Joe know a little of what I could see. He was the only person I shared anything of my life with, but I was afraid to tell him about the angels in case he would think I wasn't all there.

"Let's walk further along the riverbank," Joe suggested.

He got up and started to walk ahead of me, and an angel whispered in my ear about angels helping us to do *everything* we do in life—even walking, breathing, talking, and laughing—they are always helping us with every physical action we make with our human bodies. Angels also help us to sort out problems within our own minds, all the questions we have. All the time they are whispering to us, putting answers into our minds and thoughts, but most of the time we are so busy asking questions that we don't stop to listen for the answers. I heard Joe calling, "Hurry up," so I ran and caught up with him.

Walking along the riverbank in Celbridge, we had gotten to know an elderly couple. Their names were John and Mary and we met them quite often as they walked their dog, Toby, a "Heinz 57 variety" mongrel, but very lovable. The couple had lived in Celbridge all their lives and had just celebrated their thirtieth wedding anniversary; their children were grown up and had left home, and now they had all this time to themselves, and they were cherishing it.

One evening we met them and stopped to talk. Toward the end of the conversation John said to Joe in a mischievous tone, "When are you going to propose to this young lady?"

I blushed. I was so embarrassed I didn't know where to look. I didn't dare look at Joe, so I don't know how he reacted.

Mary said, "Don't be embarrassing the young couple!" She took John's hand and started to walk on.

Joe and I walked on further up along the river and sat on some rocks. I took my sneakers and socks off and put my feet in the water. Joe suddenly got up off the rock and stepped fully clothed into the water and got down on one knee. The river was about one foot deep and Joe was on one knee in a strong current. He was really wet. I giggled.

"I am trying to be serious," he said. "I want to propose marriage to you!" He had one of his hands on my knee, trying to keep his balance. "Will you, Lorna, accept my proposal of marriage?"

All I could do was laugh. I laughed so much that I fell off the rock into the water. Joe caught me in his arms and we were both soaked. We were both roaring with laughter. As Joe helped me to my feet I said, "Yes." I was laughing too much to say anything more.

We climbed back up onto the riverbank and we were still laughing, squeezing the water out of our clothes. Thanks be to God it was a warm evening. As we were walking back along the riverbank, Joe stopped. "I have to ask your da for your hand in marriage. What if he says no?"

I thought for a moment and, remembering what the angels had always said about Joe and me getting married, I said, "Don't worry, Da will not say no. I know he will be happy for us."

As we walked back along the riverbank people passing gave us funny looks. A child said to its mother, "Mummy, they must have fallen into the river because all their clothes are wet."

A group of men fishing shouted at us about going for a swim with all our clothes on. We must have looked like drowned rats. We waved to them and laughed. Just then a thought dawned on me. I said to Joe, "I hope the keys for the car are still in your pocket and not on the riverbed!" Joe put his hand into his pocket and shook his head. We must have lost them back up the river where he had proposed to me.

"Okay, give you a race. Let's see who gets there first and finds the keys," I said, as I started to run.

Joe called me and I stopped and looked back. There he was, standing with the keys dangling from his fingers and laughing at me. I ran back to him and grabbed the keys, saying, "Race you back to the car." Joe reached the car before I did, not surprisingly, seeing that Joe's legs were twice the length of mine.

As we drove back to my home Joe and I talked about our wedding. We decided we would say nothing to anyone until Joe had talked to Da. When we reached our house Joe would not come in; he said he would be embarrassed to be seen in wet clothes. We kissed good-night and he drove off.

The next day at work, just before lunchtime, Aunt Sara came into the store and asked me if I would babysit for her again that evening. It was unusual for her to come into the store like that, and it was clear that she and her husband were very anxious to go out. I agreed, even though that was the evening we had decided Joe would talk to Da.

Aunt Sara was delighted. She told me she and Uncle Paddy were looking forward to having dinner and going to a show afterward. I promised I'd be at her house as early as I could. We said good-bye and as I watched my aunt leaving the department store she was beaming, with light all around her. I knew she was happy.

When lunchtime came I went to the back entrance of the department store to use the pay phone. I rang the garage and when Da answered the phone I said, "Hi, Da, can I talk to Joe?"

"Joe is outside. I'll call him," Da replied. I could hear excitement in my da's voice. I said to him, "You sound very happy today."

My da gave a little laugh and said, "Here's Joe."

I spoke to Joe for a few minutes and told him that my aunt needed me to babysit that evening. I asked Joe whether he had talked to Da about our getting married.

"No," he said. "I'll leave it until tomorrow. I'll pick you up after work. We will talk and then go to your house about nine and I'll talk to your da and ask him for your hand in marriage."

"Joe, I could hear excitement in Da's voice when I was speaking to him just now. Are you sure he doesn't know anything?"

"No, I haven't talked to him, or anyone else," said Joe, "but your da is in a great mood today. Maybe he has had some good news."

"I hope Da can't hear you now," I said.

"No, he's gone out to the mechanic."

Someone came into the office just then so we said our good-byes and hung up.

I had an hour for my lunch so I planned to go out to enjoy the beautiful sunshine. When I turned to walk away from the pay phone I bumped into an angel and then I stepped into her. She was all around me; she was big, huggable, and beautiful. It was the Angel of Mother's Love. She had hugged me many times before when I was a child, but this time the feeling was stronger than ever.

The Angel of Mother's Love is round like the sun and enormous. Her wings wrap around her but open out, a little like a mother hen. Her arms are always ready to embrace you in a big hug. Her coloring mingles cream and white, and this time there was a hint of pink.

She is translucent and you can see a very bright light reflecting from within her, but you cannot see through her.

Her face radiates love, her eyes are big like saucers, sparkling with the light of a mother's love, and she has soft curls of creamy white hair. She radiates hugs of love all the time. You just want to fall into her arms and hug her and be hugged by her. No matter how much love you receive from your own mother, if you have a mother, this angel always enhances a mother's love.

That day I was worried about my mother's reaction to Joe and me getting married, and the Angel of Mother's Love knew I needed to feel a mother's love at that time, to feel more love, perhaps, than my mother was able to give me.

I was so happy and excited about our engagement that I constantly had a smile on my face. Valerie asked, "What's up? You seem very happy." She kept badgering me all day, trying to get my secret out of me. Toward the end of the day, when we were sorting a rack of trousers together, she blurted out: "I know! You and Joe are getting engaged! That's it!"

I blushed. "Shhh, it's a secret," I said to her. "Don't tell the others." I didn't want anyone to know until I had a ring, but I was still pleased to be given the chance to tell someone.

"Where's your ring?" she asked.

"We don't have one yet; that is what I am trying to tell you. Joe and I haven't looked yet. Maybe in the next few weeks, I don't know. We've many things to work out. Joe has to talk to Da first. Promise you won't say anything to the other girls? You'll be the first to see the ring and make a wish."

Valerie agreed. We stayed there chatting and sorting clothes for a little while and then she went off to work the register. She kept looking over at me with a grin on her face, but she didn't say anything to anyone.

After work I got the bus to my aunt's house to babysit. On the way

I asked the angels not to let my excitement show, as I didn't want Aunt Sara or Uncle Paddy asking questions. The angels kept me very calm and my aunt and uncle never noticed anything. The next morning I got the bus to work. The morning seemed to be very long, so at lunchtime I went for a walk around the back streets and lanes around the department store.

I always found these back streets an oasis, a place where I could be by myself, get my thoughts together, and escape for a brief moment from whatever the angels were asking me to do at that time. I would sit on a low wall, a box, or even on a doorstep. There was one lane, though, that I always avoided—the one where Mark had been gunned down.

When work was over I rushed down to the cloakroom, got my coat, went back up the stairs and out into the car park. Joe was sitting in the car waiting for me. I was so happy to see him. We drove to the Phoenix Park, parked the car, and sat and talked. Joe said that if I liked we could go looking for an engagement ring that weekend. I said that would be nice—but just to look at rings, not to buy. The angels had already told me that Joe would find the ring for me, but not in the normal way.

Joe asked me if I would like to tell his mother about the engagement. I said no, I would rather wait till I had an engagement ring. We both agreed on that. Joe said, "When we walk into the house with an engagement ring on your finger, she'll be so happy for both of us."

We also decided that even though we weren't planning to get married for a year or so, we would start to look for a place to live.

As we pulled up outside my house, the hall door was open. Da came out and gave us a wave before going back into the house and leaving the door open. That made Joe feel a little better, a bit more welcome. We went straight through to the kitchen. Mum was there. Joe greeted her and I started to make tea.

"What's up?" Mum asked.

"Joe wants to talk to Da," I replied.

"I've been waiting for this day," my mother said with a look on her face; it was clear she disapproved.

"Your da is in the dining room, reading the paper," she said rather dismissively. "I'll tell him Joe wants to see him."

Mum went into the dining room and closed the door behind her. This made Joe much more nervous. "Why can't this be simple?" he said.

Mum was back in a minute or so and told Joe that he could go and talk to Da. Mum stayed in the kitchen with me while I was making the tea and putting butter and jam on some bread. She didn't say a word. She soon left the kitchen and went into the dining room.

About five minutes later, when I had the tray ready, I carried it into the dining room. I felt Joe needed support, so I didn't wait for him to come back out into the kitchen, and anyway I was dying to know my father's response.

As I opened the door to the dining room I could see Da and Joe were sitting together on the sofa, and Mum was standing nearby. She hadn't sat down. I smiled when I saw Joe and Da together. They both looked very happy. Da was all smiles; he got up from the sofa and gave me a big hug and congratulated me. I was no longer worried. I was so happy. Even my mother's reaction didn't have the power to spoil the moment.

Da was thrilled that I was getting married, and to a nice reliable man. In some ways he was probably relieved that now he wouldn't have to be responsible for me, and I felt Mum was relieved too, even if she had difficulties showing it. At some stage that evening Da said, "I never thought I'd live to see this day."

Even though I was now engaged to be married, I know that they were still apprehensive, because of the way they looked at me. Da started to ask Joe and me lots of questions about our plans. Mum, who had said nothing until then, asked if we had a date in mind for the wedding, and we both replied no together.

"Maybe August next year," Joe suggested.

"We'll have the wedding reception in the house," Mum said.

I didn't say a word; I was horrified at the suggestion. Da said, "We can talk about it all later."

But that never happened. We finished tea, Joe said good-bye to Da and Mum, and we walked out to the car. Joe said, "Don't be worried—if you don't want the reception in the house, we can find a hotel."

That weekend Joe and I went looking at engagement rings, but I saw nothing that I liked in any of the jewelers. I told Joe, "I would really like something different. All the engagement rings look more or less the same, no matter which jewelers you go to. I am willing to wait until I find the ring I really want."

"Are you sure?" he asked.

About six weeks later I was working late one evening and not expecting to meet Joe as he was meant to be doing stocktaking at the garage. I was going to catch the eight o'clock bus home, but I got a great surprise when I saw Joe standing by the car in the car park when I left work.

"Come on, let's go for an ice cream," he said.

"You're in a wonderful humor," I said to him. "I'm still in my uniform. How can I go for an ice cream?"

"That doesn't matter." Joe said. "You look beautiful to me. Now let's go and get that ice cream."

We walked hand in hand to the ice cream parlor and sat facing each other in one of our favorite seats. I ordered a banana split and Joe ordered a sundae. Halfway through eating, Joe reached into his jacket breast pocket, saying, "I have a big surprise for you." He took out a little box and opened it. I couldn't believe it! There was a fabulous engagement ring shaped like a rose with petals in gold and a diamond set in the center. It was so different from all the other rings I had seen. Joe held my hand and, slipping the ring onto my finger, said, "I love you. I want to marry you and grow old with you."

Hearing these words from Joe filled my eyes with tears. I was happy and yet I remembered what Angel Elijah had said to me all those years ago. That we would marry, Joe would become ill, I would have to look after him, and that we would never grow old together.

"Don't cry," Joe said as he kissed my hand. I looked into his eyes and saw his happiness and forgot about the future. I leaned across the table and gave Joe a big kiss and asked him where he had found the ring.

"You wouldn't believe it," he said. "In the garage! We were very busy and I went outside to help at the gas pumps just as a car pulled in with a flat tire. I removed the wheel for him and brought the wheel around to the back to be repaired. As I was standing by his car, telling him the wheel would be ready in twenty minutes, I noticed the backseat of his car was covered with cases like little cabinets."

Joe had asked the man about the strange-looking cases and the man had told him he was a jeweler. Joe continued, "I told the man I was looking for an engagement ring, but something completely different. The man said he had a small box with new designs of different kinds—some were rings. He opened the box and I saw this ring and I immediately knew it was perfect for you. I asked him if he would sell me the ring, and he said he would have to check with his boss. We went into the office to phone him, and when we were there I showed your da the ring. Your da said I had done well and that this ring would make you happy, that it was a lovely ring. The man came off the phone and told me I could buy it."

I gave Joe a big smile. "I don't want you to tell me how much it cost. I don't want to know that. Thank you for finding this beautiful engagement ring for me."

I was thrilled; I was walking on air as we went back to the car park. "I'm dying to show my ring to Mum and my sisters and brothers," I said. I don't remember the journey home, but I do remember walking in the back door into the kitchen with Joe right behind me. The kitchen was empty, and I opened the door into the dining room. Da said, "What took you so long to get home?"

"Well! I needn't show you my engagement ring, seeing as you have seen it already," I said. Da laughed and came over to me and gave me a big hug. I showed Mum my ring and told her to make a wish. Mum gave me a hug too and said, "It's very dainty."

Joe had a cup of tea before heading home and I said, "Don't tell your mum about our engagement until after work tomorrow. We'll go to your house together, as usual, for dinner and then surprise her. Let's see if she notices the ring on my finger."

The next day that is exactly what we did. We were sitting at the table, and as Joe's mum was putting my dinner in front of me she let out a scream, saying, "Lorna, you have an engagement ring on! Stand up so I can hug my future daughter-in-law." Joe's mum always made me feel so welcome.

I was fascinated because within what seemed like only minutes the members of Joe's family who lived close by started to call in to congratulate us. Within about an hour family who lived further afield also started arriving. I was being fussed over—something that rarely happened to me. I loved the excitement.

At about eleven o'clock I told Joe he had better drive me home because I had work in the morning. I said good-bye to Joe's mum and she gave me a big hug. I could feel the happiness and joy in her. She was more at peace within herself now that she could see her dream coming true—her youngest son was engaged. Her hug was so tight I could feel and see her guardian angel hugging me too. As Joe's mum stood at the hall door waving to us as we drove away, I could see her guardian angel standing in the doorway waving and gleaming with light.

As we drove up the road I turned in the car seat, not wanting to lose sight of Joe's mum and her angel. Actually, all I could see was the light of the angel. Joe laughed at me. "What are you trying to do? Turn the seat around altogether?"

"I am just trying to see your mum waving to us for as long as I can," I replied.

As we drove on Joe said, "You're a bit quiet."

"I'm just thinking about tomorrow," I said, "about going into work with my engagement ring. If the excitement is anything like what it was in your mum's house, I think I will be embarrassed. I feel very shy and nervous about it, but on the other hand I can't wait to show the girls my ring."

I was home in no time. Just as I was about to get out of the car Joe said, "Get back here and give me a kiss. Enjoy work tomorrow, showing all the girls your ring. I'll see you after work.". We said good-bye. I went into the house. It was in darkness. I crept slowly up to my room, not making a sound, and got into bed. I didn't sleep well that night; I was too excited. I thought the morning would never come, but it did.

I got up a bit earlier in order to catch an earlier bus to work, hoping to arrive before the other girls from my department and hoping that Valerie might be there so I could share my excitement with her and show her the ring. But I was very shy. As I reached the back entrance of the department store I took a deep breath and went in.

I went down the stairs to the cloakroom and clocked in for work. The cloakroom was a square shape with lockers all around the walls and a set of lockers dividing the room. I walked around the lockers and there was Valerie. As soon as she saw me she jumped up from the seat and said, "I know by the look on your face. Let me see your engagement ring."

"I told you I would keep my promise," I said to her, "just as you kept yours. You can have the first wish."

Valerie took the ring off my finger gently, put it on her own, and started to turn the ring toward her three times with her eyes closed and her lips moving silently. I could see her angel clearly, but only part of mine because my guardian angel was behind me. Then as I looked up I saw both angels' heads touch, and as I looked down their feet touched and the angels started to wrap around each other. My guardian angel's wings seemed to stretch out to Valerie's angel's wings and they started to intertwine to make an oval shape. The floor beneath us disappeared. I watched Valerie as she opened her eyes. I could feel a wonderful peace and tranquillity; I wondered if she felt anything of it. She took a deep breath and gave me a wonderful smile saying, "Thanks, Lorna."

More girls came in and I was surrounded by people congratulating me and stretching out their hands to see the ring and make wishes. Pauline, in particular, was thrilled; she was very romantic and adored a good love story. She had only met Joe briefly, but she thought he was very handsome and she was very happy for me.

All the attention was very exciting. I asked the angels to grant as many wishes as possible, especially for my friends, because I knew they had many wishes—not just for themselves, but for their families and friends.

The supervisor walked into the cloakroom and said, "What's all this excitement? Let me have a look."

As she made her way through the girls who were still wishing on the ring, she asked, "Who's engaged?"

"Lorna," everyone answered her at the same time.

"I'm next to make a wish, girls," she said. She took the ring from another girl, ignoring the others who were waiting, and slipped it onto her finger and made a wish.

"Congratulations, Lorna. All you girls—off to the shop floor."

They teased her back and she started to laugh. "Lorna, it's a beautiful ring," she said to me. "Tell me his name."

"Joe," I said.

"I wish you and Joe all the happiness in the world. When is the big day?"

"We are planning August of next year, maybe. We have not quite made up our minds," I answered.

"My advice is don't make it a rushed decision," the supervisor said. "Give yourselves plenty of time. Now, we'd better get back to work."

Later that day when I was in the canteen queuing for tea, the girls behind the counter said, "Lorna, we heard you were engaged. Congratulations."

The canteen supervisor commented that everyone would be over at my table during the break to have a look at my ring and to make a wish. That's what it was like for the next week or so. I was so happy that everyone was happy for me and Joe; even the security guard in the car park congratulated Joe when he came to pick me up after work that day.

For the first time in my life I felt I was the center of attention. But Mum and Da never sat down with Joe and me to talk about wedding plans. In fact, my family didn't seem to show a great interest in my wedding at all.

After talking with Joe I decided to ask Pauline, my friend at work, to be my bridesmaid. I knew she would be thrilled and would be a great support to me on my wedding day. She was a little like me, very quiet; whereas the other girls in the fashion department frequently went to the pub together after work, that didn't really interest Pauline or me.

The next day I told Mum I wanted Pauline as my bridesmaid, even though I had not asked her yet. Mum seemed surprised and suggested that my brother Barry should be the best man. That evening Joe and I talked about our wedding. Joe knew I was unhappy about it; he wanted to have words with Mum and Da, but I said, "No, I don't want our wedding to cost my parents much money, if possible." And we were saving hard for a home so we didn't want to spend much money ourselves.

Joe gave me a big hug and said, "Let's make arrangements to meet the parish priest and set a date for our wedding."

Joe's family was completely different from mine as far as our wedding was concerned. Joe's mum asked me which friends I was going to invite and I told her that I would love to ask Pauline, Valerie, and Mary from work, but I didn't know what they would think about my having the wedding reception in the house. I told her, "Since I started work in the department store, several girls have gotten married and they all have had their receptions in hotels. Mum is set on having it in the house, and I don't want to hurt her by telling her that I am disappointed at that idea. Joe and I have agreed we don't want our wedding to cost my parents much money, if possible."

Joe's mum replied, "Don't worry, we will all chip in."

Then everything seemed to begin to fall into place. A few weeks later, in the canteen at work when I was having lunch with Valerie and Mary, they asked me if I had set a date for the wedding and I told them, "Yes, the eighteenth of August, and you're invited."

They were delighted and asked where the reception was going to be held. I told them it wasn't decided yet; I didn't want to tell them that it was going to be at my house.

Later that day I asked Pauline to be my bridesmaid; she said it would be an honor. I told her that Joe's sister Barbara would make her dress.

CHAPTER 12

Country cottage

I started to encourage Joe to look for a job somewhere else, to be independent. I said that we needed to stand on our own two feet. "Talk to Da. I know he will give you a good reference."

Joe got another job, no problem, this time working in CIE (the Irish public transport company). With the new job Joe could not pick me up after work as often as he used to, so most evenings I got the bus home. One particular evening as I walked round to the back entrance of the house I knew something was going to happen.

I noticed Da's newspaper *The Irish Press* on the dining room table. When the angels asked me to open it I was reluctant, but I pulled out a chair, sat down at the table, and started to turn the pages. My hands were trembling; I seemed to be moving in slow motion. I was afraid the angels were going to highlight something in the paper that would be distressing.

"Don't be afraid, Lorna," my angels said, "just turn the pages and we'll tell you when to stop."

I was turning the pages slowly, one at a time. I could feel my Angel Hosus's hand on my shoulder.

"Now," he whispered in my ear, "look at the houses for sale."

I looked and there were hundreds of houses for sale. I couldn't make sense of anything on the page; everything was upside down and turned around. I looked up from the paper to see a crowd of angels sitting around the table. What a sight! It made me smile.

"Hello," said Angel Elijah, sitting directly opposite me. He reached out for the paper and the tips of his fingers touched the page. "Look now, Lorna," he said. It all immediately became clear. I could see the words "Cottage for sale in Maynooth."

"Lorna, a little cottage with a big garden," said Elijah. "It's perfect for you and Joe. Read on!"

It was a tiny ad with only three lines. I read on: "For sale, by auction," and a telephone number.

"Now, Lorna, put a circle around the advertisement and tear out the page," Elijah said. I did and put the page in my pocket. "Show the advertisement to your da when you are ready," Elijah said. "He will be able to help."

There were tears in my eyes I was so happy. Angel Elijah stood up, reached forward, and, with the tips of his fingers, touched my tears. "Tears of happiness," he said. Then the angels were gone.

I showed Joe the advertisement for the cottage in Maynooth the following day as we walked along the canal.

"I'll talk to Da when he gets home from fishing this evening," I said.

I folded up the paper and put it back in my bag. Later that evening, when Joe had gone, Da got home from fishing. He put all his fishing gear on the floor and proudly took out two large, fresh, pink river trout, one at a time, from the fishing bag and laid them on the kitchen table. Mum was delighted. When Da had finished tidying away all his fishing gear, he sat down in his usual place.

"Da," I said, "I saw an advertisement in the paper for a cottage in Maynooth. It is going up for auction. How do you go about those things?"

He looked at me quite surprised; he probably thought I would have no notion of looking for a house. I didn't know what to think of the look on my da's face, but without any hesitation he said, "Show me the paper."

I took the paper out of my bag and laid it in front of him on the little table. Da asked where the ad was.

"I have circled it with a black pen. Look, there it is, Da, on the bottom of the page on the righthand side."

Da looked up at me again with a surprised look on his face—I was standing and he was sitting—and he read it very carefully before he said anything to me. Then with a smile on his face he said, "Well done," and then he asked, "Does Joe know about the ad for the cottage?"

"Yes," I said, "when I was with Joe today I showed him the paper. We are both excited, but we don't know how to go about this."

"First things first: you'll have to get a loan," Da said.

"Joe and I have money in the bank—should we go there?" I asked.

"Yes," he replied, "and there are other places you could try, such as the Council, for a housing loan, which would be cheaper than the bank. Leave the auction to me. I'll ring about that."

"Thanks, Da," I said. I was delighted Da was helping us, and I was very excited at the possibility of buying the cottage.

The next day I was off work and I walked down to the telephone kiosk and rang the local council and told them I was inquiring about a loan for a young married couple. I said we were not married yet, but we would be. The girl said she would send out the forms. I thanked her and hung up. Next thing I rang Da and he told me he had inquired about the auction. It was in two days' time, so if we were interested we needed to go and see the cottage as soon as possible. He suggested that evening.

I left a message at Joe's work for him to come straight to Leixlip. I was so excited I ran home to the house and told Mum what Da had said. "Don't get your hopes up too high," she said. "It's not that easy to get a loan, and you and Joe don't have much money."

Joe and Da arrived at the house within five minutes of each other that evening. Da said there was no time for dinner as the power in the cottage was not on and we needed to look at it while there was daylight.

We all got into Da's car, Mum as well, and drove to the cottage; it was about a fifteen-minute drive.

When we pulled up alongside the little cottage we could hardly see it, as the hedge was so tall. The gate was locked and Da called into the next-door neighbor, as the auctioneer had told him to, and got the keys. Da opened the gates and handed the keys to Joe. The garden was big, all overgrown—enormously overgrown. We walked up the path to the little cottage. Joe put the key in the door and turned the lock. As he opened the door a horrible stale smell hit us. It was musty and damp; clearly nobody had lived there for quite some time. The cottage was tiny, but Joe and I did not mind that, if only we could buy it.

As we walked around the cottage Joe and I told Da that we were concerned about the auction—what would happen if we succeeded in getting the cottage? Wouldn't the auctioneers want a deposit? Did we need to take cash out of the bank in advance, as we did not have a checkbook? Da said that if everything went well he would pay the deposit on the day of the auction and we could pay him back later. Every so often I would walk back into one of the little rooms on my own in order to talk to the angels in silence about all the things on my mind.

As I walked through the rooms with Joe, Mum, and Da, the angels kept pulling my hair. Mum asked why I was putting my hands up to my head all the time. Was I making sure there were no cobwebs in my hair? I smiled to myself at the question.

We were inside the cottage for only a few minutes; then we left and Joe pulled the door closed and put the key through the letter box next door. While driving home in the car Mum said, "It is in a terrible condition."

Da glanced at Mum and then asked us were we still interested in the cottage. The two of us said yes together.

That Wednesday morning at about nine I left home with my parents and we picked up Joe. Da stopped outside Joe's house and said to me, "You go and knock on the door." Joe opened the door, came over to the car, and asked my parents if they would come in for a minute to meet his mum. They declined. Nevertheless, I went in to her. She wished us the best of luck and said, "Another time I'll meet your mum. We will invite your parents for dinner some Sunday." Joe's mum was dying to meet my parents. She waved good-bye to us from the door as we drove off.

I sat holding Joe's hand in the car. We never said a word; we were so anxious and I was constantly praying. Before I knew it Da was parking the car.

The auction was taking place in an old hotel. We were early, so we sat in the hotel lounge to have some tea and relax a little. I recognized some people among the group sitting in the lounge; I knew them as customers at the garage; their name was Murphy and they were builders. Da got up from the table and walked over to them. I watched Da shaking hands and talking to them. They bought him a drink and there seemed to be great conversation and laughter. Da turned around and gave me a smile. From the look on his face I knew everything was going well.

I asked Joe what time it was; it was 10:45 and the auction was at 11:00. Just then Da came back to the table. We were all dying to hear how he had got on. Da asked if we wanted to hear the good news or the bad news first.

"Good news, please!" I said.

"A number of years ago when there was a gas strike I did the Murphys a favor by making sure they didn't go short of diesel or gas,"

Da said. "Now it's their turn to do me a favor. I had a good chat with them and told them that you both had your heart set on buying this cottage."

None of us had realized that there was land at the far end of the lane for sale as well as the cottage; the Murphys' main interest was in the land. They had wanted to buy the cottage as well, to use for offices and parking trucks. But after talking with Da they agreed not to go after the cottage themselves and to do all they could to help us get it.

People started to leave the lounge and walk across the hall to the room where the auction was being held. The room wasn't very bright; there were lots of chairs in rows and a desk and chair at the top of the room. There were maybe about twenty people there for the auction. We sat in a row halfway down on the righthand side, and the Murphys were on the left. There were several lots sold before the auctioneer got to the cottage; one of the lots was the land up the road, which the Murphys bought.

Eventually, it felt like forever, the cottage came up for bid; it was the last parcel. The bidding started and a woman put her hand up and said a price; Da put his hand up and made a higher bid; then the Murphys named a price; then my Da; and it went on like that for a little while. The woman gave up and stopped bidding. Da made a bid and the Murphys made one more but then stopped. "Twenty-five hundred pounds," my da said, and there were no further bids. When the auctioneer said, "SOLD!" I felt I could breathe again.

The auctioneer indicated to Da to come up to him, and Da turned around to Joe and me, saying: "You two had better come up as well, seeing as it's you who are buying the cottage."

The auctioneer asked for Da's name and Da told him with pride that he was only doing the bidding, that it was Joe and I who were the buyers. The man took our names and looked for the deposit. Without hesitation Da said he was taking care of that.

I remember looking at Da as he took out his checkbook—at that time a 10 percent deposit of £250 was a huge amount of money to me. I felt so much love and affection for my da as I watched him writing out the check; I was delighted that he would do this for us and I felt like hugging him.

Da and Mum drove us back to Joe's mother's house. When we got there his mum was standing at the railings in the garden, talking to a neighbor. Again Joe invited Mum and Da in for a cup of tea; again my parents declined the invitation. We got out of the car as Joe's mum reached the gate. My parents waved good-bye and drove away. We told Joe's mum the great news straightaway.

"Let's go inside first," she said. "Tell me the whole story over a cup of tea. I want to hear every detail, and I have just baked some apple tarts."

We went into the kitchen and Joe's mum put the kettle on. There were already cups and saucers, milk, sugar, and apple tarts on the table. Joe's mum was so eager to hear every detail that the conversation went on for some time. There was always great activity in that house, with family coming and going. They all wanted to hear the good news about the cottage. Some of the family said, "Maynooth—it is so far away. We will never get familiar with the idea that you will be living down in the country."

I laughed and said, "You would think we were moving a million miles away, instead of about twenty-five miles."

Joe's mum asked, "When can I go down and help you to clean out the cottage?"

Joe looked at me and I said, "The weekend after next is my long weekend off." Joe said he was off that Saturday as well, so we agreed to meet at the cottage on that Saturday morning. Shortly afterward Joe brought me home. We were both very excited about everything that had happened that day.

A few days after buying the cottage Joe and I decided to walk to Maynooth from Leixlip and start work on cleaning it up. We were very excited and when we arrived the gate was open. We searched for the key and it took us some time to find it. Eventually Joe found it under a stone at the far end of the cottage.

Our new next-door neighbors must have heard us, because a lady came to the gate and shouted, "Hello there, I'm from next door."

"Hello," I called as I went toward the gate, "I'm Lorna, and we're hoping to live here after we get married in six months' time."

"That's absolutely wonderful," she said with a big smile. "It will be great to have neighbors. I'm Elizabeth."

I invited Elizabeth in and we walked up the completely over-grown drive and turned to the right along the cottage wall to the main door. Joe was standing there and I introduced him as my fiancé. She was delighted to meet him.

"You look like a lovely couple!" she said.

I invited Elizabeth in to see the house and Joe turned the key. We continued talking as we went in.

"I dread the thought of your seeing how bad the inside of the cottage is," Elizabeth said. "It has been empty for such a long time now. The old lady who lived here, Mrs. Costello, died a long time ago."

"That's all right, Elizabeth," I said as we looked around the rooms.

"We'll get it looking all right in no time," Joe said. "Lots of scrub-bing, strip the wallpaper off the walls, get the lino off the floor, and get the old furniture out." Joe looked around. "Maybe we can save some of the furniture—the kitchen table looks good and perhaps those armchairs and the chest of drawers."

The truth is we had no furniture, and very little money to buy any. We were going to be dependent on what we could salvage and whatever old furniture people gave us.

"They'll clean up well and look nearly like new," Elizabeth said. "Please God, my husband will be able to give you a hand doing some of the heavy work."

Before Joe and I could say a word she rushed out the door and was gone to find him. We laughed. She was a lovely little round lady—that's how I'd describe her. She had a beautiful smile and the energy I could see around her held a lot of love and care. She was the salt of the earth.

In no time at all she was back with a tall skinny man with a very pale complexion and deep lines etched on his face—it was a face full of character. "Hello! How are ye?" he said.

"This is my husband, John," Elizabeth said, as she introduced us and explained to him that we were getting married shortly and would then be moving in.

"Well, Joe, you've a hell of a lot of work to do here," John said. "An awful lot of work!"

"Sure—you're right," Joe said. "Let's go around the back and have a look at the sheds."

The two of them went out the door and left Elizabeth and me in the main room. It was quite small, with a fireplace. We went into the bedroom and had a good look around in there. The place stank.

"God, look at the curtains. They're mangy," I said. "They are in a terrible state and we don't have money for new curtains."

"Listen, Lorna, don't worry," Elizabeth replied, "I'll take those curtains down during the week. I have nothing to do at the moment, and I'll wash them."

I couldn't believe it. I said, "God, Elizabeth it's an awful lot of curtains to wash."

"I'll wash and iron them and I'll come in and put them back up on the windows—and while I'm doing that I'll get John to clean the windows."

We had a bedroom, a little front room, a little kitchen, and another room, which one could use for a bedroom, but there was no toilet or bathroom.

"The kitchen is a good size for a young family starting out," said Elizabeth, "but you'd better turn that little bedroom into a bathroom because you'll need one. You'll probably have children."

"Of course we will," I said with certainty. After all, the Angel

Elijah had told me so. "But the outdoor loo will have to do for now. I wonder what sort of condition it is in."

We went around the back of the house to have a look. It was completely wild around there; we could hardly see anything because the hedge was completely overgrown. There were also grass, weeds, nettles, and stinging brambles that came up above my waist everywhere. We fought our way over to where Elizabeth said the loo was.

We could not see Joe or John, but we found the loo. It was just a loo in a long shed with a door. There was no toilet seat, but it was usable and it wasn't too bad. I asked Elizabeth about the building next door to it.

"It's another shed. We have the same next door."

Then we heard Joe and John. "Don't look into that shed," Joe said.

That was irresistible, of course. "Oh, I'll just have a peep, seeing as you said that," I said. I peeped in and, of course, it was piled high as a mountain with all kinds of things. "What are the other sheds like?" I asked.

"You wouldn't want to look into them either," John said. "You've got another big shed there and down past that you've got a piggery—it's a small shed with an outer wall around it and a gate into a little yard. It would be an ideal place if you had chickens. The sheds are all full of junk, but, sure, I'll give Joe a hand and we can clear some of it out when he's here next and burn it."

"God, John, you are very good to give us a hand," I said.

John turned around and said, "Well, we'd better go now, Elizabeth, and leave the two of you to yourselves."

As Elizabeth was walking away she turned around and said, "Before you go home would you like to come in for a cup of tea? We'd love to have you."

"Would you like to do that?" I asked Joe.

He nodded. "We'll be in, in five or ten minutes," he said. "We'll just have a little time looking around here and sorting out a few things."

So off they went. I was really so happy and so was Joe. "Isn't it wonderful that this house is ours now?" I said. "We have a lot of work to do but I know we can do it."

We went back into the house and Joe reached up and started to pull bits of the wallpaper off the walls, to see how hard it would be to strip the walls. It wasn't too bad. The lino on the floor was all torn, and the two of us started to lift it. We got a shock because under each layer of lino there was another. Under the bottom layer there was a thick layer of newspapers—hundreds of them all glued together. We looked at each other.

"Let's get something and see if we can move them," Joe suggested.

We got a piece of stick and we found that under all those layers of lino and newspapers were straw and clay. Eventually, under all that, believe it or not, were floorboards—quite decent ones. We found out later from Elizabeth that all the layers were there to insulate the room, to keep the heat in.

We had a lovely cup of tea with Elizabeth and John. Elizabeth told me a little about Mrs. Costello, who used to live there and how she looked like Mrs. Tiggywinkle in the Beatrix Potter story; she had a big hat, a big coat, and she always carried a big bag. She lived on her own and never had any visitors.

John invited Joe to see his house and garden. Looking through the window at them, I could see angels playing around them. I smiled.

"You seem so happy, smiling there," Elizabeth said.

"I am very, very happy," I replied. It was lovely to be there in their home, to have a happy family home right next to us, to see the light around Elizabeth and John. They also had a lovely little boy; I don't know what age he was, maybe ten.

"Anytime you need us, just give us a call," Elizabeth offered. We thanked them, and Joe and I left and walked down the road holding hands.

The following Saturday Joe brought his mum to the cottage. I was already there waiting for them. When Joe's mum got out of the car she gave us a big hug, looked around, and said, "Oh my God! From the outside you have a big job on your hands." She asked him to open the trunk of the car; she had everything needed for cleaning. We carried the whole lot into the cottage. She walked in.

"Well," she said, "This little cottage has the makings of a great home."

Over the next two days we did a lot of cleaning. Spending that time together gave me the chance to really get to know Joe's mum, and we had great fun together. Those two days were wonderful and we got an awful lot of work done. Joe's mum was brilliant. And by the time our wedding came around, the cottage was habitable—just about.

CHAPTER 13

Telling Joe

One morning down in the cloakroom at work Pauline and I were chatting about wedding dresses and she asked the supervisor if it would be possible for us to have a lunch break together so we could go to the fabric shop. The supervisor agreed and put us on the same lunch break.

When lunchtime came Pauline and I went to the canteen, had a five-minute lunch and headed out to the shops. We looked at hundreds of dress patterns and rolls and rolls of fabric. It was very exciting. Eventually, after many lunch breaks of looking, I found a fabric that I really liked and that I felt would be suitable for a wedding dress: it was cream with little wine-colored wildflowers scattered here and there. Pauline found a beautiful fabric that matched the flowers on mine. But I didn't buy anything just yet; I knew Mum would want to come shopping for my wedding dress with me.

Even with all the time we spent together looking for fabric, I hadn't told Pauline about the wedding reception being at home. I dreaded the thought of telling her and the other two girls. One day I asked the angels when would be the best time to tell my friends and they said, "Right now."

"You mean now, on our tea break?" I asked.

"Yes!" my angels replied.

When I walked into the canteen I saw Valerie and Mary sitting at our usual table. I went and got tea and biscuits and joined them. As I sat down Valerie asked: "Lorna, we are dying to know where the reception is being held." My friends were all smiles and full of excitement.

"It is being held in my parents' house in Leixlip," I said. I could see from the expression on their faces that they were shocked.

"You are joking, Lorna?" Mary said.

"No," I said. "I wouldn't joke about something as important as my wedding day."

They asked me all kinds of questions then, including why my mum and da wanted to have the reception in the house. I told them it was kind of a custom in my mum's family and that Mum's heart was set on it. Then they asked who else was coming to the wedding.

"It's mostly family. My parents and brothers and sisters, some of my uncles and aunts, Joe's family, of course, you two and my brides-maid, Pauline. We'll be about thirty in total for the meal. Some neighbors are coming to the church."

A few days later while I was sitting in the canteen having lunch with my friends Valerie said she had a few suggestions to make about the wedding reception.

"How about, Lorna, if we all leave after the meal and go into Dublin to a pub with music and dancing to celebrate?"

"It's a great idea and I'm sure Joe would agree," I replied, "considering that we won't be able to dance in the house. How are you going to get to the church in Leixlip that morning?" I asked.

"We are going to meet in Dublin," Valerie answered, "and get the bus to the church. Let's hope it doesn't rain, because we don't want to bring coats. And I hope it's not too long a walk to the church, because we will all be wearing high heels!"

"Two minutes," I assured them. "Make sure you are all early." They laughed and said they were really looking forward to their day out.

Later that day when Pauline was helping me tidy the racks just before closing time in the fashion department I said to her, "I guess it's time for me to tell you where the wedding reception will be held."

"I have already heard from the other girls that it is at your parents' house," Pauline said. "I think that is great."

I told her it was nice of her to say that.

When I got home from work that night Mum suggested we should go shopping for the dress material on my day off, the next day. I was looking forward to going into town with Mum and buying the material and pattern for my wedding dress—even though I had already chosen it and knew exactly what I would buy. I hadn't, of course, told her this. I knew Mum would enjoy going around the stores, so I said nothing.

Going in and out of the fabric departments and stores in Dublin with Mum the next morning was fun, but Mum was getting a little annoyed because I didn't like anything I saw, although she saw lots that she thought would be perfect.

"I don't want a traditional dress," I said to Mum, "and I definitely don't want to wear white! There is one more fabric store, Mum. You brought me to it once; it's down a side street beside Clerys."

After a cup of tea Mum led the way to the fabric store. We looked at lots of material on big rolls, some standing and some lying flat on counters. When we came to my chosen one I said to Mum, "I think this material is beautiful. I love the cream color and wine wildflowers scattered around it. And look, this one standing beside it would be perfect for the bridesmaid's dress."

"Yes," Mum nodded. "It is beautiful. They would go together very well." As my mum said those words, angels arrived all around us. As Mum asked, "How much does the material cost?" I nearly burst out laughing because I could hear the angels' voices, like a chorus, chanting, "No price tag, no price tag." I knew the angels had made the price tag disappear.

Mum decided to ask one of the staff the price. All the angels stopped their activity and waved their hands, indicating no. I knew then I had to stop Mum, because she was going to think the material was too expensive and try to get me to buy something cheaper. This was something I would not allow, but I didn't want to hurt her either.

"Don't worry, Mum," I said, "I am paying for the material and pattern and all that I will need for the dress. Let's look through the pattern books."

The angels took Mum's arm as we walked to the back wall where all the pattern books were. Mum opened one of the books and started to look. I suggested that, to save time, I would look at another one. I must have looked through five books before I found the pattern I had seen before. I called Mum over. "Look, this pattern will suit the material I have chosen beautifully."

Mum was very good at making clothes, and she knew how to read the back of the pattern and see how much material I would need for both dresses. When Mum had finished calculating the amount of material that would be needed, we went to the counter and I asked the assistant for it. She got the two bolts of material, laid them on the counter, and measured the material out, yard by yard. It piled up on the counter and the girl folded it perfectly and put it in a bag. She also put the patterns and all the trimmings we needed into the bag.

"That's £25.99 in total," she said.

As I was handing the sales lady the money, Mum said she wanted to pay for the material for my wedding dress. I was pleased by her offer but said, "No, Mum. It's too much." But Mum kept on insisting, so I let her pay. She seemed very happy and proud as she handed the assistant the money. We said thank you and as we were leaving the shop one of the angels was standing at the door. I thanked the angel in a whisper, and then we headed home. As we walked to the bus stop, carrying the bags, I thanked Mum.

I was like a little child, full of excitement, wanting to show Joe the material and to bring it over to his mum's house. That evening Joe's mum said, "I will have to meet your mother and father. Will you ask them can they come to dinner on Sunday?"

When Joe dropped me home that night I went in the back door as usual. I was surprised my mum and da were still in the dining room, so I seized the opportunity.

"Hello! I was not expecting to see you up. By the way, Joe's mum has invited both of you to dinner on Sunday at five o'clock."

Mum was not too impressed, but Da said, "Of course we'll come. Tell Joe's mum we'll be there at five on Sunday." I was delighted and offered to make them a cup of tea. Da refused and said, "Go off to bed." I said good-night.

The next day after work I caught the bus to Joe's mum's house and I told her that my parents would come to dinner on Sunday. She was delighted, if a little nervous. I knew she would go to great trouble to make a perfect dinner.

When I arrived with my parents for dinner at Joe's that Sunday Da knocked on the door and I was glad to see it was Joe who answered it. Joe welcomed Mum and Da in and gave me a hug. We went into the dining room; the table was set for a queen. It was fabulous. Joe introduced his mum, his sister Barbara, her husband, and their children. One funny thing happened at the beginning, though; Barbara kept on insisting Mum take off her coat, and Mum kept saying, "No, it's fine."

I pulled Joe out of the room and whispered, "It's not a coat; it's a coatdress. Tell Barbara to stop asking or I will burst out laughing."

Joe said he never heard of a coatdress before, and when he went back into the dining room, his sister was asking my mum again, could she take her coat. Joe just interrupted and pulled out a chair for Mum to sit down.

We had a fabulous dinner of roast beef with roasted potatoes, cabbage, and carrots. For dessert we had Joe's mum's wonderful apple pie and cream. I've never had any apple pie that was better than hers. Joe's mum had really done us proud; everything went well.

⁂

All through the summer before our marriage the angels had been telling me to let Joe know a little about my secret. I told them many times I was apprehensive. I wanted to be able to share my secret with someone, and especially Joe, but I was scared of his reaction—what if he did not believe me?

"You should only share part of your secret," the angels told me. "A little at a time, no more than that. Keep in mind, Lorna, that you will never be able to share your entire secret; some of it can never be told. Next time there is a suitable opportunity we will help you."

A few nights later, as Joe was taking me home, he suggested going for a drive up into the mountains.

"It's going to be a beautiful night," he said. "There is a full moon and I hope the sky will be full of stars. I know a place where we can park and have a wonderful view of Dublin and the sea beyond."

When we got there, there were lots of other cars. "Let's go for a little walk and maybe sit on the wall over there for a little while," I said.

The wall was only a pile of scattered rocks, but we sat and Joe held me in his arms. We kissed and I felt safe. I don't know how long we sat there, but all of a sudden I noticed the sky was full of stars. Then some of them seemed to spin and fall, and as they came closer to the earth I saw they were angels. I could hear the angels say, "Now is the time to share a little of your secret with Joe."

I turned in Joe's arms and said I had something to tell him. He looked at me and asked was it something to do with the wedding?

"No," I said. "It is actually about me. Let me explain something. I see things that other people don't normally see. Sometimes I see angels."

A look of complete disbelief came over his face. He looked at me and laughed. "Lorna, as far as I know only nuns and priests see angels. This is ridiculous! Ordinary people like you and I don't see angels."

I looked at him nervously; this was just as I feared. I silently called "Help!" to the hundreds of angels who were around me.

He gave me a hug and said no more about it.

"Let's go. It's late and we both have work tomorrow," he said.

The journey home was silent except for a few words. Joe glanced at me now and then while driving as if to say, "What have I got here?"

I was scolding the angels, saying, "Joe's not responding well to this at all."

When we pulled up outside my house, Joe said, "Lorna, you have asked me to believe in something that I haven't ever thought of before." But I felt a little bit reassured when he hugged me and gave me a kiss.

As I walked round to the back door I was still scolding the angels. An angel said, "Don't worry, Lorna, this is just the beginning of Joe getting to know you."

I wondered how I was going to be able to get him to believe me, but I soon had an opportunity.

Although Joe no longer worked with Da he sometimes helped him out in the garage. One Thursday evening as I finished work I had a vision—I saw lots of glass, large windows; light seemed to be shining on them and blocking my vision, and yet it seemed to be dark. "What's all this about?" I asked my angels.

The angels said, "Tell Joe."

"I really don't want to," I replied.

"Remember your vision, Lorna," the angels said. "Now do you see where it is?"

"Yes, it's the garage."

That evening I told Joe. "That does not mean anything," he replied.

No more was said, but I was worried. On Friday I had the vision again. This time I saw Joe in a car, as if he were driving it to the pumps for gas; I saw men approach the car and Joe wind down the window. Then the vision was gone.

I told Joe I had the vision again and explained in detail what I had seen. "I don't want you getting hurt. It's a warning."

"I don't believe in that kind of thing," Joe said. "Your da rang and left me a message. He needs me to work the weekend; the man who does the night shift has left, so he has no one for Saturday and Sunday, for the shift from midnight to seven in the morning."

I had the vision again and I was shown more still. I saw Joe wind down the window and one of the two men punch him in the face. Then I saw Joe in the police station, and the police believed the other men, not Joe. I couldn't make out what it was all about; I was upset now and arguing with the angels.

"Joe will have a bloody nose," the angels said, "but otherwise he will be okay. Remember the vision, Lorna. The police may not believe him, but it will all be sorted out eventually." After work I went to Joe's mum's house and Joe and I went for a walk around the housing estate. I pleaded with Joe to believe me. I was mad with him. I said, "Why won't you listen to me?"

All the time his guardian angel was whispering in his ear. I wanted to shout at Joe, "Your guardian angel is trying to tell you, but you won't listen." Because I seemed to be so upset Joe promised that he would be very careful over the weekend.

That weekend the vision unfolded, and it all happened just as I had seen.

One evening Joe was repairing a customer's car and went to fill it with gas. A friend of the owner of the car was passing and believed Joe had stolen it. He yelled at Joe and when Joe wound down the window the guy punched him in the face, then called the police. The police did not believe Joe and arrested him. Da bailed him out and everything was sorted out, but that evening Joe got another insight into who I am.

Two weeks before my wedding, Pauline, Valerie, and Mary took me on a hen night to celebrate. I had never been out after work with them before. They took me first to Smyth's, the pub that Valerie went to most Friday evenings, which was full of people who worked in the department store. Valerie and Mary seemed to know everyone in the pub, and there was a lot of laughter. They were used to drinking, but I was not. They encouraged me to have a glass of wine; it went straight to my head, and my friends thought that was hilarious. One glass was more than enough for me, as I could really feel its effect, and after that I stuck to 7Up.

We went from one pub to another, on foot, until we ended up in Mary's favorite pub, Murphy's. There was a great atmosphere there. The place was very basic—the floor was concrete with potholes, there were no tables, only stools at the bar, and the place was packed with people singing Irish rebel songs. I loved the music and singing and we all joined in. Afterward we went back to Mary's bedsit in the city center and had a cup of tea and some biscuits and chatted about the evening. My friends teased me about tricks they could play on Joe and me on our wedding day; we had a good laugh. It was a great night, but I was glad to get home eventually and go to bed.

It was getting closer and closer to our wedding day. Almost everything was ready and my wedding cake had arrived at the house; one of my aunts had made it as a wedding present. It was fabulous, three tiers tall. I still have the decorations belonging to it, too; they have been put away in a box somewhere.

With two days to go the house was spotless, both families were ready, and, on the eve of the wedding, the neighbors called in at the house to see if they could help with any last-minute things. Anne, our next-door neighbor, assured me that she would be over early in the morning to do my hair.

It is wonderful to see the happiness that weddings can bring to family, friends, and even neighbors—to see all the excitement that is inside everybody come to the surface. Whenever there is a wedding planned, I ask all the angels of the universe that the wedding can bring happiness and excitement to all involved.

Finally, my wedding day arrived! The eighteenth of August 1975. I hardly slept the night before and I was up early—as was the whole house. I was too excited to eat breakfast, so I just had a cup of tea.

One of the most precious moments was when Da escorted me to the car and sat beside me in the backseat. He did not say a word, but just held my hand. When we pulled up to the main entrance of the church Da said, "Don't move," and he got out of the car. The driver had come around to open the car door, but Da insisted on opening it. As I got out of the car the smile on Da's face made me happy. He took my hand. Just as we entered the church to walk down the aisle he told me in a gentle voice how proud he was to walk down the aisle with his beautiful daughter on her wedding day.

As I walked toward the altar on Da's arm I could feel my guardian angel ruffling my hair, which my neighbor had spent so much time on that morning. I could see Joe standing at the top of the aisle, look-ing in my direction. He looked so handsome. Beside him stood his guardian angel with a big smile on his face. Angels then started to ap-pear on the altar: Michael, Hosus, Elijah, Elisha—all the angels who have been with me over the years. The altar was packed with angels. The priest stood there waiting.

Joe and I walked to the altar and stood before the priest, and the ceremony began. As Joe put the wedding ring on my finger, Hosus tugged at my dress and joined me in saying, "I do."

Outside the church there were lots of photos taken, and back at the house we had a wonderful meal with my friends and family sitting around one big table.

Later that evening we all left the house, and Joe and I went with our friends for a drink in the local pub. It was packed, though, with no space for a bride and groom, so we made our way into a pub in the center of Dublin. Joe and I didn't stay long before we headed to Maynooth where, in the early hours of the morning, Joe carried me over the threshold of our little cottage.

CHAPTER 14

I never knew I had a guardian angel

Sometimes the angels do not give me any warning before an event. One evening when Joe and I had been married three months something strange happened. It was about eleven o'clock and Joe had gone to bed and was reading a book while I was tidying up and getting ready for bed. We had no bathroom in the cottage at this time, so I was washing myself in front of the fire. I was only in bed about five minutes when I needed to go to the loo, so I climbed out over the end of the bed.

I opened the bedroom door and I got a shock. I nearly walked into someone.

"Oh my God, what are you doing here?" I exclaimed.

Mrs. Costello, the old lady who had lived in the cottage until she died, was standing in front of me! She looked just as Elizabeth had described her. She was dressed in her coat and a wonderful hat with netting and what looked like fruit on it, and she carried a big bag under her arm.

"Good-bye," she said. "I am off now."

She smiled at me. She looked beautiful, perfect, just like Mrs. Tiggywinkle. I don't know why she needed to say good-bye to me, but if that's what she had to do then that was fine with me. She had given me such a start though!

I turned round and got back into bed.

"What's wrong?" Joe asked.

"I nearly walked into her," I said to Joe, forgetting that I hadn't yet told him that I see spirits as well. "I just met the old woman who lived here before us," I told him. "She just came to say good-bye."

Joe sat up in the bed and looked at me, startled. He told me to get back in bed and under the blankets.

I did so quietly, hoping that Joe wouldn't think too much of the incident. He didn't—he turned around and went back to reading. Clearly my angels were working hard! Joe never mentioned it again.

I lay in bed talking to the angels, asking why Mrs. Costello had nearly let me walk into her. I don't like walking into a dead person, a spirit that has not yet gone to Heaven; it feels unpleasant to have electrical shocks sent through my body. A spirit that has not yet gone to Heaven has not yet been purified and feels completely different from a spirit that has gone to Heaven and come back, like my brother Christopher. With spirits who have returned from Heaven, I feel the life force of their soul.

The angels told me that for some reason that they never explained Mrs. Costello was unable to leave the cottage until she had made contact with me, and that she needed that contact in order to be able to go to Heaven. I can't explain this, but frequently I encounter souls who have not yet left this earth and gone to Heaven, and for some reason I have a role to play in their passing over.

A few months later I became pregnant. Joe decided he would sell the car in order to be able to afford all the extras we would need with a baby on the way. So we were back to traveling by bus, and we both laughed about that.

I found the pregnancy hard and I complained to the angels and God all the time. The angels just laughed at me and told me to rest.

My baby decided to come into the world a few weeks before his time—he was a beautiful baby boy almost seven pounds in weight. We were so happy. I had told Joe long before about my baby brother Christopher who had died as an infant and my desire to name my first son after him. So we had already decided we would call our baby Christopher.

I never told Joe about my encounters with my spirit brother, though; I have never been allowed to share those encounters until writing this book. I asked Joe not to mention to my parents the reason I wanted our son to be called Christopher. When my parents came to visit me in the hospital after his birth, Mum said we should name our son Christopher—after her da, my grandfather. I smiled at Joe and said we had already chosen the name Christopher. Joe squeezed my hand.

When I brought Christopher home from the hospital I was like any young mother—nervous and fussing over him. He was strong and healthy, but one time when I was looking after him the angels appeared around me and told me he had a little problem.

"I notice he's not digesting the milk properly. Am I right?" I asked.

"Yes," said the angels. "Wrap Christopher up well, put him in his stroller, and walk down to the telephone box."

I did as I was asked, and when I got there I was glad to see there was no one on the telephone. I rang the doctor and asked him to call to see Christopher. The doctor called that afternoon. It was a very cold day and lashing rain. The key was in the hall door and the doctor called out, "Anyone at home?" as he walked in. I was sitting by the fire with Christopher on my knee, feeding him. I smiled at the doctor because all the angels followed him in. He sat down on the chair and said that it was lovely and cosy, and he heated his hands by the fire. He played with the baby for a minute and then asked me what was wrong. I told him I didn't think Christopher was digesting his milk properly. He looked at me strangely. The angels behind him told me to be careful about what I said.

"He throws up a lot," I added.

"Lorna," he said, laughing, "all babies do that."

As the doctor pulled his chair closer to examine Christopher, one of the angels touched Christopher's tummy and he threw up. The milk went flying across the room. The doctor looked at me and said, "That's not normal."

The doctor put a stethoscope to the baby's tummy and commented that anytime he had seen a baby do what Christopher had just done, they always turned out to be celiac. He then gave me a letter to see a specialist in Temple Street Children's Hospital in Dublin.

Christopher was indeed celiac, so from then on he was on a special diet. This meant there were a lot of visits to the hospital and sometimes Christopher had to stay in for a few days, which was hard on him and on us.

Joe worked on the garden every spare moment he had, and I must say it was really starting to take shape. One day when I was watching Joe working in the garden his guardian angel appeared for just a brief moment and then other angels appeared around Joe, as if they were supporting him. I could see that the light around him was very weak.

I started to cry, saying to myself, "No! It's not fair."

I knew the angels were showing me that Joe was going to become sick.

He did. He became very ill with a gastric ulcer shortly afterward, and he was much sicker than most people with the same condition. This was to be a pattern with Joe. For some reason that I never fully understood, when he got sick with something he became much sicker than other people.

Despite a special diet and lots of medication, Joe was very ill and unable to work for six months. As a result he lost his job with the transport company and we had to depend on the state social welfare to survive.

It was a very difficult time for us, and, although I didn't know it then, this was a pattern that was going to continue for the rest of his life.

One day when Christopher was about eighteen months old I brought him out to the front garden to play, locked the little gate, and walked back into the house to make the beds, leaving the front door open. Angel Elisha appeared for just a moment.

"Hello, Lorna, I'm just letting you know that you are going to have a visitor."

Before I could say a word, Angel Elisha had disappeared. I laughed and said, "That was a quick visit."

Elisha did not reappear; I did not give it another thought and continued making the beds, every now and then looking out the window to check on Christopher. When I walked into our little front room I noticed a flash of light on the doorstep and heard a little laugh. The spirit of a little girl walked into the hall. She had long, wavy black hair with dark blue eyes. She was dressed in a coat with a black collar, a hat and kneesocks with black shoes. She danced into the kitchen and smiled at me. I followed her into the kitchen.

This little spirit still had her guardian angel with her. I have rarely seen a spirit with its guardian angel—they normally stay with us only for a little while after death because a spirit doesn't need the help of a guardian angel after it has passed through the gates of what we call Heaven.

The little girl appeared as in flesh and blood, just like you or me. She had lived sometime in the past but I did not know quite how she had died. Her guardian angel was transparent, like a raindrop full of life; he reflected all colors and he surrounded her. All guardian angels are similar in appearance, despite having distinguishing characteristics—a little like the way brothers and sisters are similar to each other but have different characteristics. I have no difficulty telling a guardian angel from another type of angel.

I could see the little girl's guardian angel moving around her, as if protecting her from the human world and everything in it; he did not even let her feet touch the ground. Sometimes he turned and smiled at me then put his finger to his mouth, indicating I was not to say a word.

The little girl turned around and skipped out of the kitchen, into the hall, and through the front door and they both disappeared in a flash of light. Over the next few months the little girl appeared with her guardian angel on many occasions. She only visited when the front door was open, but that was 99 percent of the time. The first time she spoke to me she told me she had been all alone when she died. Then she looked up at her guardian angel and said, "I really did not know I had a guardian angel. I never knew you were there."

The little girl's eyes seemed to fill with tears, and her guardian angel reached down and took the tears away. I could feel great love and emotion, and my own eyes filled with tears. The little girl said no more and skipped back out the door.

Another time she told me her name was Annie. I never seemed to get a chance to ask her questions because her guardian angel would always put his finger to his lips, indicating for me not to say a word.

One morning Angel Elisha appeared again. "Don't you dare disappear on me like you did last time," I immediately said.

"Let us sit down on the doorstep," Angel Elisha said.

"Elisha," I asked, "why are the spirit of this little girl and her guardian angel coming to see me?"

"Lorna," she replied, "Annie needs to know that someone loved her when she was alive. She died alone and she thought no one loved her, not even her mum and da—she could not find them when she was dying. Her guardian angel has brought Annie to you so you can be a parent to her. It's a big thing to ask of you, Lorna."

"You know, Angel Elisha," I said, "it is working. I look forward to seeing Annie, even though she is a soul and not flesh and blood. I am finding I have an attachment to her. I know her guardian angel is making that attachment grow into love between us both. Thank you, Angel Elisha."

"Good-bye now, Lorna," Elisha said as she disappeared.

Annie's visits became more frequent—almost every day. Then one day she used my name.

"Lorna," she said, "you know I died in a fire. I couldn't find anyone. I called out but no one heard me. Where were my mummy and daddy? My mummy and daddy didn't care; they didn't love me. I remember lying down and crying and when I woke up I was in Heaven."

"Annie, when you go back to Heaven," I replied, "you will meet your mum and dad and you will know they love you."

As I spoke these words Annie reached out and touched me for a moment. In that hug I felt her physical body.

"That's all I need to know, that I was loved in the human world," she said, and she turned around, with her guardian angel, and ran out the door.

I thanked God. I felt happy to know that Annie was now settled in Heaven with her parents.

Sometimes it seems that God and the angels can't convince spirits that they were loved when they lived. So God sent Annie to this human world of ours with her guardian angel, so that she could be told that she was loved when she lived. It's hard to understand, but she needed to know that she was loved.

CHAPTER 15

The power of prayer

I became pregnant again. I was twenty-five and Christopher was two and a half years old, and this time the first three months of the pregnancy were great; I had no morning sickness. One morning I decided to stay in bed, with Christopher beside me, after Joe had gone to work. I woke an hour or so later. Christopher was fast asleep and I gave him a kiss and slipped quietly out of bed. I walked into our little front room and there was Angel Hosus, sitting in a chair. He told me to sit down.

"Angel Hosus, don't tell me something is wrong," I said.

"No, Lorna, it's nothing serious. There is a mark on the baby's left side. The doctors will be concerned and will send for a specialist from another hospital. You must remember it will be okay, your baby is perfect, but it just wants to be born in a hurry. That little baby is impatient for you to hold him in your arms. We angels and your baby's guardian angel will do everything to keep your baby where it is meant to stay for as long as possible—right in there, Lorna." Angel Hosus reached out and touched my tummy and I could feel the baby move.

"My baby knows you have touched my belly," I told Hosus. "I felt my baby move when I was six weeks pregnant, but my doctor said that was impossible. I know it's not. When I stand in front of the mirror I sometimes ask God for a peep and then I can see all the energy, spinning in a whirl. Sometimes it opens for a moment and God shows me that my baby is perfect."

I asked Angel Hosus, "Why does my baby want to come before it's time?"

He didn't answer my question, though; instead he told me, "You are going to have a hard time from now on, and you will spend most of this pregnancy in the hospital."

A few days later I went to the hospital for a scan and I could see my baby.

"You seem to have a very active baby," the doctor said. "Everything looks fine. He's no bigger than my thumbnail but his legs and arms are moving. He even opened his eyes and put his thumbs up to his mouth."

The doctor decided that I should stay in the hospital for a few days' rest and I was brought up to a ward. Joe went home but returned that evening with the bits and pieces I would need. I ended up staying in the hospital for a week, and when the doctor said I could go home, I felt very happy and well.

I was home for only about two weeks before I was back in the hospital again. Mum took care of Christopher so that Joe could continue going to work—he had recently got a job with the local County Council. Christopher fretted a lot and it was not easy for Mum to console him, but Joe would call to my mum's house after work before coming to the hospital to visit me, and at weekends Joe kept Christopher with him.

Back in the hospital I was on a drip and not allowed out of bed. The doctors couldn't understand why I kept going into premature labor. I spent the remaining months of the pregnancy in the hospital. During the week before Christmas, when I was seven months pregnant, the wards were emptying and everyone was sent home who could be. It didn't look like they were going to let me go home, but I kept praying to God that I could go so I could be with Christopher and Joe for Christmas. Christmas Eve came and, just before lunch, one of the doctors came over to my bed and told me I could go home for two or three days, on the condition that I came straight back if I felt unwell.

That evening Da drove Joe and Christopher to the hospital to collect me, and I was feeling great. When we arrived at the cottage it looked so homey: Elizabeth, our wonderful neighbor, had kept the fire going. Before Da left he told us that we were invited for dinner on Saint Stephen's Day, the day after Christmas, and that he would collect us at about twelve. Christopher went out with his father to close the gates as his granddad drove away, and when they came back in I was sitting comfortably by the fire. Christopher sat on my knee and I gave him a big hug while Joe made us tea. I really don't remember much about that particular Christmas, nor do I know how Joe managed. I only remember hugging Christopher by the fire that evening and then being at my mother's on Saint Stephen's Day, saying I wasn't feeling too good and asking Da to take me back to the hospital.

He did and two weeks later, as I was going into the eighth month of pregnancy, my second son, Owen, was born. Believe it or not, he weighed almost eight pounds—despite being four weeks premature.

I don't know how Mum and Da became involved in prayer groups, but they did and the prayer work seemed to have a great effect on my da. He started to help people. He always had done, but now he helped people even more than before. If he heard anyone was in trouble, he would do what he could to help.

One particular evening Da came up to the cottage and asked us if we would like to come to the prayer group down in Maynooth College that evening. Maynooth College was one of the biggest seminaries in Ireland at that time, so there were always a lot of priests and student priests around.

I looked at Joe and we both nodded. I was thrilled at the opportunity to get out of the house, and I was also fascinated at the prospect of praying in a group. I have always loved churches and I went to Mass whenever I could.

"What are these prayer groups like?" I asked.

"We have the use of a room in the grounds of Maynooth College," Dad replied. "We pray together and read passages from the Bible; then we can ask the group to say a prayer for our families or for someone else who's in trouble. After the prayer meeting we usually have tea and biscuits and a chat and socialize with each other."

"And make new friends," I said.

Elizabeth said she would babysit for us, and from that day on Elizabeth babysat for us every time we went to the prayer meeting.

I loved that first prayer group, even though, to be honest, I was so nervous that I remember little of it. We did, however, become regulars and we tried to go as often as possible.

Prayer is extremely powerful: when we pray we don't pray alone; our guardian angel always prays with us and so do any other angels who may be with us at the time. Even loved ones who are already in Heaven join with us when we pray.

Nothing is too small or trivial to pray for, and no prayer is too short—whether it is just one word or many words. We can pray anywhere—driving in our cars, when out walking, during a meeting, in a crowd, or on our own. Sometimes we pray without even realizing we are doing so, especially when we are thinking of a loved one who is sick or a friend with difficulties. When a prayer comes from the depths of our being it is incredibly powerful, and a person's religion or creed doesn't come into it: God hears the prayers of all his children equally.

Prayer is especially powerful when a group of people pray together in the same place, as we did in the prayer group, or if people from all over the world pray for something specific at the same time. Such prayer causes a tremendous intensification of spiritual power.

We always enjoyed the walk down to the prayer group; Joe would talk about different things that were happening in his job at the County Council and we would also talk about the prayer group. One Wednesday as we were walking down to the meeting I talked to Joe about my hope that it would be a big group that evening—it was usually about ten people and sometimes, especially in the summer, it was even smaller. When holiday time was over, the prayer group would start to grow in numbers and sometimes because of this it would be moved from one end of the campus to the other.

Da went to a lot of prayer groups, but he had been to only a few in Maynooth. He had brought us to our first one but he hadn't been often since, so this evening I was delighted to see him and hurried over to say hello. We walked up the steps together and through the door and into one of the rooms on the left. There were some people there and about twenty chairs in a circle. We said hello and sat down. Almost all of the chairs were taken.

More people then came in, followed by a priest who introduced himself as Father David; he then asked whether the group minded if some seminarians and nuns joined the prayer group that evening. We all said in chorus that they were welcome. As there were already about twenty laypeople in the room, he suggested we find a bigger room. Within minutes he was back, saying we had a bigger room in a building that wasn't directly attached to the college and we should bring the chairs—including the ones stacked against the wall. Everyone got up to help.

The next room was much bigger. Soon a lot of young seminarians started to arrive, together with some priests—maybe about seven of them. Some nuns arrived, too, along with a young girl who was staying in the nuns' house on the campus. More laypeople also arrived.

The room was very vibrant and full of light. I saw several angels, although not very clearly, and my soul was jumping with joy. My angels were whispering in my ear that someone very special was coming. "I know," I said, "I know who's coming." I wanted to jump for joy and tell everybody, but the angels stuck my feet to the ground so I could not move. "No," they said, "they would not believe you."

I was standing to the right, inside the door, with my feet held fast to the floor, watching the chairs. The chairs were arranged in concentric circles, and as the group kept getting bigger and bigger the chairs kept being moved around. I could see the original idea of circles of chairs was now out of the question, and instead an oval shape was being formed, with five or six ovals of chairs starting from the center and getting bigger by the minute. People were still coming in carrying chairs.

Joe called to me to come and sit down beside him. There were now six complete ovals of seats around this large room. The angels released my feet so I could move. I could see the empty chair beside Joe, but finding my way in was a problem. Some people got up off their chairs and moved them back so that I could get through and eventually I got to my seat and sat down beside Joe.

John, one of the laypeople, welcomed everyone to the prayer meeting. Then everyone started to praise God out loud, in their own words. (People prayed in the way they felt like, in the way that was meaningful to them.) The atmosphere became highly vibrant and electric, and with the beating of the angels' wings the light was also becoming radiant. I praised God with my whole heart and soul and I wanted to close my eyes, but the angels said no. As they shaded my eyes I could also feel angels' hands under my chin, holding my head up. I was starting to go into ecstasy. Everyone around me had their heads bowed; they were all in prayer and giving praise. In front, behind, and at both sides of each person, angels glimmered. The room was enveloped in angels from the floor to the ceiling—I do not think there was any space that was not filled by an angel.

Then one angel whispered in my ear, "Listen to everyone, Lorna."

I did and it was unbelievable. I could hear everyone individually: some were praying in tongues, others were repeating prayers over and over again, and some were singing hymns and praising God from the depths of their being, from their souls.

Slowly the angels allowed my head to bow a little and I could no longer feel the chair underneath me. I asked the angels not to let me close my eyes as I gave praise and thanks to God. The angels whispered in my ear that they would close my eyes only a little. Then the room grew silent. The angels fell silent.

A cloud of brilliant white light, alive with life, gradually engulfed the room, surrounding everything and everyone, purifying and cleansing everyone and everything in its path. From this cloud in the center of us God as a young man materialized and became visible; I recognized the very powerful presence as the one I had encountered that day as a child in Mountshannon, as I walked to my granny's house.

The young man—God—was dressed in a white robe. The tip of His toes had a golden appearance. His arms were down by His sides, His hands open, pointing downward, and beams of gold light flowed from His fingers. His face shone and His eyes were bright, radiating the eternity of life. His hair came down to His shoulders and was curly and bronze in color. But how can I hope to describe a brilliant, radiant light—all life itself—full of love, compassion, and hope?

God turned slowly to face everyone. Without movement, as we know movement, God moved among the people sitting in the inner oval circle. The people were giving praise and thanking God in silence, in meditation, in prayer, oblivious to Him. As God moved among the people sitting behind me I could feel Him; His presence was extremely powerful. I was filled with the peace that dwells in God. My prayer was this: if only God could stay and walk among us like this all the time.

When I finished my prayer I felt the touch of His hand on my shoulder. God touched my soul physically in this radiant light. How can I describe what my soul saw? Purity, in all infinity; clarity in full.

Then in a flash of light God was gone and the room was normal again. My eyes were fully open and I saw that the cloud of beautiful radiant life—the radiance of God's presence walking among us— was gone. I smiled with tears in my eyes.

A moment or two later everyone stopped praying and lifted up their heads. Someone spoke and said that praying and meditating in a big group filled them with unbelievable joy and peace. Then a young priest (I don't know whether he was a priest yet; he might have been a seminarian) spoke. He had light brown hair, was not very tall, and had a bit of a beard. "Did anyone feel it?" he asked.

I knew exactly what he was going to say, and I asked the angels, "Can I say it as well, that I felt it too—so that it would help him?" But they said no.

"I felt God walk among us," he said. "And I felt Him touch me. Did He touch anyone else?"

I so much wanted to say, "Yes, He did, He touched me too," but I was told no, that I was to be quiet. And the sad thing was that no one else had the courage to say, "Yes, God touched me"; no one else had the courage to acknowledge God. God had actually touched them! We are so afraid to say that God is in our lives; we are so afraid to acknowledge God openly, to speak openly.

I don't know who the other people were whom God touched, but I do remember that young man, and even to this day I hope that whatever he is doing he keeps on acknowledging that beautiful thing.

When the prayer meeting was over we had the usual tea and biscuits. Meanwhile I slipped outside to the car park with my drink in my hand. I went over and walked between some small trees—I was still shaking with excitement—and angels walked around the trees with me.

"I know that young man desperately wanted acknowledgment," I said to the many angels around me, not talking to any one angel in particular. I asked the angels and the young man's guardian angel to help him to keep his faith, his belief in God, regardless of whether he became a priest or not. I asked them, "What if I share with Joe about God walking among us and touching some of us?"

"No, Lorna, that would be too much for Joe to understand," the angels replied. "A time will come when you will share more with Joe, but you must remember, not everything. This is one of the things you will never share with him."

I felt a little sad. As I walked back toward the entrance the Angel Elisha appeared and held the door open for me, smiling. "Don't be sad," she said, and as she said that my sadness left me.

I met Da in the corridor and he said he was ready to go. I said I would find Joe and meet him at the car. We were home in a few minutes, and neither Da nor Joe said anything particular about the prayer meeting, so I believe they saw nothing.

CHAPTER 16

The tunnel

By the time we had been living in the cottage for five years the garden was in good shape. We were growing plenty of vegetables and we had some hens—the only difficulty was finding where the hens had laid the eggs! Eventually we fenced off the part of the garden with the big shed and used it as a henhouse, and after that it was no problem to find the eggs. Joe also built a long clothesline for all the washing; I can still remember the day he made it—him standing on a step ladder using a sledgehammer and me holding the pole. We laughed so much.

One afternoon Christopher and Owen made a tent from poles, a blanket, and some string and were having great fun playing in it while I was down in the garden hanging out the washing. Suddenly a big beam of light landed in front of my feet and hit me like a little slap—and I nearly fell over. It was Angel Hosus, of course! I laughed, knowing Hosus was doing this for fun.

"Lorna, I have something to tell you," he said. "It will be happy and sad. God is sending you a little baby soul. You will become pregnant in the New Year, but this little baby will not stay; it will return to God."

"I am sad already," I said. "Why are you telling me this, Angel Hosus? Why don't you just let it happen and say nothing? It would be easier for me not to know."

"Joe will be delighted you are pregnant, Lorna," Hosus said, "and when this little baby goes back to God, Joe will share in this in a little way that will help him understand your gifts."

"Do you think he'll understand?" I asked.

"Yes, he will," answered Hosus. "He'll understand—he'll find it a bit unbelievable in some ways, but as time goes on he'll know that it's all true because of other things that will happen in your lives. It's now time for you to talk to Joe again."

"Okay, I will," I said. "Maybe when I go for a walk with him later."

The children were still playing in their tent and running around in the front part of the garden when Joe came home from work that evening. He opened the gate. Christopher and Owen ran to him and he picked them both up in his arms and carried them into the cottage. Later that evening I asked Elizabeth to mind the children while Joe and I went for a little walk.

As we walked down by the canal we talked about all kinds of things, and I said, "I have something I'd like to share with you. Something that the angels show me."

I explained to Joe a little about the energy I see around plants as we passed wildflowers growing along the bank of the canal.

"Hold my hand and maybe the angels will help you to see the energy around these flowers," I said as I held his hand tightly. "Look at that flower there. Do you see the way balls of energy are coming out of it? The flower is throwing off its own energy. Can you see the different colors—yellow, white, and blue?"

I turned, still holding Joe's hand and still asking the angels to let him see.

"Look at that red poppy. Can you see the spirals shooting up from the base of the plant about a foot into the air? They're like fireworks exploding, one following another, only lasting for a few seconds."

Joe looked, but it was obvious from the expression on his face that he could see nothing, and that he even doubted that there was anything to see. My heart sank.

"Come on," said Joe, "let's go home."

Suddenly angels appeared as if they had come out of the air above the canal. The angels blew gently in the direction of the flowers. Joe started to walk away. I grabbed his hand and said, "Look at the breeze blowing the flowers. Can you see now, Joe?"

He stood in amazement, as if he was glued to the ground, and said, "I've never seen anything like that before."

He described for me what he was seeing. I smiled happily. *This was the first time I had ever been given confirmation that others saw the same things I did.*

Joe stood smiling at me in wonder. "Some things are hard to believe, but I know I shouldn't doubt you." He turned and looked again and seeing that the energy around the flowers had disappeared he was a little disappointed.

"I never understand it myself," I said to Joe. "It is almost as if the energy turns on and off, only to be seen physically with the human eye at certain times."

We strolled contentedly home, hand in hand. Joe and I put the children to bed and later that evening we sat and talked. Joe asked me a lot of questions, and some I could not give answer to.

As time went on Da became involved with different prayer groups in Dublin and around where he lived, including the "born-again Christians." Occasionally when the children and I would be up visiting my parents we would arrive as a visitor from the prayer group was leaving. One particular day just as we reached the gate of my parents' house the hall door opened and a man stepped out.

He looked at us and then turned to Mum and asked, "Who is this?"

Mum replied that I was her daughter and these were her grandchildren. He suggested to Mum that she bring us along to the prayer group one Sunday. I said hello but kept walking with the children around to the back of the house. I asked Mum who the man was. She told me he was one of the preachers from the born-again Christian prayer group in Dublin. I didn't ask any more questions, and Mum didn't give any more information.

Later the children and I caught a bus back to the cottage in Maynooth. As I was washing up in the kitchen I was keeping half an eye on Christopher—who was playing with toys on the dining room floor while Owen slept on a blanket. I was thinking about our invitation to this different prayer group. At that moment the kitchen door gave a little creak and opened. Instantly I knew it was Angel Michael.

Angels do not usually intervene with something material that is happening in our world, but for some reason they frequently do with me—often in small ways, such as when Michael helps me to lift things and Hosus blows on the washing. One woman who I met years later described how she couldn't get a key to turn in a locked door when she was trying to help her elderly mother who was inside. This went on for some time and she was desperate. She prayed to God and asked her angels for help, and suddenly the locked door opened without her touching it. This is what we call a miracle: we have no explanation for it, but we know we couldn't have done it ourselves. This is rare, but it is happening more frequently as people are evolving spiritually and are reaching out to the angels.

"Is that you, Michael?" I called, without turning around from the sink. As he entered the kitchen he touched my shoulder.

"Lorna, you called me!" Angel Michael said.

"I didn't realize I had, Michael," I replied.

"You have not realized yet," he said, "but for a long time now you have not needed to call us by name when you want us. All of God's angels are with you all the time."

"How did you know then, Angel Michael, that it was you I wanted to talk to?" I asked.

"Lorna, your human mind and soul are connected," Michael explained. "Your soul knows ahead of your consciousness that the human side of you needs to talk to me."

I laughed at the idea of my soul knowing ahead of me, and Christopher called out, "Mummy, what are you laughing at?" As he got up and walked into the kitchen, Christopher put his hand over his eyes and said, "Mummy, where did that bright light come from?"

I tickled him and didn't answer his question; then I sent him back to play with his little brother.

"Michael," I said, "you know one of the things I love is going to the prayer group in Maynooth. I have met wonderful people there."

Angel Michael gave me a big smile and said, "Tell me now what is really on your mind."

I took a deep breath and told Michael about being in my mum's house in Leixlip and about the man who had invited us as a family to this prayer group of born-again Christians in Dublin. "You know, I always feel nervous about having to go somewhere new," I said.

Angel Michael started to laugh at me. He reached out and took my hand. "Lorna, you won't have to stand on your head or do anything like that," he said. "Don't worry." We both laughed. Michael continued, "Just remember, when you go to the prayer group in Maynooth you pray and praise God. Do so the same way; just be free, Lorna, in your prayer and praise. There will be a lot of families there, so in this way it will be different. When the time comes, Lorna, you will go as a family to this prayer group with your parents, but it won't happen for quite some time."

As always, Michael was right. It would be many years later that we all went together and when it did happen it was a turning point in my life that brought me much closer to my father.

Christopher peeped in the kitchen door. "I can see the light again, Mummy."

Angel Michael disappeared. I picked Christopher up and we played wheelbarrow for a little while.

In the New Year, just as the angels had said, I became pregnant. Joe and I were very happy about the pregnancy, even though my heart was heavy because I knew that this little baby wasn't going to stay.

When a woman becomes pregnant, the baby's soul already knows if its mother will miscarry—if it will be aborted, stillborn, or deformed. Regardless of what happens, the baby's soul still loves its parents and will always be by their side—it will be there to help them through life. If you have ever lost a baby, never forget that that little baby's soul chose you to be its mother or father. It actually chose you before it was even conceived; that little soul loves you and was full of joy that you were able to conceive it.

In the Bible you read sometimes that God already knew you before you were conceived; this is because we were already spiritual beings in Heaven, where we were all queuing up to leave Heaven and be born on earth.

We have an awful lot of abortions in the world, but one must remember that even if a mother decides to have an abortion, that little soul already knows that its mother may do this, and even knowing this that soul has already chosen this woman to be its mother—even if that means that the baby is only conceived and never actually born. The little soul has chosen that mother and will love her no matter what. It is unconditional love. I would like every mother to remember this, particularly any woman who has had an abortion. Maybe a young girl had an abortion because she was afraid of life, of the world out there, or maybe she was scared of her parents or felt she had no one in whom to confide, or who could help her. Remember, that baby's soul loves you and never for one moment holds it against you that you did not give birth to it. It already knew what would happen, and still it will pour its love onto you.

Some years later people started to come to me for help, and I remember a woman who sought me out. At one stage she said to me, "I had a few miscarriages."

"Yes," I said, "the angels are telling me that." I looked toward my kitchen door and there, sitting on the floor, were five little children, five little souls surrounded by light, and they were beautiful—beautiful souls and beautiful little children. They turned and smiled at their mother. She couldn't see them, but I told her what I could see and she was filled with joy. I was able to tell her that some of them were boys and some were girls, and also what they looked like. That made her so happy. The little souls told me to let their mother know that they have always been around her and would always be with her.

"You know, I've always felt in the past that they were around me," the mother said to me. "Sometimes I even thought I felt their little hands touching my leg. I can even feel them now, touching me."

I had to smile, because at that moment they were up around her chair and they *were* touching her.

"Yes, they are," I said with a smile, "and you are blessed that you can feel the touch of your own little children whom God has sent to visit you. Remember, when the time comes for you to pass over, those five little souls will have their hands stretched out to you to bring you to Heaven as well."

"Thank you," the woman said. "I never told anyone about the presence of my little babies around me, and I never told anyone that I felt them touch me. I was afraid to tell anyone. I was afraid that people would think I was mad."

One thing people must remember is that there are millions of people who are actually having spiritual experiences, but they are afraid to say so. There are plenty of people who believe that angels are there helping them, and who actually sometimes feel them, but often they say to themselves, *Maybe I didn't see them; maybe it was my imagination.* It is wonderful to acknowledge the angels and to say, "Yes, I do believe in angels. Yes, I do believe in God." Many times we don't do this. Many times we only admit these things when we are bereaved, very ill, or desperate in some way. Only then do we turn to God and pray. We are often afraid to acknowledge God and his angels. As you grow spiritually you will find that you won't be afraid to acknowledge God, his angels, or any spiritual being that has come from the heavens.

During the first few months of my pregnancy, Joe did not look well. He complained of a lot of pains in his stomach, and the doctors sent him to the hospital for tests. They said it was a rumbling appendix, but that he was not sick enough to operate, so he was sent home with medicine. Joe continued to be in a lot of pain and, unable to keep food down, he lost a lot of weight that he couldn't afford to lose.

I could see the deterioration in him: the grey around his internal organs that I had seen before we married had gotten darker, and around the area of his appendix I could see a swollen mass of red.

I told the angels that it was so unfair that Joe had to suffer like that for months and months on end. I begged them to help. The doctor said he could do nothing; he apologized to Joe but said that the hospital wouldn't remove his appendix unless he was critically ill.

I miscarried at three months. For about a week before my little unborn baby left, the angels kept touching my belly and beams of light would flash straight out. Many times I asked, "Can my little baby not stay?" But I was always told no. Sometimes Joe asked me why was I sad, and I would tell him it was just the hormones and to take no notice of me. I never told him what the angels had said.

No matter how sick Joe was he always tried to help around the house. On that fateful day, I had been helping Joe stack turf in the shed and I told him that I wanted to go in and lie down on the couch, that I was tired. I fell asleep for a while and Joe came in and said the job was done—all the turf was in the shed. The children stayed outside playing. I was going to get up to make tea, but Joe said he would make it instead.

Joe was in the kitchen only a minute when I started to feel horrific pain; I could feel the life going out of my body. I called out to Joe urgently. He came immediately and sat beside me on the couch and said I looked very pale. He went into the bedroom to get a pillow to put under my head.

I felt my soul holding my baby's soul and rising out of my body, going toward a beautiful light. I knew my baby had died *and that I was dying too.*

I was rising toward the light, carrying my baby. The pain had gone. I was traveling through a tunnel of silver and gold, an enormous tunnel made of shiny white angels. I couldn't see the end of the tunnel as its path curved. I knew without being told that I was on my way to Heaven, and I felt no fear, just tremendous joy.

I could see other souls on their way to Heaven, too. They looked human in appearance and were dressed in brilliant white robes. I call the color white because I don't have any other word, but it was much more brilliant than the color we call white. Through their robes I could also see the light of their souls; it radiated up through their faces, making them look more pure and radiant than they ever had been on this earth.

When I got to a particular point a beautiful angel stood in front of me and stopped me from going further. I knew without being told why she was blocking my way, but she spoke to me in the sweetest, gentlest, and most compassionate of voices.

"Lorna, you should not have come with your baby. You must return."

"I don't want to go back," I said to the beautiful angel, but deep down in my soul I knew it was not my time to go to Heaven.

"Turn around, Lorna, and look back down the tunnel," said the angel.

As I turned I could see Joe holding on to my still body lying on the couch, trying to feel a pulse, a breath, shaking me, saying, "Come back, come back—you can't die on me." He was praying as he spoke.

I turned back to the angel and said, "No matter how much I love Joe and the children, I still don't want to go back to the human world. Why would I go? Here I am in the presence of God. Here I am perfect in every way. I feel unbelievably alive; I feel no pain and no sadness of any kind. Why do I have to go back?"

"You have no choice," said the beautiful angel. "You have to return, Lorna."

I looked at the soul of my little baby in my arms. He smiled at me; his blue eyes sparkled and he was radiant with life. The beautiful angel in front of me put out her arms to take him.

A powerful authority entered my soul. I knew I had no choice, that I had to go back, that I wasn't meant to be there.

I kissed my baby, holding him very tight, and then very reluctantly I put him into the beautiful angel's arms. I really did not want to let him go, even though I knew that someday I would see him again, and that in the meantime this beautiful snow white angel would take care of him.

As soon as I had handed over my baby, it was as if God took hold of my soul and brought it back gently through the tunnel, back to the house in Maynooth and to the couch where my body lay.

My soul started to enter my body slowly, but the pain was horrific. I felt every pore, every organ, every bone, every bit of flesh and muscle. Life was being poured back into a body that had been dead for a few minutes. It was horrific pain, but for some reason I am unable to understand I couldn't cry out; I couldn't make a sound.

Eventually I heard Joe's voice.

"Lorna, thank God you are alive. I thought you were dead."

I managed to give him a weak little smile.

I lay there for hours with the angels holding me, and I wouldn't let Joe leave me, even to call a doctor or an ambulance. Deep down inside I knew I was going to live, that I was meant to live. I never told Joe that I had died for those few minutes; he did not need to know that, and it would only have frightened him worse than he had been already. Eventually Joe went to the phone booth and called my parents and they came up to the house.

I asked Joe not to say anything about what had happened. All I told Mum and Da was that I had been feeling unwell all day and had started to bleed. Joe and Da brought me into the hospital and Mum stayed and minded Christopher and Owen.

At the hospital they were very concerned that I seemed so weak, and of course I didn't tell them all of what had happened earlier that day. They did a scan and said they could see nothing—there was no sign of the baby. The doctor came to see me and he held my hand and said he was very sorry.

"You lost your baby. It must have happened before you got to the hospital."

As the doctor was leaving Da walked in on his own and said, "I'm so sorry you lost the baby. I know how much this baby meant to you." He had tears in his eyes as he talked with me. I had never seen my father so upset over something to do with me.

The doctors said I needed to stay in the hospital, and when I was settled in the ward Joe and Da went home. A few days later they did an operation to clean out my womb.

Joe came to visit me every night. He was worried about me and sad that we had lost the baby. Two weeks later I was discharged, but

I was still very weak and spent a lot of time in bed. I was so glad to get home and hold my children in my arms and hug and kiss them.

It was years later that I told Joe more about what had happened that day; the day that I died and went some of the way to Heaven and back. I told him as a way of consoling him in the last few months of his life.

Many of us have a fear of death, but there is no need for it. At the moment of death there is no pain, no discomfort; some people may have pain right up to that last moment, but then there is none. You have no fear and anxiety—you go freely. Death is like birth; I know you might think that's a strange thing to say, but you are being born into a new life. You actually don't "die"; it's only this physical shell that you leave—like an empty eggshell.

I know there is a place called Hell, that it actually exists, but God has never shown me anyone being sent there. I can only go by what I have seen myself, and from what I have seen, God forgives everyone—no matter what they have done. I know this is hard for us to understand. A lot of the time we look for justice and revenge, so it is very hard for us to understand, but when our soul stands in front of God after death, it feels so much love and desire to be with God that it wants so much to stay there and it asks forgiveness in a very deep and real way, forgiveness for all that was done on this earth out of the frailty of the human condition.

And God in his infinite mercy forgives his child. We are all nothing but children in the presence of God, who is our Father.

Your soul is perfect; when your soul is free of your body it can travel through the universe to places you could never imagine. How can I help you to understand how wonderful this feeling is? There is no way to express it; no way to tell you, unless you have experienced it yourself. And most of us have to wait until we die to do this.

When you die you are not on your own; you are accompanied all the time by angels and those spirits who have gone before you.

You won't want to come back. Why, when you have no more pain, no more tears, no more sadness, would you want to get back into a human body? That is why when people die they do not want to return, and the only thing that brings a soul back to a human body is God sending it back, because it is not yet time.

We have become very materialistic as a society, and so frequently we look at death and ask, "Is this it? I rot away and there is nothing more?" I assure you there is more—much more. I hope that through the books I write I can communicate this and help people to understand. Believe what I say. Believe that, yes, there is more, much more, even though I may not be able to prove it or show it to you now; it is proven to everyone when they die. Some people feel that then it's too late—if they have to wait to die to see the proof. People are given proofs while they are alive, but sometimes they have to look or listen very hard to recognize them.

CHAPTER 17

Three knocks on the window

A few days after I got out of the hospital the weather started to get very cold. Joe was back working with the local County Council, even though it was only a temporary contract. I was out in the shed getting turf for the fire when I heard my name being called. I turned around but saw no one. I brought the bucket of turf into the house and there, sitting in the chair beside the fire, was an angel.

He startled me because he was very striking, very different from any other angel I had ever seen. It was as if he was made of jagged glass, of perfect shattered splinters that were all identical in size and all reflected light. His face and his features were very sharp, and as he stood up he was about twelve feet tall, the ceiling seemed to have disappeared to allow him space to stand there. Very unusually, music seemed to come from every part of him—enchanting, soft, mellow music, quite unlike anything I have ever heard before. It wasn't human music, but the sort of music I could imagine hearing in Heaven.

"Hello, Lorna," he said in a very soft voice. "My name is Kaphas. Something special is going to happen for you and Joe, but particularly for Joe."

"Angel Kaphas, can you tell me when?" I asked.

"Soon, Lorna. You will know when the angels descend on your home." Then Angel Kaphas rose out of the chair and was gone.

Weeks passed, I don't know how many, and the weather got colder still. Joe remained very sad about losing our baby, and I was too, but I had known in advance and so I had had more time to get used to it. The weather was getting very bad and it was ice-cold outside—really, really cold—and it was snowing extremely heavily. On his way back from work Joe decided to get extra groceries, and I always remember him arriving at the door with his arms full of bags of shopping. As Joe walked in he started to say, "God, it's cold . . ." but as soon as he said the word "God," angels descended on our little home.

It was as if angels were coming through every part of the house—through the roof, through the walls, even up through the floors. Every atom of the house seemed to be full of angels. Something like this sometimes happens—when something very special is about to occur. I knew this was the something special Angel Kaphas had spoken of—something special for Joe.

Joe continued " . . . You never know, tomorrow morning we might not be able to get outside the hall door with that snow." It was stacking up pretty high outside, and there were reports on the radio about roads blocked and traffic not being able to go up to Leixlip because the road was covered in snow and ice.

That evening we had the fire going—there was a power outage, so the fire was our only light—and I remember feeling nice and snug in our little cottage. The children were in bed asleep, we had plenty of fuel and food in, and it felt lovely; it felt safe. Around ten o'clock Joe and I were sitting by the fire enjoying tea and sandwiches and talking about the baby we had lost. As we sat there we gave him a name.

The room was shining with the angels and I noticed some angels going into our bedroom. When they came back into our little living room I heard them say of Christopher and Owen, "They are sleeping peacefully, like little angels."

Everything became silent; there wasn't a sound. I got up out of the chair and peeped out the window; it was pitch-dark outside, except for the snow, which left a glow in the darkness. I was a little anxious and excited. I did not know what the angels were going to allow to happen, but I knew it was going to be special.

The next minute there came three knocks on the window—of course, Joe and I nearly jumped out of our skins. He said, "Oh God, somebody must be outside."

As he was getting up out of the chair, three knocks came on the door as well. I said, "They must be freezing. Maybe it's Mum and Da; maybe they had to come up for something."

"They are out of their minds to travel on a night like this," Joe said.

Joe was surrounded by a whole host of angels, but, of course, he didn't realize it. Suddenly I knew what was going on and started to laugh.

Joe said, "Why are you laughing?"

"There is no one outside the door," I said. "I know who that was."

"Who?" asked Joe.

"It was our baby," I said. "He was saying good-bye. He was just giving you a physical sign to help you to believe, by knocking."

"Go away out of that! Don't be talking such nonsense," Joe said.

"Go out and open the hall door and you won't see any footprints in the snow."

I had to laugh again at the expression on Joe's face. The room was full of angels. I knew angels had brought my baby's soul to knock on the window and now he had gone back with other angels. I didn't need to see him, our little son—he had done this for his dad, to help him to believe.

Joe opened the hall door. The snow was up against it; it was nearly a foot deep and it fell in onto the mat; the freezing cold air came in, too. Joe looked out and he could not believe it—there were no footprints in the snow. He looked and he looked to see if he could find any footprints in the snow—of animals, birds, footprints of any kind. He stepped out into the snow. Joe went white in the face; he couldn't believe it. He looked at me and shook his head, saying, "Oh my God, that's just too much!"

Eventually he came back in, closed the hall door, and I said, "Don't worry, sit down by the fire and get warm. That was your son, our baby, saying good-bye. He was leaving with all the angels to go to Heaven, off to where he should be. Now you can let him go."

Joe cried there at the fire; we held each other in our arms and we both cried. We were very peaceful, though.

"Wasn't it wonderful that our little baby did that for us?" I said to him. "That the angels allowed something like that to happen so we would know that our baby's okay, that it's all right. That was our child thanking us for being his parents."

Da had a habit of dropping in to see us out of the blue—mostly in the evening. I always loved this. One day I was out working in the garden, pulling weeds and hoeing between the rows of potatoes—we were now growing most of our own fruit and vegetables—and Christopher was helping me. Although he was only about five, he was always anxious to help.

As I heard Da's car pull up outside the gate, I turned around. The two boys cried out "Granddad." Christopher ran through the potatoes and tried to open the gate, with Owen toddling behind. The gate was tied with string, so I picked Owen up and helped Christopher to untie the knot. The gate opened and Owen wiggled in my arms to get down. Christopher greeted Da as he got out of the car. He was in fishing gear and wearing his favorite hat—a tweed hat with colorful fishing flies in it. He'd had the same hat for years, he wore it every opportunity he got, and he always treated it with loving care.

Da greeted the kiddies with a pet on the head—he always did that, and sometimes I would say to him, "They are not dogs you are petting, Da!" and he would laugh at me.

"The garden is looking great," said Da, as Christopher pulled him in the direction of the potatoes.

"When the children are finished showing you all the vegetables we're growing come in and I'll have tea ready," I said.

Owen, who was now about three, was first back into the kitchen and arrived with a tumble and roll. He had been born prematurely and as a result of not having developed fully before birth his hips swiveled much more than normal. He could move so fast that I would hold my breath as I watched him, and he could tumble over three or four times and still end up back on his feet. It was as if he was double-jointed from the waist down. Many times when I saw Owen tumbling and I was holding my breath I would see flashes of angels spinning around him in every direction, protecting him. Seeing the way he tumbled you would expect him to break bones— but he never did. The doctors in the hospital said that Owen's hips wouldn't develop properly before the age of seven, and I often said to Joe that I couldn't wait for Owen to reach that age so that I could breathe easily.

"Lorna," my father asked, "would you and Joe and the kiddies like to come on holiday with your mum and me in the summer— down to the little cottage in Mullingar?"

I was delighted. My parents had recently got enough money together to buy a little cottage in Mullingar—fifty miles from Dublin. Joe and I had never had a holiday; we had never even gone on honeymoon. I was thrilled at the idea of a break.

"That would be great," I said. "Of course we'd love to come. I hope Joe can get the time off."

Joe had recovered from his appendicitis, but I could still see the red mass of energy around his appendix, so I knew it would flare up again. He had recently gotten a job at the local carpet factory—it was hard physical work in unpleasant conditions, washing and dying wool—and most of the time he worked the night shift. This work couldn't have helped his health, but we needed the money.

One of the few benefits of this job, other than the small, but regular, income, was that Joe had access to cheap undyed wool. I had done little knitting as a child, but now that I had access to this wool I took to knitting with a vengeance, even though all the jumpers I knitted were the one color—the color of sheep! I knitted Aran sweaters for the children, for Joe, and for Da. My da loved his sweater and wore it a lot of the time he wasn't working.

This day Da and I sat down and had a cup of tea and talked for a few minutes. The children were delighted, too; they asked their granddad so many questions about where the cottage was, what it was like, whether there were trees in the garden.

"The garden is wild, with lots of trees and grass as tall as you. There are lots of little lanes as well, all overgrown like a jungle. You'll have a great time."

"When can we go?" they kept asking, and I told the children, "Not until your granddad and dad get a holiday."

Da had his tea and then went outside into the garden with the children for a little while. "See you, Lorna, I'm going now," he called out.

The day before we were due to go on holiday was a really warm, sunny day with hardly a breeze, but as I was hanging washing on the line this strong wind suddenly came up. I knew it wasn't an ordinary breeze and I started to laugh.

"I bet that is you, Hosus!" I said. "What are you doing blowing away my washing on me? What are you up to?"

Then he just appeared. As usual, he was playing tricks and trying to make me laugh. Then he disappeared again, just like a light evaporating into the air. He is a wonderful angel. That day I caught my son Christopher standing there, looking in the same direction and staring, and I knew by his eyes that he saw what I saw. He never mentioned it then, nor since; maybe he has forgotten about it; maybe, though, when he reads this book he will remember—that I don't know; I will just wait and see.

The day we were off on holiday I was worrying how we were all going to fit into the car. Da's car was not big, and we had a lot of luggage. The children were out in the garden watching anxiously for their granny and granddad, and when the car pulled up to the gate the children let out such screams of joy.

Christopher and Owen immediately climbed into the car with their toys, and Da and Joe somehow managed to fit everything into the trunk. Off we went toward Mullingar, in County Westmeath, some forty miles from Maynooth. Joe talked quite a bit, but I stayed quiet within myself and played with the children.

We got to the cottage late; it was almost getting dark, but there was a beautiful full moon and a bright sky packed with stars. The little stone cottage was lovely—nice and cosy. I just felt happy to be there. Mum and Da slept downstairs and we all slept upstairs. I slept really well that first night.

During that holiday Da and Joe did a lot of fishing on different lakes around the area, and Da brought the children and me out in a boat, too. The children were so excited about being on the water and the boat bobbing up and down, even though we only went a short distance from the shore and back in again.

Da had had an accident in the garage a few years before, and since then he had been unable to do heavy physical work. Even though Joe wasn't particularly well himself, he did a lot of work on the cottage that holiday that Da couldn't do. I helped too. We put up dry wall to protect the walls from the damp, which was a difficult job as one of the walls was very high and the dry wall was very heavy. On a couple of days we worked all day until the evening but by the end of the holiday we had succeeded in finishing the job.

On a few evenings Joe and Da went fly-fishing. One evening I told Joe I'd like to go for a walk on my own and I asked him to stay with the children. I wanted to be by myself so that I could really talk to the angels, not just quietly, but aloud, so that they could actually walk beside me in a physical human form. It was about eight o'clock in the evening when I went off. I knew there wouldn't be that many people down by the lake at that hour. I crossed the main road and took a left turn down a minor road to reach the lane that leads to the lake. Instead of turning left for the lake I decided to go straight on, and as I walked I said to the angels, "Now you can walk alongside me. I know you are there in spiritual form, but I need you to appear in physical form so that I can talk to you."

Angel Michael appeared beside me and walked in time with my step. He put his hand on my shoulder, and that felt good. As we walked along the road Angel Michael said, "A little further up the road, Lorna, there is a forest to the right. Let's go for a walk there."

When we reached the forest it looked overgrown and very dark. "I can't go for a walk in that forest," I said. Michael took my hand and as we walked the brambles moved apart and we had a path. We came to a little opening in the forest, looking down across the fields and the lake. Sometimes it is nice just to walk and know that the angels are right beside me and that I have nothing to fear, but that night as I walked through the forest with Michael I had a vague sense of something watching me.

I didn't give it much thought, though, and I didn't ask Michael about it.

Next morning, after breakfast, Da invited Joe to go fishing with him again and off they went with their fishing gear. I called after them to bring some fish home for our tea. Da said he'd try, but he couldn't promise, and they headed off down to the lake. Mum was busy out in the garden, doing something or other with flowerpots, so when I had cleaned up I went off with the children down the boreen and where the trees were; it was a wild place and they loved it there.

Later Mum and I went off walking with the children down toward the lake, enjoying the last day of our holiday. We talked to people we met on the way; some were vacationers like ourselves and some were local people Mum had gotten to know. When we got down to the shore of the lake there were a lot of families there. The children and I played in the water; they enjoyed picking up stones, throwing them, and watching the splash and feeling the ripple of the water hitting their legs. There were tears when it was time to head back to the house.

Shortly afterward Joe and Da arrived home with some trout. Da took the trout outside and showed the children how to chop off the head and the tail and clean them out.

"Ugh," the children went. "Ugh!"

"That's an easy thing to do," I told them. "I learned how to clean out fish and cook them as a child. It's great to know how to do it, particularly when you can cook them over a campfire."

No sooner had I said this than Christopher wanted us to build a campfire to cook the fish. Unfortunately we had to say no because we were going back to Maynooth that night. We did eat the lovely trout, though, but we cooked them in the kitchen. As soon as we were finished tea we had to clean up and then pack the car. We arrived back at Maynooth and Mum and Da went home—the holiday was over.

We never had very much. I used to ask the Lord, "How on earth do we survive?" But we did. I always seemed to manage on a shoestring. I would count pennies and grow vegetables to make things stretch. There was no such thing as buying new clothes for Joe or myself. Every now and then my mother would say she had a bag full of clothes—I don't know where she got them from, but they never suited me; they were always too big and made me look like a granny. Sometimes, but not always, there might be trousers or jumpers in the bag that would fit Joe. We would laugh and say, "Beggars can't be choosers."

Many times my engagement ring was a godsend. Pawnbrokers were a blessing for us, as for many families in Ireland at that time—there was almost always a queue. I remember occasions when we went into the pawnbrokers and came out with money in our hand, feeling like a millionaire. On occasions when we didn't have money for bread and butter to put on the table, Joe would thumb a lift into Dublin with my engagement ring in his pocket and head straight for the pawnbrokers. He would get maybe ten pounds for it and then, over time, we would save up to get it back again. What a lifesaver that ring turned out to be!

Joe was given a bicycle by a neighbor, an old man down the road who had asked Joe to help him clean up his house and garden and out of gratitude gave him his old bicycle. It only needed cleaning up and a few minor repairs. I thanked God and the angels for the gift of the bicycle, and the old man for listening to his angels. Joe could now cycle to work at the carpet factory.

Despite the shortage of money those years were great; they were wonderful times when it was lovely to be alive, to see my children smiling and to see Joe being able to enjoy life for a while.

The summer after I lost the baby Joe had a great idea. He went off to the bicycle shop in Celbridge and made a deal: in return for two weeks of cleaning the bike shop and sorting out all the bicycles and bits and pieces in the yard every evening he would be paid two bicycles—an adult's and a child's. Then, with Owen on the back of Joe's bike, we could all go on outings together.

So every evening after work he went to the bicycle shop, and by the time he got home it was after midnight. But it was worth it—at the end of the first week he brought home a child's bike. It was badly in need of repair, though, and in many ways it looked like a piece of junk. Halfway through the second week the man in the bike shop gave Joe the adult bike and this one looked much better.

Christopher was very excited about getting a bicycle and with his help eventually we got the bikes all fixed up. Christopher, who was a very skinny young lad at the time, was out there helping his dad, learning how to oil the chain and fix spokes and all that kind of thing. He also learned how to cycle very well.

I always remember the first day we decided to cycle to Donadea, some six miles away, for a picnic. Joe said six miles was a long cycle for a five-year-old, so we'd have to see how far we got before Christopher got too tired. Joe had a seat on the back of his bike for Owen, and I had the bags with the picnic on the back of mine.

I was worried about Christopher, but I shouldn't have worried, as he was well able. We did stop every now and then to have a little rest, though, or walk a little with the bikes.

After that we went to Donadea for a picnic as often as possible and had lovely times. The place had a stillness and peace, particularly in the evening time when everyone had gone home. There was also what many people called a lake—I called it a pond—with ducks, and there was a little bridge to a tiny island that had four trees and a few picnic tables, but no grass.

On arriving we would light a little campfire and make tea. The children loved sitting at a campfire on the island with the water all around them and the ducks coming up beside them, looking for bread. We would have our tea and our sandwiches and look at the stars. I know we weren't really meant to light a campfire there, because of the forest, but we were always very careful. Da had taught me a lot about campfires and other things to do with nature when I was a child; he had taught me about lighting fires, about walking safely along a riverbank, about swimming and currents in the water; he had told me that there were rules about everything.

One evening when we were there the stars were shining and there was a full moon in the sky, so it was quite bright. There was no one else around, just us and the ducks. We had lit a little fire and the children were eating their sandwiches and playing around—the little boys doing all kinds of things. I told Joe I would like a few moments on my own and I asked him to keep an eye on the boys while I went for a walk. For some time I had been aware of something watching me from very far away. I wanted to talk about this with the angels.

Joe protested that it was dark. But I replied, "I'll take the torch with me."

I walked across the little wooden bridge onto a little path in the direction of the old castle, then right again to where there was a fair-sized lawn with a lot of trees around it. I went around the big oak tree so that Joe couldn't see me. I really wanted to be on my own and I knew that he would be watching for me.

Angel Elijah appeared, like a vibrant light among the trees, and walked out into the clearing, calling my name. As Elijah reached out toward me my hands lifted toward him and he enveloped them in his hands.

We communicated, but there were no words. "Lorna, he walks in the darkness," Elijah told me. "Don't be afraid, he cannot come any closer unless God allows him. Do you know who I am talking about?"

"Yes, Angel Elijah," I said. "Satan. Is that who has been watching me in the dark? I have been conscious of someone, or something's presence, on the outskirts of my life—beyond the circle of light that surrounds me, millions of miles away in another circle of darkness where he hides. For the last six months I have been scared, even though I know that God and all of you angels are protecting me."

"Lorna, this is happening because one day God is going to test you by putting you in the presence of Satan," Elijah said.

"Where will God be when this is happening?" I asked.

"God will be on your right and Satan will be on your left," said Elijah.

"God will be with me to give me the strength," I said; "that is all that matters." But inside I was filled with an enormous dread and terror. Then Angel Elijah let my hands go, and as they fell to my side I was filled with a feeling of peace and love. Elijah, smiling, gestured to me to look behind me, and then he disappeared.

Joe came up behind me with the children. Christopher had his bike and Joe had the two bikes and Owen as well.

"Lorna, we have to go now. It's really getting late." He spoke in a quiet voice, as if not to wake any of the creatures in the forest.

"I didn't notice the time pass," I said.

I took my bike and we walked along the paths and out onto the road. I felt very quiet and very still, very detached from the human world, and my family. From that moment I could feel that Satan was on his way toward me; it might take months or even years for him to come to me, but I was certain that we would meet.

CHAPTER 18

"Isn't Lorna lucky . . ."

One winter evening Joe and I arrived at the prayer group in Maynooth. There were already about twenty-five people in the room, a lot of them young men. Johnny, a very spiritual person, welcomed everybody, and we all started to pray together and sing, which I always loved. Then everybody, including myself, went into silent prayer. You could have heard a pin drop. An angel whispered in my ear, "Lorna, open your eyes and raise your head. Do you see the young man to the right?"

"Yes," I whispered back.

"Lorna, you are going to share that young man's vision. Lower your head now and close your eyes," the angel whispered.

I went into the young man's vision immediately. I was walking beside him, along a winding, dusty road, full of stones and holes; I could not see very far ahead because there was always another turn. He was walking for some time but he always managed to avoid the stones and the holes. He seemed to be lost, but he wasn't really because around the next turn was a building with steps leading up the lefthand side. With great effort the young man made his way up the steps—it was as if they became steeper with each step. Slowly, he approached the door.

As I watched his vision it was as if the building had grown. From the road it had looked a normal size, but now it was gigantic. The young man stood back in amazement. The door now in front of him was very big and heavy, and he was tiny by comparison. He wanted to go in, but it was going to take great effort. Using all his weight he eventually succeeded in pushing the door open and squeezed inside into an enormous empty hall that was filled with a great light. He sat down on the floor and began meditating, a tiny speck in this massive place.

I felt the touch of the angel's hands on my head, and the connection between the young man and myself was broken.

"It is time for sharing," Johnny said.

One by one people started to share. Eventually, the young man who had had the vision started to speak. He described the vision as he had experienced it—it was exactly as I had seen it. This was the first time I had ever shared another person's vision in this way and I was very excited about it. At the end of his description the young man said he didn't understand what the vision meant.

The angels asked me to speak; they told me that I must tell the young man the significance of his vision, in order to give him courage to continue with his journey.

I was nervous; I was terrified!

"I can't do this," I said to the angels. "They won't listen to me—I'm just an ordinary person."

The young man stopped speaking. The angels kept telling me I had to do it, and I kept giving them reasons why I shouldn't. Then another young man spoke and the angels told me to pay attention and listen to what he had to say.

"There is someone at the prayer meeting to whom God is talking. This person is afraid and nervous." That is all he said. God was asking me not to hide anymore.

I took a big, deep breath just as Johnny said, "If that is all the sharing, we will say a prayer together."

"No, I have something to say," I said. I turned to the young man who had had the vision and explained to him that the vision related to his fear of becoming a priest. I told him that there would be a lot of obstacles on the path that God had laid out for him, but he would overcome them. He would make a big difference, not just in Ireland, but in other parts of the world. He needed to have faith and belief in God and in himself, and he should take up his bag and go on his journey. I explained this was the message that the angels had given me for him.

Then Johnny started to pray and we sang and praised God. I really enjoyed that part. I was told by the angels that I had more to do at future prayer meetings, but I told the angels that I was dreading the thought of what they would ask me to do next.

The prayer meeting ended and we had tea and biscuits before Joe and I walked home. Joe made no comment about my having talked at the prayer group.

A few months later, at another prayer meeting in Maynooth, Johnny said, "Let us all pray and ask for the healing that is needed within our families, or for our friends or anywhere in the world."

Everyone shared, one by one. Some people had problems in their families, or their friends had problems. People prayed for family members or friends to get well, or for a daughter's success with an exam; there were also prayers for help with a much needed holiday and a decision about a car. Miracles were asked to achieve world peace, for governments, for help for priests and nuns and different charities—for so many things. It seemed a lot of miracles were needed. All the while the angels kept tapping on my shoulder and saying, "Now, Lorna. You know what to say."

I took a deep breath. "There is someone here," I started, "who needs a lot of prayer for her family. She has a brother who is married and he suffers with an alcohol problem and is abusing his wife and children. This person loves her brother very much. There is a court case coming up to do with something else and there is an awful lot of stress. God is saying to you that there is no need to be ashamed. Come and talk to Him. Have faith and pray for everything to be all right."

I finished. No one said anything else.

Sometimes in prayer groups certain people will lay hands on others and pray with them, sometimes out loud. Johnny then asked whether anyone wanted to be prayed over, and he called out the names of those who would pray over other people.

I was not one of them—I never had been—but that's not the way it turned out that day. God had other plans.

People got up and walked around the room, chatting, and some went off to make tea. A nun walked to me; I smiled at her and said hello. It did not dawn on me that she was going to ask me to pray with her, but she did.

"Would you mind praying with me, Lorna? It was me you were talking about and I need to talk to God through you."

I nearly lost my voice. "Yes, of course," I said, "but not in here with everybody. Can we leave the room and go somewhere else, where we can be on our own?"

"Of course," she said. We went out into the corridor and found an empty room three doors down. We went in and sat down together, just the two of us—little did she know that I was shaking. "Oh my God, what are you doing?" I kept praying.

Angels appeared all around us, whispering in my ear, "You are in God's hands, Lorna."

I prayed over the nun and I thanked God for the wonderful things that would change in her life. Then I said to her, "It's time for you to talk to God."

She started to talk; she must have talked for about an hour. At the end we prayed together. Every now and then the angels told me to open my eyes and look at her. The angel who was with her, her guardian angel, was beautiful. I called her guardian angel "the angel of peace and tranquillity." I never told the nun I could see her angel or that the angel had her wrapped in her arms with her wings around her, that her angel was merged with her. I smiled, closed my eyes again, and praised God more. Then the angels told me to go back to the other room.

When we got back to the other room almost everyone was gone. Joe and I walked home. He said he was very surprised that I had spoken, and I told him I found it very hard because I was so nervous, but that I had to do what God had asked me to do, with the angels' help. That was the first time I had ever prayed "over" someone. I had, of course, prayed for many people before, but I always did so secretly, without their knowing.

Joe's work at the carpet factory kept him out most nights. Many times after the children were in bed I would sit in front of the fire, take a deep breath, close my eyes, and when I opened them again there would be lots of angels sitting around the fire with me. I would talk to them about everything. I would tell them that one of the most wonderful things was that I could talk to them, no matter where I was, and know that they were hearing my words. I talked to the angels constantly—they were my companions, my best friends.

When it got late I would tell the angels that they had better go because Joe would be home soon and I had things to do. The angels would then disappear physically, but I would still feel their presence; sometimes I would even feel an angel brushing against me. One particular evening, that is exactly what one angel did—brushed against me—and then appeared, just for a moment. This angel smiled at me and touched my belly, saying, "God has granted your desire for another baby." Then the angel disappeared.

Shortly afterward I discovered I was pregnant. Joe was thrilled;

he said it would be lovely if the baby was a little girl. I did not seem to have too many difficulties during the pregnancy this time, and I thanked God for that.

After Christmas we decided to look at names for our unborn child. Joe said there was no point picking a boy's name this time; he was sure it was going to be a girl. We decided on the name Ruth. I went into labor about ten days early and was admitted into the hospital. Then the labor stopped for a while. During this time Mum and Da came in to visit and brought me some fruit. Da said he was looking forward to another grandson and Joe told him, "It won't be a boy this time! Wait and you'll see—it will be a girl."

When Mum and Da were leaving the hospital I decided to walk with Joe to the main entrance. Mum and Da were ahead of us as my grandparents, Mum's parents, walked in through the doors of the hospital. Mum and Da stopped to talk to them and Joe and I said hello. We were standing about two feet away from Mum and Da when my grandmother said to my parents, "Isn't Lorna lucky her boys aren't retarded like herself, or even worse! We expect this baby will be, though."

Her guardian angel appeared behind her—there were tears in the angel's eyes and he reached out and touched me, giving me strength. But I was devastated. I could see Joe, too, was shocked to overhear this comment. My grandparents had spoken to my parents as if we did not exist. I moved away, with Joe's arm around me.

"Don't mind them," Joe said, "they are ignorant people."

He walked back to the ward with me. I was crying. Angels appeared all around my bed and filled Joe and me with peace and love. I asked Joe not to mention to my parents what we had overheard.

What upset me most that day was that my father didn't defend me. I was deeply upset that he did not rebuke my grandparents, although I think I know why. He knew my mother's parents didn't fully approve of him either—they felt that Mum had married beneath her, despite all the progress Da had made. Da loved Mum very much; he felt he had caused a rift between my mother and her parents, and he was anxious not to widen it.

I understood why Da hadn't defended me, but it still hurt, and I lay there that night crying my heart out.

Years later I discovered, accidentally, that Granny, my mother's mother who had made those dreadful comments, had had a baby with Down syndrome. The baby had a bad heart and lived to be only six or seven. For all her short life she was kept in a bedroom upstairs, shut away from all the neighbors. I was told they felt ashamed to have a "retarded" child.

In the early hours of the next morning I went into labor and our little daughter, Ruth, was born on March 25—on Mother's Day and my own birthday. What a great birthday present!

The day we were discharged from the hospital Joe arrived with Christopher and Owen. The boys ran over to my bed but Joe walked slowly. There were angels around him, supporting him. His guardian angel came forward and told me Joe was not well. I wanted to cry, but I knew I had to smile. Christopher and Owen were both fussing over their new little sister, wanting to hold her, and Joe took our little daughter out of the cot and let her little brothers put their arms around her. I asked Joe if he was okay and he said yes—though I knew it wasn't the truth, and he knew it too. I told the angels that I was really worried about him and I asked them to do anything they could to help.

About two months later Joe was working on the night shift when he got bad pains in his stomach. He went to his boss and told him he was feeling unwell and asked if someone could take him home.

"No, you look fine to me," his boss said, and sent him back to work.

The thing was that Joe hardly ever looked sick because he was tall and strong-looking. Eventually, though, he told his boss that he was going home anyway, that he was too sick to work. About two in the morning the angels woke me, saying, "Lorna, get up. Joe is not well; he's on his way home. We are sending him help."

I got up straightaway, turned on all the lights, put on the kettle, and then got myself dressed. I stood at the window looking out, praying to God to get Joe home safely somehow.

Joe told me later that about halfway between Celbridge and Maynooth he had collapsed along the side of the road. He remembered coming round and crawling on his hands and knees when suddenly the lights of a car shone on him. It was a neighbor from Maynooth who stopped, turned his car around, and got out to help. At first the neighbor assumed it was a drunk and could not believe his eyes when he recognized Joe. Joe explained he had a lot of pains in his stomach and the man offered to drive him home.

An angel tapped me on the shoulder. "Lorna, go and open the gates. Joe is almost here."

As I opened the gates the neighbor drove the car in. I helped him bring Joe into the house and put him into bed. He told me he would ring the doctor.

"How can I ever thank you for being so good?" I asked.

He told me that he hadn't been able to sleep and had decided to go for a drive, and now he was glad he had. I made Joe a cup of tea and about ten minutes later, when the doctor arrived, Joe was sitting up in bed, feeling much better. The doctor laughed at Joe when he saw him.

"I hope you haven't got me out of my bed for nothing. I was told you had fits of pain and that you were found crawling on your hands and knees on the side of the road."

"All the pain is gone," Joe said. "I feel fine now."

They talked and joked for a few minutes and then the doctor

said, "Lie down flat on the bed there. Maybe your appendix is acting up again." He put his hands on Joe's stomach and instantly Joe shot bolt upright in bed, screaming with agony.

"You are in trouble, Joe," the doctor said. "I'm going to send for an ambulance and write a note for the hospital."

The angels continually amaze me: who else do you think they were talking to that night but my da! They told him to get up and go to our cottage. Da pulled into the drive behind the doctor's car just as the doctor was asking where the nearest telephone was.

Da walked in asking, "What's happening?"

The doctor told him that Joe needed to go to the hospital and that he was just about to call an ambulance. Da offered to take Joe to the hospital, but the doctor refused and said he needed an ambulance. Da went out and moved his car out of the way and the doctor went down the road to where there was a public telephone. He was back in two minutes, saying that the ambulance was on the way. The doctor went back out to his car to write a note about Joe for the hospital, and I went into the kitchen, leaving Da with Joe.

I was filling the kettle with water again when I felt the gentle hands of the angels caressing me, taking the anxiety out of my body, whispering that Joe would be all right, that he would have a tough time but he would pull through.

The doctor came back in, saying the ambulance had arrived. Da told me he would follow the ambulance in his car and be there for Joe. I, of course, had to stay with the children as I was still feeding Ruth. I gave Joe a hug.

"Don't worry," he said, "I'll be home in no time."

They had gone. I walked back into the bedroom; the children were fast asleep, their guardian angels watching over them. I smiled back, knowing the angels had kept the children asleep while all the commotion was going on. I thanked them and turned around. Angel Hosus was standing in front of me.

"Lorna, go to bed now," he said. "We're going to put you to sleep."

I got into bed and did not wake until ten o'clock the next morning, and the children slept too. While I was getting breakfast ready, Christopher came into the kitchen asking where his dad was. I explained that he was in hospital and that as soon as everyone had had breakfast we would ring the doctor to find out how he was.

I was feeding Ruth when my da called in. The children were delighted to see him. I thanked him for last night and asked him how Joe was, and how long he had stayed with him. Da had been in the hospital with Joe all night; Joe had been rushed into surgery, but he was now all right, although they had feared for his life for a while.

"I will take you in every evening to see Joe," Da offered.

I protested that that was too much to ask of him, but he insisted and said that Mum would look after the children.

When I saw Joe that evening he looked dreadful. He spent two weeks in the hospital, and then a few weeks later he was back in the hospital again for about ten days with an infection. After that he was off work for almost six months.

One day when I was approaching the checkout in the local supermarket the guardian angel of a little girl sitting in a shopping cart called me over. I knew the mother by sight but I didn't know her name.

I said hello to the little girl, and her guardian angel told me that she was unwell and asked me to touch her. I touched her little hand as I greeted her mother and told her she had a beautiful child. The mother said good-bye and moved on with her daughter.

The angels told me that a connection had to be made between me and the child so that she would get well. This is something that often happens, although I don't fully understand it. A year or so later

I bumped into the same mother and daughter, and again the child's guardian angel called me over to her. The mother told me her little girl had been unwell; she had been in the hospital but now she was better.

As the mother walked away with her little girl the angels told me, "The little girl is going to get very sick, Lorna, but because of your touch the strong spiritual bond that was made will give her the strength to pull through this illness. From now on until she fully recovers you will constantly see this little girl's smile directly in front of you."

During the following months I would regularly see this little girl's smiling face in front of me, and I would physically feel her sickness and her tears. Each time I would say a prayer for her and I would ask God and her guardian angel to make her better. I know this little girl was critically ill. I was the child's lifeline; somehow spiritually I kept her alive. I was by her bedside in spirit every time I was needed and I did not let her soul leave her body.

Suddenly, though, I stopped seeing her face and I knew she was well. I thanked God and the angels and gave it little further thought. Years later I saw the mother and daughter walking down the main street of Maynooth, their guardian angels walking hand in hand with them. The little girl was now a teenager and was healthy and strong. I smiled, thanking God and the angels.

One summer day when Ruth was a few months old I was out wheeling her in her stroller, enjoying the sunshine, when suddenly I felt the atmosphere change. There was an incredible silence. The air grew very still and it seemed to get brighter. I knew that an angel was coming. I was walking, but my feet didn't seem to be touching the ground. I felt I was moving yet nothing around me was moving. I felt a presence behind me. I stopped and turned around but I could see no one. I walked on. No sooner had I taken a step than I felt the presence again.

"Whoever is walking behind me, please make yourself known." I said.

There was no reply.

"Don't do this. I hate it!"

I walked on very, very slowly, and then I felt a little tap on my shoulder. I turned around and there was an angel there. He was just like a light—the same glowing and shimmering effect as if you were looking at a star, but many times brighter. I just said, "Hello." No reply. Sometimes I feel a little shy talking to the angels—and I think sometimes they feel shy talking to me. Communication is as important in the spiritual world as it is in the physical world, and sometimes just as hard, so I told him that it would be easier for me to talk to him if he made himself a bit more human-looking.

It was only when he did so that I realized it was Angel Michael. He turned himself into a very handsome man, maybe in his forties, about six feet tall or possibly a little taller, with sharp blue eyes and long, dark, flowing hair to his shoulders.

"Well, this time you've certainly made yourself handsome," I said and we both laughed.

We started to walk along the road, with me pushing the stroller with the baby asleep in it. He told me he had come to talk to me about a book, a book he said the angels needed me to write, into which they wanted me to put certain things. I replied that deep inside I had known for some time that I had to write a book, but I admitted to him that I was scared to do so as I was afraid of being ridiculed.

"Lorna, the day will come when you will do it for us," Angel Michael replied. It's now many, many years later, but the day has finally come, and this is my first book.

Since the first time I saw him in my bedroom as a young child,

Michael—that beautiful angel—has come and visited me regularly. He comes in and out of my life; sometimes he comes and walks with me or sits down at my kitchen table; other times he sits by the fire with me, saying he needs to get himself warm. I laughingly tell him that angels don't feel the cold, but he always says that he can imagine how it feels because he has been around so many humans.

We talk as if he is a human friend. Sometimes we talk about ordinary things and sometimes we talk about very important things. Michael tells me that fewer and fewer people are asking for angels to help them, so we talk about the extraordinary fact that there are millions of angels out there who are unemployed.

That's why this book is being written, so that people will realize that angels are walking beside us, that they are there all the time, that we just need to reach out and let them help. It's as simple as that. I listen to Michael and he tells me what to write; he tells me to write from my heart.

God is pouring these beautiful angels out on this world for us, and yet many of us are ignoring them. We need to reach out and ask them for help. It's as simple as that.

CHAPTER 19

"I'm here, I'm here—here I am!"

One morning when Ruth was a few months old I took her down to the health center for her checkup. When I got home and was feeding her I felt the presence of a spirit, a ghost, gradually approaching the cottage. I said a little prayer but thought no more of it.

As the days passed I started to notice the presence of that spirit visiting quite frequently, getting closer; I was feeling a drag on my body, forcefully pulling me down. It was as if he was dragging me down to the floor, sometimes with quite a lot of force. I said more prayers and asked God to take the spirit, whoever it was, to Heaven. Then one day when I was at the kitchen sink with the cottage door open I watched the spirit come into the hall. He was a faint presence and I couldn't see him clearly, but I had a sense that he was male and taller than me, but I had no real idea of what he looked like. I stopped doing what I was doing. Before I could physically feel him I asked, "What is it that is wrong? How can I help you?"

The spirit clung on to me saying, "I'm here, I'm here—here I am!" Over and over, again and again, he was saying these words, but I could not understand why. I knew he meant me no harm, but that he was desperate so was pulling at me physically. He was very strong, and he was pulling me downward. I became oblivious for a moment and when I came to I realized I was clinging onto the side of the sink, trying to hold myself up. The spirit left suddenly, and when he did I called my angels and I prayed. Then I heard a knock on the door, even though the door was open. I turned around and there at the door were three of my angels: Michael, Hosus, and Elijah. Hosus walked in doing his imitation of a clown's walk, which made me laugh. I thanked him because I needed a laugh.

"What is wrong with that spirit?" I asked.

Angel Michael came toward me and reached out and took my hands. Angel Hosus went to my left side and Angel Elijah went to my right.

"Michael, that spirit almost pulled me down to the floor!" I said.

"Lorna," Michael replied, "we will give you the physical and emotional strength for you and the spirit, but we cannot tell you any more, not now. Remember, we will be with you all the time; you will never be alone."

"Michael, I hate it when you do this. Why can't you make it a little easier?"

"Sorry, Lorna. We can't tell you any more because then you would not be able to help the spirit." As Angel Michael finished saying this he withdrew his hands from mine.

Every day the spirit came. I never knew if it would be morning or night; each time he pulled me down, crying in a voice of desperation, "I'm here, I'm here—here I am!"

As the months passed I became more and more exhausted. Joe was back working in the carpet factory and never seemed to notice how tired I was. He was quite well during this period, but I could always see that grey deterioration around his organs.

Eventually I was able to discern from visions that the spirit was a young man, aged between seventeen and twenty, called Peter, and that he was in water, but trapped and struggling to get out. He seemed unable to use his hands; he could not hold on to anything.

At times the water seemed to be muddy and there was what seemed like a shelf of earth above him. This young man's spirit was pulling, struggling. He tried and tried to escape: "I'm here, I'm here—here I am!" He would say this over and over, again and again. My body somehow became intertwined with his spirit, and I felt everything physically as he struggled for life. I also felt all his emotions: he wanted to be found; he wanted to go home; he wanted his parents and family to know where he was. I just prayed to God that he would be found where he was.

I asked my angels if I could tell Joe, and they said yes. One evening Joe came in from the garden and looked at me and said, "What is wrong? You look awful! Are you sick?"

"No, Joe," I said. "I need to share something with you." I still told Joe little about my spiritual life, but this time the angels told me I really needed his help.

We sat down and I continued, "There is a ghost of a young man who comes to visit me. He needs my help. It's wearing me out physically and emotionally; I need your support, your help—just to look after me when I need it. Sometimes I need to feel your arm around me." Joe put his arm around me and looked at me. He didn't understand what was going on, how could he?

"I'll do my best," he said.

During one of the ghost's visits I was shown a vision: it appeared as if through his eyes, through water—I was being shown what had happened to him, seemingly from under the water. He was out walking along a riverbank with a path of some kind beside it. He was with two or three other people and they were pushing him around. He was very frightened. They were blaming him for something he hadn't done and he didn't know what they were talking about. He was trying to talk his way out of it; he was telling them they were making a mistake. One of them shouted back at him, "No, we are not making any mistake."

They beat him and kicked him to the ground and were really hurting him. He was being punished for something that someone else had done. Suddenly the vision ended, and I saw no more.

One Sunday afternoon when Ruth was about eight months old and all this was going on I heard a knock on the door. It was my brother Cormac's new wife, Sally. I had never actually met her; I had been in the hospital when they had married a short time before, and Joe had gone to the wedding with the children but without me. I greeted her and told her to sit down by the fire and get warm. "Is Cormac not with you?" I asked her.

"No," she replied, apologizing that she couldn't stay long. "I just wanted to say hello and give you some photographs from the wedding."

Joe made her a cup of tea, and as we sat by the fire she talked, telling us how happy she was to meet us and see our new baby daughter. Then just before Sally left as we were walking to the door she stopped and told us her brother was missing. She was surprised that we hadn't heard, that no one had mentioned it. She said he had been missing for some time now; that one evening he had left to meet his girlfriend but had never arrived. Sally said that her parents were very worried about him; they thought maybe he had gone to England so they were in touch with the Salvation Army and all the hostels over there. He was on the missing persons list, but no one understood why he would just leave like that.

"I'm sure he will turn up soon," I said to her, and we said our good-byes. "Don't be a stranger, Sally, you're always welcome."

I can be quite slow at times, and it was only later that I realized that through a series of strange coincidences I had made eye contact with that young man several years before. One afternoon we had gone to visit my sister Aoife and her husband, Alan, in their new home. The house was in the city center, with a tiny front garden with silver railings. Joe had opened the gate and lifted Christopher up so that he could reach the door knocker. Aoife opened the door and gave us a great welcome.

We went into the dining room and were introduced to Aoife's mother-in-law, a lovely elderly lady, and she welcomed us with open arms. The house seemed very small; maybe it was because there was beautiful old furniture there that left hardly any room to move. In the corner of the dining room was a fireplace with two chairs, one to the right of the fire and the other in front of the fire. The fire made the room very welcoming. There was a little pathway through the furniture from the hall to the fireplace and out into the tiny kitchen beyond.

I was sitting at the fireplace with Owen on my knee, feeding him, but I was the only one sitting and all the rest were standing. There were seven of us in that crowded dining room and little kitchen. Then there was a knock on the door and some more people squeezed into the room. I could not see who had arrived, and I continued feeding Owen. It was, in fact, my brother Cormac and Sally—the girl he would later marry—but everyone was busy talking and I could not even see my brother or his girlfriend—that's how crowded the room seemed to be. I noticed a light for a brief second and tried to see where it was coming from. No angels made themselves visible to me, nor did I see anything special. It all happened so quickly. The laughter and chat continued and obviously I could not talk openly to the angels there, so I tried to communicate with them without words. They didn't answer me.

I looked up a second time and I saw the light again through the standing bodies, as if somebody within the group, half blocked by the others, was giving off this light. People appeared to fade and it was as if everyone had moved their heads slightly to the left or right, creating a little pathway through which I could see across the room. I saw the side of the face of a young man, a man I didn't know. He turned his head and looked in my direction. His face glowed like a soft light and he gave a little smile. I smiled back. His eyes sparkled and I saw him for a fraction of a second more. Then people moved and he was blocked from my sight again.

The next instant everything went back to normal. Later I asked my sister Aoife who the young man was. She explained that it was Sally's younger brother, Peter. I never gave the incident another thought.

Joe didn't make the connection either—that the spirit was Sally's missing brother. Perhaps we weren't allowed to. It had to be God's doing; Joe had a very inquisitive mind and under normal circumstances he would have figured out that the ghost was Sally's brother's. But that was not God's plan. It was not time for Peter to be found.

The young man's spirit continued the horrific struggle beneath the water, not knowing where he was, struggling to take a breath, and not knowing what was above him—that darkness, the odd, faint flicker of light. He was trying to suck in air but instead he was sucking in water—drowning. He desperately wanted his family to know it wasn't his doing; he wanted to be found, and he wanted them to know he loved them. He continued to visit me. "I'm here, I'm here—here I am." These were his words, over and over again. I called on the angels and God many times to give me strength. I prayed so hard, constantly, that this young man would be found, that his spirit would be free and at peace. I prayed that his family could bring his body home and grieve for his loss, that they would know the truth, that he had not run away and that he loved them.

I was sitting at the fire, exhausted, one evening and Joe looked at me and said, "My God, you're so pale! The ghost of that young man has been here again. It's taking too much out of you. You look as if you're dying, just like that young man. This has to stop!" Joe was very mad with God.

"Joe, please don't be cross," I said. "I cannot cope with you being cross just now. Just support me and comfort me. The young man will be found, please God soon."

Joe held me in his arms and I must have fallen asleep, because when I woke later I was still in the chair by the fire, with a blanket around me. The children were all in bed; Joe smiled at me then got up and made me a cup of tea.

Sitting by the fire with a cup of tea in my hand I said to Joe, "You must not get cross like that again, Joe. I need you to support and comfort me. And I particularly need your support when God and the angels allow me to share with you the supernatural things that God allows to happen in my life. Joe, I need your help, especially when I'm exhausted."

Joe gave me a hug and kiss. Holding hands in front of the fire, we prayed together for the young man's spirit, that he would be found soon, that he would be free and that I would be free too. Joe knelt down in front of my chair and put his hands on each side of my face, saying, "If God asked me to do the things that you do, I would have to say no, because I would not have the courage, or strength, or your strong faith."

Family life went on as normal and then it happened—all of a sudden I was free. Don't ask me what day it was or what time it was, because I don't know, but suddenly I felt normal; I felt human again. I was so delighted, I was jumping for joy. I knew that the boy's body must have been found. I ran to tell Joe. "He's been found! I know they have found his body, because he's gone from me." I praised and thanked God while dancing around the cottage. Joe gave me a hug, and later that day we went down to the church and lit a candle, and I thanked God for Peter's spirit being freed to go to God.

God had allowed Peter's spirit to stay here in this world until his body was found, and I was used as a connection between the supernatural and the physical world. Without that connection I believe he would never have been found.

Miracles happen all the time, and when they do the usual flow of cause and effect does not matter—sometimes the miracle is put in place years before. This was a miracle that God and the angels arranged in advance. I know Peter's guardian angel, and the guardian angels of those involved in his death, must have worked hard to stop this young, innocent life being taken in a wrongful act of revenge, but the men who killed Peter did not listen to their angels. That made me feel so sad.

Peter was a very beautiful spirit, and when his body was found and his spirit had gone to Heaven he did something I did not expect him to do. He sent his sister to tell me.

A few days after I felt him leave me Sally arrived at the house. It was as if she had been running; she seemed very excited and jittery and said she felt the need to let us know that her brother's body had been found, that it had been in the canal, under a shelf in the bank of the canal, and that his hands had been tied together with rope.

It was only then that I realized that this beautiful spirit was in fact Sally's brother, the boy with whom I had made eye contact and a spiritual connection with all those years before.

Sally was sad, but happy now that the search was over, and that the family could now lay him to rest. When I looked into Sally's face as she stood before me telling me all of this, I saw Peter's spirit. Unbeknownst to her, he had sent Sally to us with urgency, so that she could tell us that he had been found. Sending Sally as a spiritual messenger was Peter's way of thanking me. To this day Sally has never come to visit me again.

CHAPTER 20

The golden chain

One cold winter's morning Joe was back from the night shift but hadn't yet gone to bed. He told the children that they were going to give their mum some time off, that he was going to take them down to the canal to see the ducks. I never saw the two boys and their little sister, Ruth, get ready so quickly; they put on their coats and hats and off they went.

No sooner had they gone than I got a flash of a vision of my parents. I saw them standing together in conversation and there seemed to be a strong breeze blowing around them. It was as if they were standing together but my da wasn't really there—he looked like a spirit. As quickly as it appeared the vision was gone. I knew I was being told that Da's life was coming to an end. It was like a bolt of lightning hitting me.

I cried. I argued with God and the angels, because I loved my father. It was as if only a few minutes had passed and then Joe and the children came back through the hall door. The children were all excited, telling me about what they had seen down by the canal. As I made some tea, Joe said, "What's wrong? You look very pale and you've been crying."

"I had a vision," I told Joe. "my da is going to die!"

"Maybe you misunderstood," Joe said. "What did the angels say?"

"They said nothing. They just showed me the vision," I said. "I was so upset and then you and the children came home. It was as if you were only gone a few minutes."

Joe gave me a hug and I felt a little bit better. I tried to put the vision at the back of my mind. I would have liked to have gone and seen my father there and then, but I couldn't. I had three young children to mind and we had no car. Fortunately the following day Da came to visit. I was delighted to see him, but I couldn't tell him why.

Often I am able to see illness in a person's body: sometimes bones will flash and I will see them, or sometimes the heart might come forward in someone's chest, or sometimes I will see an organ with a dark shadow around it. I looked hard at Da but I couldn't see anything wrong, and that confused me a little.

A few weeks later the weather had improved and I went for a walk down to the Maynooth College grounds while Joe looked after the children. Walking through the apple orchard and the groves of trees I gave praise and thanks to God. I was enjoying my walk, feeling the breeze—that cold fresh air—on my face. Seeing the birds and the squirrels, all of these creatures made me smile; I was seeing them not only in the ordinary way but I was also seeing the light of the energy around them.

I said hello to the people I passed—a priest and a mother with a baby in a stroller. Suddenly the Angel Michael stepped into stride beside me. He put his hand on my shoulder and then he touched my hand. Immediately I was filled with peace. "Thank you, Michael," I said, "that makes me feel good."

Michael was walking beside me in human form. As usual he was tall with dark hair, but this time his hair was short. He wore a black suit and black coat and could easily have been mistaken for a priest. I looked up at him and smiled, saying, "I admire your priestlike appearance!"

He gave himself a little shiver and turned up the collar on his jacket. "How does this look?" he said. We both laughed.

A few priests passed by with prayer books in their hands and said hello; Michael nodded his head in acknowledgment. I smile now as I recollect a neighbor, whom I didn't know well, saying that she had seen me out walking again with my friend. I never walked with anyone other than my family—it was the Angel Michael she had been seeing. (I can think of three occasions when people have said to me that they had seen me out walking with someone, when I knew I was alone, and I realized they had seen me with an angel in human form. It's possible that this has also occurred more frequently but I haven't realized it.)

Angel Michael said, "Let's stand under that big oak tree for a few minutes, while there is no one around, and I will explain to you the vision about your father."

"Michael, before you say anything," I said, "I want you to know I am cross."

Michael laughed at me, saying, "Lorna, you are such a character."

"Sometimes," I said, "I think God and all you angels forget I am human. Why do I have to know about my father's death? Michael, I would rather not know!"

Michael looked at me with sadness in his eyes, held my hand, and said, "Your father needs you to help him pass over."

I took a deep breath. "I love my da."

Angel Michael said, "Let's walk for a little while." Still holding my hand as we walked, he continued. "Remember the vision you had of your da the day Joe brought the children down to the canal? That was the time that God connected your da's soul and yours— joining them together. Your souls have been intertwined, Lorna. In a few days it will start: you will see your da's life from the moment he was conceived; it will be like a television screen in front of your eyes and in your mind, continuous every day. When it stops you will feel the sudden shock of your da's soul breaking away from your soul as he leaves his human body to be taken by the angels to God."

I walked beside Michael and cried my heart out.

"Lorna, let me wipe away those tears." As Angel Michael raised his two hands to my eyes I realized that we were not walking; we were standing in a circle of light. Sobbing, between words and gulps of breath, I said, "This is really going to be hard."

"Lorna, remember God and we angels will help you," Angel Michael said to me, as he again slipped his hand into my pocket and touched mine. "I will walk to the end of the path with you, and then I must go."

We walked in silence; it was only a short distance and I could feel Michael giving me strength. Then he squeezed my hand and was gone. I walked on home and never told Joe about my meeting with the Angel Michael.

Within a few days, as Michael had foretold, my da's life started to roll in front of my eyes and in my mind. It was constantly there—sometimes very rapid, sometimes slow—but never ceasing. I saw the scenes over and over again. I saw Da as a little child playing with another child in the mud, looking skinny and scrawny sitting at a school desk, as a young man with jet-black hair sitting by a riverbank with a good-looking young woman who I knew was Mum, Da mending bicycles in the dark shop in Old Kilmainham, the despair on Da's face when the little house we lived in collapsed, the loneliness as he took the boat to England to get work . . .

Da now started to visit us more often, sometimes even early in the morning. He would say he just wanted to call in for a cup of tea or a little chat and stay for a few minutes. I wanted to tell my Da what I knew, but how could I? You cannot tell someone that you know that he is going to leave this world; that your souls have become connected in order to help him pass over. That would be too frightening. We have not evolved spiritually enough yet.

Da was coming to know God now; he had grown so much spiritually in recent years. I always remember my father saying to me some years before, "Why did it take me so long to find God?" He had become fascinated with God, and it was wonderful to see my da's soul growing as he made his journey to God, his transition from the human world to the spiritual world. This is a journey we all have to take, regardless of our religion or belief in God. For some of us this journey will be short; for others it can be much longer—years, or even a lifetime.

On one of Da's visits he invited us to the born-again Christian family prayer group the following Sunday morning in Dublin. Joe and I said okay together and Da said he would collect us.

Later that day I went for a walk down along the canal banks. The children ran ahead to play so I had a little time to myself with the angels. I said, "Hello angels," and laughed as they tickled me, pulled my hair, and filled me with tingles. I asked the angels if they could tell me why it had taken so long for us to go to this group. It had been several years since that day at my mother's house when the preacher had suggested to Mum that she bring us along some Sunday.

The angels spoke to me in one voice: "Remember, Lorna, you're sharing something very spiritual with your da—the partnership between your souls. Your da feels within himself the need for you to share this prayer group with him. Now is the right time."

Owen called, "Mommy!" and in a flash of light the angels disappeared.

The two boys were standing together smiling as I walked up to them, and Ruth was asleep in the buggy. I knew by the expressions on their faces that they had seen me talking with the angels.

"Don't say anything," I said.

"I won't," replied Christopher.

We had fun that day, we fed the ducks and then we headed home.

On Sunday morning Da and Mum arrived at the cottage at about a quarter to twelve and we all got into the car. Sitting in the back of the car on our journey into Dublin, I found it heartrending watching my da; all the time I could see golden light surrounding him.

The church was big, more like a cathedral. There were a lot of families there and children running about, and food was being served. I felt very light; I could feel the angels carrying me and it was as if I were in a trance—as if I was on the outside looking in. Da walked over to me and said, "Come, the prayer meeting is about to start."

Da walked ahead of me and sat in the second row from the front, with an empty seat beside him. I know he meant for me to follow him, but the angels had other plans. About three rows back a man moved in a seat and invited me to sit down beside him, which I did. This chair was about one foot out, not in line with the other rows of chairs, and I could see my da clearly.

The meeting began with a prayer and then we sang hymns. Da stood up in front of his chair, like everyone else, and in that moment I knew this was what I was to share with my da—to see him in prayer. I could feel the power of the angels all around me.

What happened was beautiful and pure. I could no longer hear the singing. Da got brighter and brighter, until he glowed golden and became more and more radiant. My da's human body stood at the front of the church, and levitating about three feet above him was his guardian angel.

I saw Da's soul rise out of his body. I have seen other souls appear in this way but this was my own father's soul. It was glorious to see it. His soul was in the shape of his human body—it was transparent and wrapped in capes of golden light. It rose upward, accompanied by his guardian angel, and grew, becoming an enormous presence of bright light about four times the size of a person. It was shimmering and moving gently all the time.

Then his soul turned and faced me from afar, smiling love down on me. I could also see that Da's soul had great love for the human part of my father's life. It was then that I saw what looked to me like a golden chain dangling from my da's soul, which entered my father's head from above and encased his whole human body. To my surprise I saw another part of this golden chain coming from my father's physical body and slowly moving through the air toward me. As the angels bowed my head I could see how this golden chain entered my body, in the center of my chest, connecting Da's soul with mine.

The angels lifted my head and I watched Da's soul descending carefully and entering his body. Normally a person's soul is fully within the area of the body, but Da's soul did not reenter his body fully; it stayed partially out, partially above his head, for the short period of his life that remained.

Someone tapped me on the shoulder from behind and asked if I could sit down. It was only then that I realized I was still standing and everyone else was sitting, including my da. I was starting to feel human again and I took a deep breath. All of a sudden I felt the touch of all my angels. Silently I thanked them. I was sad, but yet I was full of joy.

It always amazes me when God and the angels tell me that someone is going to start their transition from this life through death and to what we humans sometimes call the supernatural world. I may be told about someone whom I may have met casually years ago, or only heard of through someone else, or maybe a person who is well known in the world.

To see how another human being changes their life and their beliefs makes me smile. We never seem to realize when this is happening, that we have begun the journey of rebirth. I always remember my da asking why did it take so long to get to know God.

One morning in March after leaving the boys at school I was walking home with Ruth in the buggy when I turned toward the gate of the cottage and who did I see but the Angel Michael sitting on the doorstep. I was delighted and called out as I opened the gate,

"Angel Michael, you're gleaming like the sun." No sooner had I said those words than Michael was by my side.

"Hello, Lorna," he said.

Ruth started to awaken and Michael put his finger to his lips with a radiant smile. He touched Ruth on the cheek with the tips of his fingers on his right hand and beams of light came out, her eyes started to close slowly, and she fell back asleep. When Michael moved his hand away I could see my baby's energy and Michael's intertwined. Then breaking away gently Angel Michael said, "Lorna, you know it's getting closer to the time for your father to leave this world."

"Yes, Michael, I know," I said. "When I saw you on the doorstep I was delighted to see you, but I was sad, too, because I knew in my heart why you had come this time."

I looked over at Ruth as she continued to sleep. Michael laughed, "She won't wake up until I leave." Michael reached out and took my hand and I started to cry. He gave my hand a little squeeze and I looked up at him. His beautiful radiant light enveloped and protected me. A wave of tranquillity came over me.

Michael said, "Lorna, let the love you have for your da help you now. Over the next two weeks, your souls will separate slowly and gently. That golden chain coming from your da's soul and connecting to yours is becoming weaker and will eventually break."

I was still crying but I was also listening carefully to Angel Michael's words.

"Michael, it has begun to weaken already; I can feel it."

"Lorna, you must understand," Michael said, "that when the time comes for the final break you must not try to hold on."

"I know, Michael," I said. "I won't."

"Remember, Lorna," Michael said, "all your angels are with you, all the time, even when you cannot see or hear us. You keep us all employed."

Michael raised his hands to my eyes, saying, "Let me wipe away the tears. No more crying! Be happy now for your da."

"Michael," I said, "I need to ask you a question before you go."

"What is it, Lorna?"

"You know," I started, "the way I have been seeing Da's life from the moment of conception, the way I have been feeling his emotions and pain and seeing everything? Am I cleansing his soul? Is that what I'm doing?"

"Yes," Michael replied. "No more questions, Lorna, I must go."

Michael disappeared and at the same time Ruth woke.

"Two weeks!" I said to myself. "That's not long," and I took a deep breath.

The vision of my da's life never ceased for one second: it was never ending, continuous, heartbreaking for me. Da called in every day. He would have a cup of tea and talk, and I would listen and smile to myself. He talked mostly about the past, sometimes about what life was like when he was young, or about his parents, or about his best friend, Arthur Mason, who had died years before. Sometimes he talked about himself and Mum before they were married.

As the days went by I felt worse. It was horrific knowing there were only a few days left until my da would be gone from this world. One afternoon before going down to the school to collect the boys I called on all the angels; I cried out to them from the depth of my despair. Angels Michael, Hosus, Elijah, and Elisha appeared directly in front of me, and behind them was a host of other angels. I was enveloped in their love, which gave me the strength and courage to let go of my da's soul and not to hold on.

They spoke gentle words: "You're not alone, Lorna. Go down to the school now and collect the children." Joe was not at work that day; he was out in the garden. He came in at that moment and said, "Lorna, you look very pale." I told him I was okay, but Joe said he would go and collect the children so I could rest.

"No," I said, "I really am okay. Let's go down together." I was tired and upset but the angels had told me to collect the children from school. Walking through the main street of Maynooth on the way back home I had a big surprise: we met Da! This was the first time I had ever met Da in Maynooth, and I knew it was the angels' doing. Da was wearing his favorite Aran sweater that I had knitted for him and his hat with the fishing flies. He seemed a little disoriented, not quite sure where he was going. He looked a lot older than his fifty-six years. But he was delighted to meet us and I gave him a big hug.

Da suggested we go into the tearooms nearby. As I sat with him I saw that the light around him was almost invisible; there was just a slight flicker, like a thread of light broken in a hundred places. His guardian angel stood behind him, much taller than him, supporting him and holding onto his human body—holding his body and soul together.

Over tea Da mentioned to me that he didn't feel well, that breathing was difficult. This was the first indication he had given me that he was having physical problems. Every second with my da was precious now. We walked him back to his car and I gave him a big hug. I thought it would be the last time I would see him alive.

The following day I was washing vegetables at the kitchen sink when an angel whispered in my ear, "Your da is coming to see you for the last time." I hadn't even had the chance to call my angels when there was a honk of a car horn at the gate. Everything was in slow motion. I was surprised to see Da already out of the car, standing at the gate, looking as if he didn't want to open it, not wanting to come in.

My heart was beating fast. He called out to me to say he was very tired but had a strong need to bring this vacuum cleaner to me. I went to open the gate for him to come in, but Da said, "No, Lorna, my lungs feel like turnips. I must go home." He stood at the far side of the gate and I stood inside. I didn't open it. His guardian angel was carrying him in his arms and I could see only a tiny trace of light around him.

I know you could ask why I didn't open the gate, but I was respecting Da's wish that I not do so. A connection had to be broken for our souls to separate; that is why Da would not let me open the gate. Spiritually he knew we had to stay on opposite sides of it, that the gate was not to be opened, but how much more he knew at that time I don't know. I smiled at my da and reached out and held his hand. We said our good-byes and Da went home. I told Joe later that evening that Da was dying. He didn't say much but just held me in his arms.

Two days later our souls completely separated. It was the morning of Saint Patrick's Day: March 17, 1984. Joe was not feeling well, so I told him not to bother about coming with the children and me to the Saint Patrick's Day parade and to stay in bed. We all had breakfast and I got the children ready to go to the parade in Maynooth. Down in the town the parade was in full swing. The children were given sweets and shook hands with the clowns and everyone was having a great time. I was trying to smile and be happy for the children so as not to spoil their fun, even though at times I thought the parade would never end.

I was relieved when Angel Michael appeared beside me as I walked home with the children. I could feel his hand on my shoulder to comfort me. "You're not alone, Lorna," he whispered in my ear. I was trying not to cry, knowing that if the children saw me they would be upset too.

"I feel so empty," I whispered back to Michael, "and my da is gone! I can feel no connection with him. He's gone."

"Your da will come to you spiritually in the future," Angel Michael whispered back, "but not for a long time. Remember what you both share together—the connection, the partnership between your souls."

"I know, Michael," I said, "but just now my human part is really hurting."

Angel Michael strolled alongside me in silence, the two boys ran ahead of us, and Ruth was in the buggy as her little legs were tired. A short distance from the gate of the cottage Michael slipped his hand into mine. "Lorna," he said, "you know the connection you have with God and your angels can never be broken."

I stopped and looked at my angel. "Michael, thank you. I needed to hear that."

A car drove up the road and Michael disappeared. We were only home about a half an hour when my brother Cormac drove up. I looked out the window and Cormac was standing at the gate. I smiled, because he didn't open the gate either; he waited until I opened the gate for him. My brother was unaware he was playing a part in a spiritual blessing for our father, that he was taking the place of our da at that moment as he walked through the gate. A beam of light appeared for a brief second, and I knew it was Da saying thank you.

"I know, Cormac," I said, "our da is gone."

Cormac said, "I am trying to tell you that Da has died."

"Come in and have some tea," I said. An hour or so later we all went down to see Mum.

CHAPTER 21

I need some miracles

Even when Joe was working, money did not seem to stretch very far. Many times the electricity was turned off because we had not paid the bill. Also Christopher needed a gluten-free diet, which meant I could not buy any cheaper brands of food. So I would frequently thank the angels for the garden, as growing our own vegetables helped a lot.

In the back of my mind I still had that vague feeling of being watched, and I sometimes thought fearfully of what Elijah had said to me the night of the picnic by the lake in Donadea about my being tested by Satan. I'd try to put it out of my mind and hope it wouldn't happen, but deep down I knew it would.

Joe was eventually laid off by the carpet factory. They said they were letting others go, but I believe it was because of his health and his long absences. He got a temporary job back in CIE, the Irish public transport company. Joe used to go down to the main road and thumb a lift to work; sometimes he was lucky but other times it took him hours to get to work, so he always had to leave home early in the morning.

One morning he got a lift from a driver who got into a crash; the driver was okay, but Joe had a serious concussion. He was in the hospital for a few days and while there he was diagnosed as diabetic. All that Elijah had shown me was starting to unfold. Joe never went back to work at the transport company.

It was the end of November, getting closer and closer to Christmas, and we had barely enough money to put food on the table and to keep the fire alight. One day I was out in the garden breaking brussels sprouts off stalks and putting them in a bag while it was lashing rain. I was soaked and felt completely miserable. I was really cross with the angels. "We can't live on vegetables alone!" I shouted at them. I was in tears. Suddenly I saw a hand of light go into the bag. I looked up and there was Angel Hosus; he looked as wet as I did, which made me laugh, and that made me feel a bit better.

"Hosus, do you not realize how bad things are?" I said. "I have nothing for the children for Christmas. I need some miracles; there's no food other than vegetables, and the electricity has been cut off again. I don't even have my engagement ring to go to the pawnbrokers. My ring is already pawned, and I can't see Joe and me ever being able to get the money together to get the ring back."

Angel Hosus reached out his hands and held my face. Looking up into his eyes was like looking into Heaven.

"Lorna, we are whispering in people's ears," he said, "but it's very hard sometimes to get them to listen."

"Why can't people hear the angels like I do, Hosus?" I asked.

"Lorna," Hosus replied, "people hear the angels talking to them but they frequently think it's a silly thought and disregard what they are being asked to do. If a person shows any signs of listening to our whispers about helping someone, even with the simplest of tasks, we will inspire confidence within them. People are always afraid they will make fools of themselves, but they never make a fool of themselves by helping someone."

"Hosus," I said, "I am going to pray that people will listen to their angels."

Hosus disappeared and I went back into the cottage. A few days later, with only two weeks to go till Christmas, I was walking down the hill to town to collect the boys from school when a car passed and stopped. There was a man and a woman in the car and the man wound down the window and said hello. At first I thought they were looking for directions, but when I looked into the car I could see their guardian angels faintly.

"We know you've got two young boys," the man said.

At that his wife got out of the car, opened the trunk, and took out a large white bag saying, "These are from Santa Claus. Our boys have grown out of them."

I was dumbfounded. I couldn't believe it! Before I could say a word, the woman got back into the car and they started to drive away. I called after them, "Thank you!"

The car lit up for a moment as I watched them going up the hill. I was laughing and jumping with joy, saying, "Thank you, angels. Those people listened!" I was so happy. I opened the bag and looked in to see a variety of toys for young boys.

I hurried on my way so that I could give myself time to call in at Jim the butcher's and leave the bag with him so that the boys wouldn't see it. Waiting for the boys in the schoolyard, I was so thrilled, so delighted; I couldn't wait to tell someone what had happened. I nearly burst waiting to tell Joe.

At the first chance I got when the children were out of earshot I told Joe the whole story, describing every detail. He tried to work out who the man and woman were as he knew a lot of people in the area, whereas I knew hardly anyone. In fact, until recently I have never really been allowed to make close friends. For some reason the angels seemed to need me to be quite solitary. I did have my family, of course, but at times I would have loved to have friends.

Joe thought our good Samaritans might be a couple he knew from Leixlip. If it was, though, he was never able to thank them because we were never sure.

"Don't you know it is the angels' doing?" I said.

He laughed and said, "Thanks, angels." I laughed too; I was so relieved.

Christmas dinner was another matter. There were two days to go until Christmas, and Joe and I could still see no way of being able to buy a packet of biscuits, never mind a turkey. Yet the angels kept appearing, constantly telling me not to worry, that something was happening, that someone was listening.

Christmas Eve arrived and the children were so excited; they couldn't wait for Santa Claus. I've always loved Christmas myself; I think it is a wonderful time. Throughout the Christian world the birthday of Jesus is the time to reach out to others, to share and build understanding, to break down boundaries, to bury our hatred and let our strong innate desire for love and peace rise up.

I went to bed that night thinking that there would be no Christmas dinner, but I thanked all my angels for everything they had done already and told them I was looking forward to seeing the children's excitement when they saw their presents in the morning.

Next morning, Christmas day, the children woke at six. There were still some hot cinders in the fire, and Joe was heading to the shed to get some sticks. He hadn't even opened the hall door when he called me and walked back into the front room holding an envelope in his hand. There was nothing written on it.

Joe tore open the envelope and at that moment angels filled the room and the light around them seemed to flicker. Joe drew out two £20 notes. I couldn't believe what I was seeing—I was exhilarated. I threw my arms around him. The children asked what was going on and Joe and I spoke as one. "Santa Claus has given us a present, too!" We ended up with the children hugging our legs.

Imagine someone putting two £20 notes into an envelope, coming to the house on foot or in a car, opening the gate gently, tiptoeing up to the door, and sliding the envelope under it! It must have been very late when it was delivered, because it had been after midnight when Joe and I went to bed. Whoever it was had given completely anonymously: there was no note, no card, and they expected nothing in return. It was a godsend. They made our Christmas. I thank whoever they are for listening to their guardian angels.

I have always told my children that the name Santa Claus comes from Saint Nicholas, and that Saint Nicholas works through people and inspires them to give presents to others. Saint Nicholas had clearly been at work here, as well as the angels.

Forty pounds was a huge amount of money at that time—about eight weeks of grocery money. We felt like millionaires! Joe wrote a shopping list: lemonade, biscuits, a few sweets, and other bits and pieces, and, most important, a chicken, so the children could pretend it was a turkey. In the meantime, before we could shop, we had great fun playing with the children.

As we got ready for Mass and walked down to the church, I felt wonderful. As we all walked in through the church door I said to Joe, "I hope the shopkeeper will have some cooked chickens." Joe made me laugh by saying, "What a thing to be thinking of going into Mass." But during Mass I prayed for a cooked chicken! I thanked God and the angels for everything, and particularly for whoever had slipped the envelope under our door.

When Mass was over we headed straight to the only shop in Maynooth that was open on Christmas morning—Barry's, on Main Street. As we were walking from the church we turned the corner onto Main Street and I saw Angel Hosus standing in Barry's doorway, radiating love. Joe and the children walked ahead of me. I hesitated for a brief moment in the doorway of the shop. Hosus touched me on the shoulder and I said, "Thank you for your radiant gift of love."

"Can you smell the chickens cooking?" Hosus asked, and then disappeared.

The shop was crowded. People were buying bits and pieces and wishing everyone they met a "Happy Christmas and a Prosperous New Year." Joe was at the counter talking to the shopkeeper, Mrs.

Barry. She said she had a few orders for cooked chickens, for old people mainly, and that we were in luck as she had put on a few extra chickens to roast.

Mrs. Barry had a big smile on her face, and I know she was happy that she had put on the extra chickens. For a brief instant her angel appeared behind her and I nodded and said a silent thank you to her angel, and to Mrs. Barry for listening to it.

"It won't be cooked for about another half an hour," Mrs. Barry said. Joe said that was okay and gave her the rest of the shopping list.

We walked around the town, looking in the shop windows and entertaining the boys, while Ruth fell asleep in the buggy. When we walked back into the shop, the smell of the chickens was gorgeous. Mrs. Barry said we had timed it well, as she had just taken the chickens out of the oven. She wrapped one up well and put it in a bag, while the rest of the shopping went into a box. Joe paid her and we thanked her and wished her a happy Christmas.

Joe took the box and I carried the warm bag back home to the cottage. In the kitchen Joe put the box of groceries on the table, and the children, all excited, helped to empty it of the sweets, biscuits, and lemonade. It felt like a banquet.

I checked the chicken and turned to Joe. "I can't believe it. It even has stuffing in it—it was very good of Mrs. Barry to do that—not only cooking chickens on Christmas morning, but stuffing them as well."

When the rest of dinner was ready the candles were lit and the chicken was put in the center of the table. The meal was gorgeous; that chicken tasted nicer than any turkey I have ever had before or since. We had a great Christmas.

The next few months were cold; we even had snow. One day we were all out in the garden throwing snowballs. The children had started to build a snowman and I was watching my younger son, Owen, rolling a snowball, when an angel whispered in my ear but didn't appear.

"Is that you, Angel Hosus?" I asked.

"No, I am Owen's guardian angel," the angel replied, still not showing himself. "I want you to watch your son. I'm going to show you something."

At that moment Owen called, "Mummy, look at the snowball." His big brother, Christopher, ran over to help, and in no time at all they had rolled a snowball nearly as big as Owen. "You have made that big enough for the body of the snowman," I said, as I turned and walked toward the cottage. "Now you just need to make another snowball as big as a football for the head, then find stones for the eyes and mouth and a carrot for the nose."

But then Owen's guardian angel called out, "Where are you going, Lorna?"

I had thought that the angel just wanted me to watch the two boys pushing their enormous snowball; I turned around and there he was. Owen's angel had revealed himself to me. He was extremely tall, his eyes were a stunning emerald green, and he radiated a smile. It was as if he was saying to me, "Look at what you nearly missed by turning your back on me, Lorna." He was dressed in a suit of armor that was very fine and looked like silver, but then a moment later it changed color, into what looked like the color of a fiery flame, in stark contrast with the white snow all around. His feet seemed to be embedded in the snow and glowed under it, yet I know his feet weren't actually touching the ground, or even the snow. Just looking at Owen's guardian angel made me feel very happy.

"Lorna, look at your son," the angel said. As he said these words Owen stood up from pushing the enormous snowball and turned toward me with a big smile, looking very proud of himself. The next moment I saw a magnificent, beautiful energy emerging from

Owen's chest, getting larger by the second. As it formed it looked like a shield, but then it took on the shape of a beautiful heart. This heart was full of life: in colors of emerald, green, and blue, like running rivers mingling. It was floating in front of my little son's chest, directly connected to it. I was astonished! It was breathtaking in every way.

"What does that mean?" I asked.

Realizing that Owen's guardian angel was standing at my left side, with his hand on my shoulder, I wanted to turn around to face him, but he told me not to. I did as he said and didn't turn to him. He continued, "The heart is the symbol of the shield of life; the giver of life and love, the protector of the earth, of what is right and wrong."

I smiled and said to the angel, "That's an awful lot for a grown man to represent, let alone a little child."

I asked Owen's guardian angel to help Owen on his journey, to guide him and protect him.

"Lorna, when Owen grows up you can tell him what you saw on this day and you can tell him that my name is Angel Traffikiss."

I watched as Owen pushed another snowball with his brother. The shield in front of his heart slowly diminished in size and I felt the touch of Traffikiss's hand on my shoulder withdraw. For a brief instant I saw Traffikiss standing over Owen, and then Owen fell to his knees laughing and called out to me to help him.

$\mathcal{S}atan$ at the gate

Some years ago, at the picnic by the lake, Angel Elijah had told me that God was going to test me in the presence of Satan. One day Elijah came to visit again and told me that Satan would reach me soon.

"I can feel him getting closer," I said. I was terrified, afraid for myself and for my children.

"Don't be afraid," Elijah told me. "Prove your faith in God."

It's hard to describe, but from the time Elijah had spoken to me by the lake I had been able to feel Satan traveling toward me. Imagine, I could feel him a million miles away, then I could feel him when he got within a thousand miles of me, then within a hundred. It took years from the time that Elijah said that Satan was coming for him to get near me, but I could feel him getting closer all the time. And now Elijah had confirmed that Satan was near.

Satan got closer and closer. One day, around midday, Angels Michael and Hosus and all of my angels came and formed a half circle around me, in front of me. They said this was to help prevent my feeling the great evil that comes from Satan. Then my angels disappeared and I couldn't see them anymore. As I walked back into the cottage and closed the front door I knew Satan was standing at my gate. I felt cold and frozen; I felt the life being drained from me; it was as if I was standing on the tracks facing a fast-moving, oncoming train and being told it would stop right in front of me if I had sufficient faith. I kept remembering what Elijah had said: prove your faith in God.

Satan must have been at the gate for weeks. I was in a permanent daze, lost in time. Then one evening as I got into bed I knew he was at the front door. I was feeling the power of Satan and it was unbelievably strong. I called on my angels, but they didn't seem to be answering me. Joe and the children were all asleep in our bedroom. God and the angels must have put them into a deep sleep.

I sat in bed with my knees up and the blanket pulled up under my neck. I was trembling with fear. I sat there for some time and then suddenly all my angels—Hosus, Michael, and Elijah—appeared and surrounded me. They told me not to be afraid, and then they disappeared as suddenly as they had come.

I could feel the presence of Satan walking into the house. He walked to the bedroom, and as he reached it everything in the room disappeared—including Joe and the children. It was as if everything had vanished into darkness, even the bed I was sitting on. I was left alone with Satan.

It was horrific to feel the power of Satan: all the evil, the terror, the horror. I can't say whether it was a he, or what he or she looked like; it just seemed to be a mass of badness, of darkness, of great strength and power. He had great confidence, and he certainly had no fear.

Then God walked into the darkness. He appeared in a human form, as a young man, just as he had done at the prayer group. He was dressed in brilliant white, his face radiant and his hair dark and shoulder length. He stood on my right and stretched out his arm to me and took my hand.

Having the presence of God on my right gave me strength. I knew God was keeping Satan at bay, stopping him from coming any closer, but I was still terrified, more terrified than I have ever been in my life. I was shaking.

I sat in bed with Satan on my left—this great darkness, this great evil—and on my right was God. I couldn't see Satan clearly; he was just a dark mass. When I looked to God the fear disappeared, but when I looked back at Satan it returned, and stronger than ever.

I realized I was being tested by God and asked to show that I was not afraid of Satan; that I was stronger than him, that I could push him away. I also knew that the presence of God and his touch on my hand gave me the strength I needed to push Satan away. Three times I repeated, "Satan, go away. I choose God over you. I am stronger than you."

Each time I said this he stepped back, and by the third time he was out the bedroom door. Then God pushed him away—out of the house, out of the area. It was as if he was pushed down a long dark tunnel into nothingness. That day I proved to God that I had the faith to push Satan away.

Satan does exist: I have no doubt about this at all. If we allow Satan into our lives he will come in. He will act as a "god" and may let great things happen in our lives. There may be great wealth, great external success, but at an enormous cost. Satan does not want us to evolve spiritually and will oppose those who try to open the hearts and minds of others and help them to see differently.

Man *is* evolving spiritually. It is part of evolution for man to change and for the body and soul to become more united and eventually become one. I see people becoming less conditioned, more questioning, and more open to exploring issues of a spiritual nature. God tests us all sometime; it's part of our spiritual growth. We all have the power, with God's help, to push Satan away. This is something we should never forget. If we push him away he will take a step back, he has to. Unfortunately, he will still be there, but his power will be less. And we can always call on God and his angels to strengthen our hands, our belief, and our faith.

Joe's diabetes was becoming chronic. He would frequently faint or feel very weak, and sometimes Christopher would rush in from the garden screaming that Dad had fallen over. It was very difficult for Joe and for us. In most cases diabetes responds to medication, but in Joe's case it wasn't so simple, and the doctors, despite their efforts, were unable to control it. His condition was also affecting his heart. Joe hadn't worked since being diagnosed with diabetes; he had gone for an interview as a security guard at Maynooth College—which would have been very handy as the college was so close to home— but at the last moment they told him that they couldn't offer it to him because of the results of his medical exam. Joe was bitterly disappointed.

One of the many times Joe was in hospital a nurse suggested it mightn't be a bad idea if we had a phone in the cottage. About six weeks later one was installed, thanks to the local health authorities, but I used the phone only for emergencies and incoming calls, as I was afraid of running up a big bill. Shortly after the phone was installed the children were playing out in the garden when a car pulled up. I was around the back cleaning out one of the sheds. (We spent a lot of time in the garden—we had a few chickens running around and a neighbor had given us a puppy.) On this day I heard a man call "Hello!" and I went around and greeted him. He was getting out of a car. Inside was a woman and child. He asked was he at the right house. I smiled and said, "I don't know. Who are you looking for?"

"The healer," he replied. "My wife is not well."

I smiled but felt unsure. I knew he was looking for me, but I had never been called a healer before. In fact, I felt embarrassed at being called this—I didn't feel good enough. I took a deep breath and said, "Yes, you're at the right house. Please come in."

We walked into the kitchen. They introduced themselves as Fintan and Peg, and their son was called Eamon. The little boy stayed outside and played with my children, the chickens, and the puppy. This was the first time someone called to the cottage to ask me for help; I never learned who had sent them to me or who had told them I was a healer. They were to be the first of many though.

Years later when I met Fintan again he told me that when he saw the cottage with the children, the puppy, and the chickens he knew he was in the right place. He also told me that his wife's health had improved enormously after the visit.

I got a call one day from a woman called Josie, who had been given my telephone number. Her son had been diagnosed with cancer and she was looking for support. She also asked me to see another family whose son also had cancer, so we arranged that they would come the following Monday morning.

On Monday morning at about a quarter to eleven a car pulled up to the gate. I opened the hall door and welcomed the family in. We shook hands as we walked into the kitchen, and the father introduced himself as Dermot, his wife, Susan, and their son, Nick. We sat down at the table in the little kitchen and Nick played with some toys his mum had brought while I talked with his parents. After a few minutes he gave me a big smile and said, "Stop talking, Mum, and let Lorna bless me and tell me the name of the angel who is going to help me to get better. Then I can go out into the garden and play."

His father told him not to be so impatient, to give me a chance, but I said it was okay. "I'll tell you what we will do," I said. "I will bless Nick and pray over him and ask for the angel's name. Nick, sit on your mum's or dad's knee." Nick sat on his dad's knee. "There is no guarantee that your guardian angel will give me his name, Nick," I said to him, "so you will have to pray with me as well and ask your guardian angel to open your mind and heart. When I am finished, you can go out and play in the garden, so I can talk to your mum and dad."

I had a look at him and I asked God to show me where his cancer was. I could see it, but I didn't tell anyone where I saw it. It was actually quite aggressive and I thought to myself, *Oh God, there really is going to have to be a miracle here if he's going to live.* There was a thought in my mind that maybe Nick was not supposed to live, that his journey in this life was to get closer to God and get to know his angel. I was also aware that this could be a part of his family's journey.

While I was praying over Nick, asking God to grant the miracle that he would get well, his guardian angel appeared for a few minutes. He told me that the miracle would not be granted, that I must tell Nick's mum and dad to spend every moment they could with their son, that time was precious. I wasn't to tell them that their son would die, as they were not yet able to cope with that information. I was also to tell Nick the name of his angel.

Nick sat very still on his father's knee while I prayed over him, and when I was finished I blessed him and he jumped off his dad's knee saying, "Tell me my angel's name!"

"Sit back up there on your dad's knee," I said, "so I can tell you its name, and what your guardian angel looks like. Nick, your guardian angel looks magnificent. He has clothes that seem to sparkle in all colors and he has a cape that is constantly moving. He has beautiful sparkling green boots, the most beautiful green I've ever seen. They come up to his knees, with big, square silver buckles. He has a gold belt around his waist and in the middle of it is another silver buckle."

Nick sat completely still on his father's knee, not taking his eyes off me. You could see his excitement as I described his guardian angel.

"His hair is red like flames of fire," I continued, "and his eyes are like stars. And he has what looks like a sword in his left hand, but actually it's a sword of light and it flashes. Your guardian angel said I was to tell you that when you're feeling unwell all you've got to do is ask and he will touch you with his sword of light and make you feel better."

Nick jumped off his dad's knee again and said, "Can I go out and play now?"

His father took him out into the garden. His mother, alone with me now, started to cry and asked, "What did the angel say?"

I find it very hard when a parent says to me, "What did the angels say?" and the news is not good. What can I say? Sometimes a parent will ask, "What did I do wrong? Have I committed some big sin? Is this God's way of punishing me?" We have to understand that this is our path, the journey our souls have chosen long before we are born into this world. Nick's soul had chosen this journey long before he was born; it had chosen that he would die young, that he would fulfill all he had to do at a very young age. The souls of his parents had also chosen the journey that they would lose a young child, even if they had no memory of this. We forget most of what we know and have agreed to at the moment of conception.

"Look at your son," I replied. "Look at the belief and faith he has. He's not afraid. He's not afraid to get better and not afraid to go to God either. Listen to your son; he'll give you many messages."

When Nick's father came back in I talked with both parents for a few minutes. I told them the angels said that they should spend as much time with their little son as possible.

I used to hear from the family regularly. Whenever Nick was in the hospital or not feeling well he would ask his mum or dad to ring me to ask his angel to use his sword of light to make him better. No sooner would his parents ring me than the pain would be gone. Nick could, of course, ask his guardian angel for help himself, but I have found with sick children that they often ask their parents to ring me. Perhaps it gives them more confidence.

One time when Nick was in remission he got his parents to bring him back to see me. He insisted on seeing me alone and told his parents they must stay in the car, that he needed to see me without them. When we were on our own Nick told me that he talked to his guardian angel all the time. He told me that his angel had told him that in the future, maybe soon, he would be taking him to Heaven. Nick said that was okay with him, that he was nine years of age now. He told me that he had told his mum and dad that he would be going to Heaven someday soon, but they had replied that they didn't want to hear that kind of talk.

Nick told me that his mummy wouldn't stop crying. "I tell Mummy that I don't mind going to Heaven and this is all right, but she doesn't listen to me."

I asked, "Nick, would you like me to talk to your mum and dad?"

"Yes, would you do that, Lorna?"

I gave Nick a big hug and said, "Let me pray over you now and bless you, and I'll talk to God and your guardian angel and ask them what I should say to your mum and dad. I will ask their guardian angels to help them to let you go to Heaven when the time comes."

We prayed together and I blessed Nick. Then we went outside to the car and I invited his parents, Dermot and Susan, to come in. Our dog, Heidi, had pups and Nick played happily with Ruth and the puppies in the garden, under the tree. I smiled as I watched them. Nick's parents fussed over him but he told them to leave him alone, that he was playing and they were to go in and sit with me and listen to what his guardian angel had said.

Susan gave me a worried look as we sat down at the kitchen table. I spoke to them as gently as possible. I told them what their son had said, how Nick's guardian angel had spoken about taking

Nick to Heaven someday soon. I asked them to try, if possible, to be strong and to listen to their son and to spend as much time with him as they could from now on. They cried, holding each other in their arms, sobbing. It was heartrending.

Eventually both parents spoke. They told me that for the last few months they had been listening to what Nick had been saying about his guardian angel taking him to Heaven, but they found it too hard to bear. They felt a little ashamed that Nick had had to ask me to get them to listen to him. I hugged both of them, blessed them, and they went home.

A few days later Ruth walked into the kitchen saying, "Mum, you remember that boy I played with in the garden the other day? I liked him; he was a really nice boy. What is his name?"

"Nick," I replied.

"I know he is sick, Mum. Is he going to get better?"

"No, he's going to Heaven," I told her.

I saw tears in my daughter's eyes as she said, "That's not fair! He is such a nice boy!"

I gave my daughter a big hug; I just held her in my arms for some time and then she said, "I'm all right now, Mum," and went off to do her homework.

A few months later Nick became seriously unwell again and was in and out of the hospital. Every so often I would get a phone call from his parents saying that Nick had asked them to ring me to ask for the pain to be taken away. It always was and I thanked God for that miracle. One day, though, Susan called to tell me that Nick had peacefully passed away the night before. I told her always to remember that Nick is a beautiful soul in Heaven, and that he is beside her every time she needs him.

It's hard to describe the effect Nick had on his family, his parents, and his brothers and sisters. They had lost a son and a brother, yet it was as if his sickness and death had woken up the entire family. Nick showed them such compassion and love; it was as if God himself shone through that child. He was different; in a way he was like an angel himself, an angel who shone for all who came into contact with him. If you go into a children's hospital you will meet children who are seriously ill, yet despite this they are happy, so full of love. Few of them have any bitterness or resentment. It's as if they are here to show us their light. I am always fascinated by the wisdom of children. Children who are terminally ill become very spiritual and so grown up, so matter-of-fact—even at as young as four. It's fascinating and very beautiful.

One other thing that's worth remembering about children is how spiritually open they are when they are very young. After all, they have only just come from Heaven. Many of them see angels, even though they generally forget this later. Many of them may often also see spirits, particularly spirits of grandparents or other relatives who have come to protect them. I have frequently come across cases of very young children saying things like "Grandda was playing with me." I've heard of parents looking through a family photo album with a child who talks about knowing someone who was dead before the child was born. The child may even have a message for the parents.

Children are fonts of wisdom, including from the other world, and we should listen to them more.

More and more people came to visit me. By this time Joe was so unwell that he was rarely out of the house, and when people came he would disappear. He was a proud man and he didn't want anyone to know he was ill. No one who came to see me knew what was going on in my life, or the difficulties that I was facing with a seriously ill husband, that I was living with the knowledge the angels had given me that he wouldn't be with me much longer.

A woman came to visit me looking for the intervention of angels. She was a medical student called Marian. She told me that she was really stressed and couldn't cope with her exams. "I heard that you talk to angels," she said to me. "I believe in God. I have faith and I believe in angels, but I really need help now, because I am under such pressure that I fear I am going to have a breakdown."

Marian was almost qualified as a doctor, but she was terrified she would not pass her final exams. She desperately wanted to become a doctor, and she knew that she could be a good doctor, but she was finding the whole process very tough. I told her that her faith and her belief had helped her through this rough period and that God had already sent her angels to give her the strength to stick it out. We prayed to God and the angels to send her angels who could teach her to pass her exams and guide her to become a spiritual, loving, and caring doctor.

We all have our guardian angel with us all the time, but the guardian angel, in its role as gatekeeper of your soul, can allow other angels to come into your life to help you with different things. I call these angels teachers; they come and go frequently and are different from guardian angels. We asked for a group of angels who would be Marian's teachers. As we prayed I could already see three angels on their way to her. They were striding toward her but hadn't reached her yet.

"All three of them are men," I said. "Not a woman among them. I hope you don't mind that."

Marian laughed and cried with relief and asked me to ask God to have the angels arrive before she left me because she really needed them. I prayed over her. I asked God for all the confidence, the courage, and the abilities that Marian needed. And I asked for hope because she needed to be able to see hope within her own life. As I finished praying over her I asked for the names of the angels who had been sent to help her. I was told that she could call the angels "The

Three Stars." They had already arrived and were waiting outside the door for her to step out into her new world.

Recently, years after she came to see me, I got a call from Marian. She is now a doctor working overseas and doing a lot to help people. She rang because she wanted to thank the angels. "I had to ring you to ask you to thank them because that way I feel the message will get there quicker," she said.

I had to laugh. I told her that with the phone call we were already thanking them. I reminded her never to forget to call on her three angels whenever she needed them. "They are still there. They haven't left you. You still have a journey to undergo and a lot of work to do," I said.

Marian had believed enough to ask the angels for help; she empowered the angels, and in return the angels empowered her.

Most of the time people came to see me, but occasionally, in special circumstances, I was asked to go to people's homes. Often if this happened someone would collect me and drive me. One day I was taken to a big old house to visit a boy of about three who was very sick. He was very run-down and had difficulties breathing; he could hardly get out of bed.

There was an old man there, and I thought he was a member of the family. It was only when he sniggered at me that I realized he was a ghost, a spirit, but he had turned his light down so that he appeared to me to be a living person. He knew he had fooled me and he was highly amused by this.

When I was having a cup of tea with the young boy's grandmother, after seeing the child, she mentioned that her grandson was so like her own grandfather, who had also lived in that house—as had generations before him. She said this a few times. For some reason I don't fully understand, the grandmother's continuous reference to the young boy being like her grandfather was resulting in this spirit staying around. The spirit was that of a great-great-grandfather of the sick child.

I knew the spirit wasn't good for the family, that he was in some way a malevolent force, and that his presence was responsible in part, if not completely, for the child's sickness. All the time I was in that house I kept watching the old man's spirit and praying that he would be surrounded by love and angels, so that he could depart and go to Heaven and leave the little boy in peace.

A few weeks later I was asked back to the house to see the little boy, who was now completely recovered and full of energy. I knew that the spirit had left.

I was amazed; the house looked completely different. The house I had been in a few weeks before had been damp and not very clean, with a big old staircase and a grimy ornate fireplace in the sitting room. Now I was in a beautifully restored and well-cared-for old house with no fireplace.

I asked the grandmother, "Where's the fireplace?"

She looked at me a little strangely and said that nothing had changed since I was last there. It had for me, though. Not only had I seen the spirit of her grandfather; I had been shown the ghost of the actual house—as it had been long ago, when he had lived in it.

CHAPTER 23

Soulmates

Joe was still unable to work, but at least he was at home so he could keep an eye on the children, and so sometimes I was able to get a job for a short while. I scrubbed floors in a school, I worked in a shoe shop, but the truth is that at that time there was not a lot of work available for which I was qualified.

The financial problems were not helped by the special diet Christopher needed for his celiac disease. Joe needed special food too. I struggled hard to feed the family with the limited money we had. We lived from hand to mouth. My daughter Ruth now laughs when she remembers that the only time she got a piece of meat was when she chewed the bones of the meat from her dad's plate.

There were some short periods when Joe's diabetes was under control and he was well enough to do odd jobs. During one of these spells he gave driving lessons, but I always looked on in fear, concerned he might take a turn for the worse. He was always very happy when he was well enough to work, but unfortunately these periods never lasted long.

We had chickens in the garden, so every so often Joe used to call on a coffee shop in town looking for remains of bread to give the chickens. He didn't say that the scraps would also help feed his wife and children, but they did. We used to go through the bags of food he would bring home to see what was edible, and we would cut off the moldy parts. Sometimes there would be a perfect cream cake or a fresh loaf of bread in the bag. I've always believed that the man who ran the restaurant guessed what the story was and deliberately put these in.

At one stage we were deeply in arrears with the loan on the cottage and in danger of losing our home if we didn't pay. I went to the state social welfare office to see if they could give any help beyond the disability pension that was being provided. Joe came with me. Although Joe was seriously ill, they didn't believe us. They asked if he was really sick; despite the medical records, they said they believed he could have worked if he had truly wanted to. After Joe died, the woman in the state social welfare office apologized to me.

In desperation we put part of the garden up for sale. On reflection it's clear that I was so desperate to make life a little more comfortable for Joe that I sold it for considerably less than it was worth. The money we got, however, did enable me to clear some of our debts.

You lose your dignity when you have to beg, but sometimes there is no choice, particularly when there is a whole family involved. One of the symptoms of Joe's sickness was that he was always cold; even in summer he would be shivering. I went again to the state social welfare, looking for money to buy him thermal underwear. Again they said nothing was wrong and refused to help. What frustrated and upset me was that I could see many other families receiving financial support. I think the fact that we lived in our own cottage, tiny as it was, rather than a council house, influenced them, as did the fact that Joe, with his pride, always tried to look good and respectable when he went to see them.

My angels kept telling me to go to a local charity. I fiercely resisted. I was tired of losing my dignity. Why would they believe me if the state social welfare didn't? Eventually things got so desperate that I rang the charity and made an appointment to see them.

I explained our circumstances. They sent a man to visit the cottage, to inspect us. The man walked around the cottage slowly, looking at everything, opening cupboards. He then turned to me and announced, "If you have a bag of potatoes and a tin of beans, then your family won't go hungry. You're not in need of our help."

I tried to explain about the dietary needs of a celiac—how Christopher needed a special diet to grow, otherwise there was a danger he would be permanently stunted (in fact, at seven years old he weighed only thirty-five pounds, when he should have weighed at least fifty-six pounds). I explained how Joe's sickness meant that there were a lot of foods that he just couldn't keep down. But the man didn't seem interested; I'm sure he believed he was right.

In the end the charity gave us little bits of support, but much of it was of no use. They would send us free vouchers for particular foods, but invariably it would be a food that Christopher and Joe couldn't eat. One Christmas we got a voucher for a turkey, and we were very pleased about that, but when I went down to collect it, the humiliation of the experience took all the good away. The committee was there calling out names as people came forward to get their turkeys. When they called my name they said, "Oh yes, you . . ." I felt they had been talking about me, and they believed we were "working the system," taking food out of the mouths of those who really needed it. Little did they know!

One day I ran into Sean, a man I had known from the prayer group in Maynooth. We no longer went to the prayer group as getting there was too much for Joe. I missed going—both the praying together and the company of the people we had met there. In fact, at this time I went out little—to do the shopping, to collect the children from school, to work the odd time I had a job for a few hours, but nowhere else. Joe's health was so unpredictable that I was afraid to leave him on his own for even a short time.

Sean was now a member of the local charity committee, and soon after I ran into him he called in one day to have a cup of tea with me. As we sat at the kitchen table I told him the truth of our circumstances. He was the only person I ever told the full extent of our financial difficulties. Sean was devastated, and he promised to get more help from the charity for us.

It wasn't that easy though. When Sean raised our case with the committee, they fought hard against giving us help and eventually refused his request. I know that this was the work of the devil. Sometimes Satan makes it more difficult for us to do what we are meant to do; on some occasions the forces of evil try to frustrate us in our lives and the work that we are doing, making life harder for us than it might be otherwise. Sometimes it's in quite subtle ways, such as distracting us from something we're supposed to do. I know this is one of the reasons I received so little help with my family when Joe was sick. In this case the devil was blinding the people to the circumstances in front of them.

I am in a constant battle with the devil. When someone has a very strong faith, the devil tries to make it difficult—and frequently succeeds in the short term—but I know that no matter how hard Satan tries with his evil forces to frustrate the work, God and the angels always win in the end.

Sean found it very hard to believe that he couldn't get more help for us. He was allowed to bring us some vouchers for food, and he was distraught when he realized how little good they were to us, given the dietary requirements. Sean took a detailed list of the foods Joe and Christopher *could* eat, and every so often after that he would bring us a small bag of groceries. I'm sure he was paying for these out of his own wallet.

As time went on more and more people heard about me and came to see me for help.

One woman who came to see me about this time was a grand-mother, not very old, but a grandmother nonetheless. She was called Mary. About ten years previously one of her neighbors had given birth to twins, one of whom had died shortly after birth. Mary told me that even when the mother was pregnant, although she was not a close friend or a relation, Mary had felt drawn to the babies. She couldn't quite understand it. When Mary first saw the baby Josie in the cot she knew there was a connection, a bond, even before she reached into the cot to touch her little face.

Many of us have heard the phrase "soulmate," and we tend to think of it mainly as a romantic concept—as the perfect partner, per-haps someone to marry. But one must remember that a soulmate could be a child in the same way that it could be an adult. People go around searching for their soulmate, but he or she may be in another part of the world. It may be that person you send a few euros to help, that man in a wheelchair, the child with Down syndrome you've just passed by in the street—anyone could be your soulmate.

As Josie grew, Mary continued to be very close to her. Anytime the child was sick or in trouble Mary would instinctively know. And it was the same for Josie, too. At times the child would tell her mother that she needed to go and see Mary, and when her mother asked why she always got the same answer: "I know Mary needs me." Her mother didn't always allow Josie to go to see Mary when she asked, because sometimes it might be dark, or lashing rain, but Josie would keep asking until she was eventually allowed to go. Josie would arrive at Mary's hall door, knock, and say, "Mary, what's the matter?" Mary would just look at the little girl and think, *My God—she knows that I'm feeling sad today!* They were soulmates: different ages, the same sex, but soulmates nonetheless; they had a very special connection to each other. Each knew how the other was feeling.

Mary is dead now. Sometime before she died she said to me, "I know Josie is my soulmate—I knew it wasn't my husband." It was an understanding that she came to, toward the end of her own life. Mary's death had an enormous effect on Josie, whom I had also gotten to know. When Mary died, Josie felt as if a huge piece of her heart had been taken away.

It's very possible that Josie will meet another soulmate during her life—as there can be more than one during a lifetime. I believe that sometimes we miss our soulmate because we don't recognize him or her—we are too busy, but that doesn't mean that the other person doesn't recognize us.

We also all have to learn that we can love someone and cherish them and give our lives for them, but that doesn't necessarily mean they are our soulmate. It's so sad to see young people, or not so young people, who say, "I won't settle until I meet my soulmate." As soon as they say that they are putting a big block on finding someone who may not be their soulmate but who may be able to bring them considerable happiness. You needn't search for that person, because if your soulmate is to pass through your life, then they will, whether it is for a brief moment or a longer time.

I remember watching the news with Joe one night. There was a report of a horrific train crash in the United Kingdom. I had noticed a picture of the disaster in the paper earlier in the day but had avoided it. Yet I knew, somehow, there was something I was supposed to see. I should have known better, though; when God and the angels want to show me something, I can't avoid it.

There was film of a man on a stretcher surrounded by rescue workers. I have no idea who the man was, other than that he was a survivor of the train crash, but I do know that, whoever he was, he had just met his soulmate on that train and that his soulmate was now dead. I knew this because I was allowed to see the contact between them. As the injured man was being carried out on the stretcher he reached up with his arm and I could see that he could see the soul of his soulmate; now dead, his soulmate was comforting him, making sure he survived. I wasn't allowed to know what gender the soulmate was, or whether he or she was young or old, but I know it was his soulmate and that they had met only fleetingly on the train that day.

I remember feeling terribly sad and thinking, "Oh my God, I hate this." Actually, hate is the wrong word. I felt such pain as I was watching and such compassion for the pain and loss the man on the stretcher was feeling, seeing his dead soulmate as he reached out, I don't know whether he would remember he had fleetingly met his soulmate. Sometimes spiritual things happen when we are in a state of pain and shock. Afterward we wonder if anything really did happen—did we see something, or was it just a flash of light?

Around this time I became very conscious of the connection between myself and a man who had murdered his wife. No matter where I went or what I was doing, this connection would appear in some way. I'd turn on the radio and hear something about the murder; I'd be walking down the road and somehow I would come across a newspaper, maybe even on the ground as I was walking past. The print would stand out, as if it were rising from the paper, and the only thing I would see in that newspaper would be something about this horrific murder. One evening, I went into the front room and turned on the television. The late news was on. I went to turn it off, but the television wouldn't turn off! I heard one of my angels say, "Lorna. Sit down and watch the news."

Reluctantly I did so. As I watched I saw film of the man who had just been found guilty of murdering his young wife in a very cold, calculated, and premeditated way for financial gain. As I was sitting watching the film, the angels showed me what he had done to his soul: he had disconnected his human self from his soul, so that his soul couldn't interfere with what he planned to do. This choice he had made had put coldness, ice, into his heart. It's hard to explain, but it was as if he had pushed his soul away, back away from him, and had then chained his soul to a wall, with chains that couldn't be broken. Sometimes we do these things to our soul because we *want* greed to rule our lives. We become obsessed with material things. It wasn't the devil or anyone else who had done this to this man's soul; he had done it himself. He had become, in a sense, a man of ice.

That was how he was at that moment; I was allowed to see his soul as he was being led off to jail. This doesn't mean that over time he might not feel remorse and his soul might break some of the chains. He'll never be able to bring back the girl, his young wife whom he murdered, and he has to pay, humanely, for what he has done, but the worst part of all is what he did to his own soul. As his soul breaks free, if he allows it, he will go through terrible torment within himself; he will try to avoid feeling it, but eventually he will break down and then he will feel deep and terrible pain.

This man had deliberately gone out and killed for reasons of greed. He had planned to take the soul from someone else's body. He had taken this soul before its time (I know some would say that if you are murdered, then it had to be your time, or it had to be retribution for an act in a past life—but this is not *always* true). He took her soul and his soul felt tremendous pain and hurt; his soul felt this because it was not able to stop him from performing this terrible act.

Her soul, that of his young murdered wife, also feels the sadness of knowing that his soul is trapped. Her soul forgives him. Souls always forgive; it's as if souls never give up. They are like the angels; one soul never gives up on another.

CHAPTER 24

Peace in Ireland and at Christmas

One Monday evening Joe was watching the news on television and he called out to me to come quickly. On the screen was a picture of the pawnbroker's shop in Dublin that we used. I couldn't believe what I was hearing: thieves had broken into the shop over the weekend and everything had been cleared out. The theft hadn't been discovered until Monday morning, and the police were saying they had no idea who had done it, but that it had been well planned.

I turned to Joe, looked at him, and said, "That means my ring has gone." I started to cry. "My beautiful ring!" I was very upset. Joe put his arm around me. "Now we won't have it to get us out of a jam anymore. It's just not fair," I said.

I felt lost without my ring. It meant an awful lot to me, even though, being honest, it had spent more time with the pawnbrokers than on my finger. I hoped that maybe the police would recover it, but as time went on that seemed more and more unlikely.

A few weeks later we got a letter in the post from the pawnbrokers. Joe must have read it about four times for me. It notified us that the receipt we had signed at the pawnbrokers when we had left the ring released them of any responsibility. They had no liability at all for the theft of the ring when it was in their care. We were gutted by this. No ring and no compensation for its loss.

Joe promised that someday he would get me another ring. I told him it didn't matter, that no ring would mean the same to me as that one. Joe gave me another hug and we put the letter away.

A few days later while I was sitting on the doorstep of the cottage Angel Michael appeared as if he were walking around from the back of the house. He sat beside me on the doorstep. "I don't feel like talking," I said to him. Angel Michael put his hand on my shoulder. "Lorna, I'm very sorry about your ring. We could do nothing." I turned to Michael and his radiance made me smile a little.

"Michael, I just wish you could have done something," I said. "Joe is sad too. He feels he has let me down. He said the other day that if he had been able to provide for us better then the ring would never have been in the pawnbrokers."

"Remember, Lorna," Michael said, "it's only a ring, a material object. Just remember Joe's love." I thought about what Michael had said for a minute; he was right, of course. I felt much better. I turned and smiled at Michael and then he disappeared. I didn't give much more thought to the ring after that.

I'm not interested in politics, but I'm very interested in peace, and at this time, in the mid-1990s, there was a lot of talk about peace in Northern Ireland. I asked Angel Michael about Northern Ireland on one occasion when he was sitting with me. He told me people would try to scupper the peace process. It was unlikely they would succeed, but peace would be a long time coming. It would take twenty years or so before everything was sorted out.

Since then I have been watching and watching. I've noticed lately how some people have become considerably more open and giving, that they have been forced to retreat from previous positions to bring about peace. Michael told me that it's very important that peace come to Northern Ireland. It's not just important for Ireland and Great Britain; if a terrorist group like the IRA can become part of a government, terrorist groups in other countries will see that they can do it too, that there is a route to peace other than by violence. I have been told that Ireland can be a cornerstone for peace in the world; the devil is constantly trying to endanger the peace in Northern Ireland, but as obstacles to peace arise they seem to be overcome.

Ireland is an example of religion fighting religion, faith fighting faith, and if Ireland can come to peace, so can other countries—the Irish peace process will even have influence on Iraq, Palestine, and Israel.

I have been shown different paths for the world. At times I have watched and been terrified. Some of the possible futures I have been shown have been truly atrocious, and if one of those comes to pass I don't want to be alive to see it. But I have also been shown many wonderful paths, where there is room for everyone to live in harmony and at peace. I believe the world in the future can be a wonderful place, but every single individual has to play their part.

All ordinary people want peace. A woman who lived in Northern Ireland came to see me; her husband had been killed in the violence and her elder son was now in jail for his role as a terrorist. It broke her heart to see her elder son destroy his life, and all the pain he had caused to others. Her younger son was now following in his brother's footsteps, and she feared he would end up dead or in jail. She could see no end to the cycle of violence. Every day she went to church to pray for peace and to pray for a normal life—that her elder son could come back and be a father to his young child, and that her younger son could marry and have children.

She told me she was fed up with going to funerals and was determined not to pass on hatred—but she saw other grandmothers who were actively doing so. "If those grandmothers would stop breathing hatred into their children and their grandchildren, it would make a very big difference," she said. She was trying, but it wasn't at all easy. My heart went out to her.

As I have said before, the angels have told me that war is easy; making and keeping peace is the difficult thing.

I had become very anxious about Joe in recent months. I could see his health was deteriorating; he was losing weight and constantly having stomach problems, and his body seemed to be shrivelling up. I called the doctor frequently, but he didn't seem to be able to do anything.

One day when Joe was at home in bed he became extremely ill and disoriented. He didn't know who he was or who I was. He was in great distress, and I was terrified I was going to lose him. When he came around Joe found he couldn't move the left side of his body, and his speech was slurred.

Joe had had a stroke!

He was kept in the hospital for months, doing intensive physiotherapy and learning to walk and speak again. For a long time after this he dragged his leg, and I used to have to cut up his food because he couldn't hold his fork properly. Fortunately, after a time his speech was back to normal, and you couldn't hear the stroke in his voice.

Sometimes while he was recuperating at home, we would go for a walk in the evening when it was dark. He was embarrassed to be seen; he was afraid people would think he was drunk. I used to tell him that it didn't matter what other people thought, and I walked with my arm around him (although he was a very tall man and I'm a small woman). The angels helped me, as I wouldn't have been able to support Joe on my own. Joe had a habit of pushing me out to the edge of the footpath and, but for the angels, I know we would have fallen.

I talked to God and the angels constantly about Joe, asking, "Why does he have to be ill? Why can't you make him better? Why can't you make life easier?" One day I was out in the garden, pretending to be doing something so that no one would see my tears. Angel Michael appeared in front of me. I almost stepped into him as I reached up to pull a leaf off the plum tree. I sobbed at him, "Michael, I don't want to believe that Joe's life is coming to an end. It's too soon. Please tell God. I don't think I could cope. I don't want Joe to die."

"Lorna, God can hear you," Michael replied. "He knows what is in your heart. Lorna, look at me, look into my eyes. What do you see?"

As I looked into the Angel Michael's eyes everything seemed to vanish—even Angel Michael. His eyes turned into a pathway full of life and light. On each side of the pathway I could see snow white angels, and there was Joe as a young man, healthy and strong, walking with angels, walking toward members of his family who had already died. Joe was on the pathway to Heaven. Seeing Joe looking so well and happy filled my heart with joy.

At the same time I cried out, "Angel Michael, no! No! I don't want Joe to die. He's too young to die; he's only in his early forties. It's not fair!"

I stood under the plum tree crying my heart out with Michael comforting me, his feathered wings wrapped around me and his arms holding me tight. After a while Michael unfolded his wings from around me and wiped the tears from my eyes.

"Lorna, be strong now. Go and take care of your family and Joe."

Angel Michael touched my forehead and in a flash of light he was gone.

A few weeks later a friend asked me to see a family that needed help the following evening. I was a little hesitant about their coming because of Joe and because the children would be home from school; with dinner, sports, homework, and all that going on in that small house, I was a little reluctant to agree, but I did.

The next evening, to my surprise, Joe got up for dinner and decided he would go and visit a friend with Christopher. I kept looking at Joe; his soul seemed to be one step in front of him all the time. I was really frightened and told him he needn't go out, that I could see the family in the kitchen. Joe said that he felt he shouldn't be there when the family was visiting, and not to worry as Christopher would be with him.

A knock came at the door. The family had arrived early. Joe and Christopher passed the visitors in the hall.

Just as the family was leaving Joe arrived back and again they passed each other in the hall. I said good-bye at the front door, and when I came back into the kitchen Joe looked extremely pale and seemed a little agitated. I put the kettle on straightaway, made tea, and put about four spoonfuls of sugar into his cup for him. I insisted he sit down and drink it immediately. I made a sandwich and poured him another cup of tea. As I stood at the opposite end of the table, watching him, I asked, "Are you sure you are feeling okay?"

"I'm fine," he replied. "There's no need to fuss."

He could have taken only about two bites out of the sandwich when the atmosphere changed in the room. At that moment, Ruth, in nightclothes and bare feet, opened the kitchen door and asked, "Mum, can I ring a friend about homework?"

I looked from Ruth to Joe and then back to Ruth. "Yes, but be quick," I replied. Everything happened in slow motion; the only sound to be heard was Ruth dialing the number and the clicking sound of the dial, then her voice saying "Hello."

Then it happened: Joe took an extremely bad turn. I had always done my best never to allow the children to see this happening.

Ruth started screaming hysterically as her dad went into convulsions. I was trying to help Joe and my daughter at the same time. I knew Joe was dying and I needed help. I cried silently, "Angels, help!," as I said to Ruth, "Go and get Christopher."

It turned out that Christopher had gone to the shops and wasn't home to help. I told Ruth to dial 999, ask for an ambulance, and give our address. Ruth spoke hysterically to someone on the other end of the phone line. After she hung up I told her to go quickly and fetch a neighbor to help. Ruth ran out the door screaming, still barefoot.

I was standing beside Joe, holding onto him and praying. I was doing all I could to help him physically, holding him up as he sat slumped at the kitchen table. No sooner had Ruth gone out the door than there was a flash of light. Joe and I, sitting at the table in the center of the room, became encased in what looked like an enormous ice cube or cube of crystal. The cube was hollow in the center and extremely cold. I could see my breath yet I felt warm. There was no breath coming from Joe's mouth; he had stopped breathing and his lips were going blue. I cried out, "Angels, I am not prepared for this!"

Snow white angels walked into the cube. I screamed and cried, "No, God! Please don't take Joe yet. Let him stay in this world a little longer."

I watched with great pain in my heart as Joe's soul moved out of his body completely, and the path that Angel Michael had shown me appeared before my eyes. I could see Joe as I had seen him before: his soul radiant, beautiful angels walking with him, and, in the distance further down the path, members of his family waiting to welcome him. As he walked toward them I was still asking God to please let him stay in this world for a little longer, for him not to die just yet, that I still needed him and so did the children.

I suddenly felt great warmth as God spoke: "Lorna, I will give him back to you only this once, but you must never ask again." God spoke with a firm voice of power and authority. I knew he was being stern with me for asking for something I should not have asked for. I felt like I had as a child when an adult was cross with me. His words stayed in my mind constantly from then on; I knew that I should not have asked and that I must never ask again.

Suddenly Joe's body sat up. He opened his mouth and it was as if life had been sucked back into his body. As his soul reentered his body the life force was unbelievable. It was only then that I noticed that it was Joe's guardian angel who had sat him up. Joe turned to me and spoke in a whispered voice: "I think I was on my way to Heaven." Then he seemed to pass out.

Only then did I become aware of the sound of Ruth and our neighbor rushing in through the hall door and at the same time heard Christopher's and Owen's voices calling out, "What's wrong?" as they ran up the drive.

When the ambulance arrived it took a little convincing to get Joe to go to the hospital. Eventually, though, he went and I followed with a neighbor in a car. Some hours later a doctor came out to speak to me and told me that Joe was very lucky. He had been in a coma when he had arrived at the hospital. "Joe must have someone watching over him," the doctor said, as he turned around and walked away. I smiled because I, of course, knew he did have someone watching over him—his guardian angel—and that God had granted the miracle and given Joe back his life.

Joe spent two weeks in the hospital. I was constantly thanking God for the miracle of giving Joe back for another little while. I didn't know how much time we would have together: whether it would be weeks, months, or maybe another couple of years. In my heart I was hoping so much that it could be years, but I knew that when the time came I could not ask God again to allow Joe to live.

Joe had been given back to me, but his health never recovered.

He stayed in bed most of the time and was never able to work again. Things were very tough. The children did what they could to help; they had had part-time jobs since they were about twelve years old, and gave some of their pay to me. Joe and I were always determined, though, that our children would continue in school, whatever our circumstances, and would get a good education. I always felt that I had lost out by being taken out of school at fourteen.

I noticed our gate was quite rusty and badly in need of paint. On a morning when I had some time to spare, and the weather was crisp and cold, I found an old paintbrush that needed some cleaning and half a tin of black paint in the shed and started painting the gate. I was working away when a young boy on a bicycle came along, stopped, and said hello. It was Paul, one of Christopher's school friends; they were around the same age, about fourteen.

"Why aren't you at school?" I asked.

He told me he was off sick but was well enough to give me a hand and offered to help. I handed him an old knife and he started to scrape loose paint off the gate. He chatted away about school and fishing, laughing and joking in between. After a while I'd had enough, thanked Paul, and said good-bye. He picked up his bike and went down the road. I watched him as he went and I saw four angels around him.

The four angels appeared to be running alongside Paul, in front of and behind him; they gave me the impression they were trying to prevent him from falling off his bike. I asked, "What are you angels up to?" I could see no reason for him to fall; to me he looked as if he was cycling perfectly. I did not see his guardian angel, but I did think it was a little strange at the time that Paul had come to visit me, because he had never done anything like that before.

I didn't give it another thought until about three days later. I was out working on the gate again when I heard someone coming. I stopped what I was doing, walked out onto the road, and there was Paul, walking toward me with his bike. His guardian angel was behind him. I knew something was wrong; Paul looked healthy and strong, but the light surrounding him should have been glowing and it wasn't. Instead it was turned down, making the light of life look dim around him. I also couldn't understand why his head was down.

I called out "Paul," and he looked up, gave me a big smile, and ran toward me with his bike. He dropped it on the ground and asked could he help. "Yes, but you're a little late," I replied, laughingly. I went around to the shed to get another paintbrush, leaving Paul standing at the gate. As I went around to the back of the cottage I was asking the angels, "What is wrong?" No angels appeared, but many spoke simultaneously as if with one voice: "All you need to do Lorna is spend time with Paul. Listen to him."

"That's no problem," I said. "I hope I can find a paintbrush for him."

I did. As I went back round the side of the cottage I saw Paul standing anxiously at the gate, waiting for me. He was glowing now, shining bright, and I couldn't understand what made him shine so brightly now, when a few minutes before the light was so dim. I could see he was happy and I was delighted. We painted the gate together and Paul laughed and joked, chatting all the time. He mentioned that it was his birthday the week after next.

When it was time to go, Paul went off on his bike. As I watched him cycle away I could see the four angels running with him again. It looked so comical and I smiled to myself. The four angels' clothing appeared to be long and loose; they ran so elegantly and they seemed to bounce lightly, like bubbles full of hot air. They were watery amber in color and they shone gently, a little like light shining on water. Looking at them was very soothing on my eyes. When I could no longer see Paul or his angels I walked back in through the gate and around to the sheds. I called my own angels and asked would they tell me about Paul, but they did not reply.

Paul was on my mind constantly. The next day I went for a walk on my own up the lane, not far from the cottage. I stopped at a gate into a field and I called on my angels. I thought they were not listening, but as I turned around to walk on further down the lane, Angel Elijah appeared, saying, "Where are you going Lorna? Come back here."

"It's about time," I said. "Where have you angels been?"

"Lorna, we have been here all the time with you," Elijah replied.

"Angel Elijah, I am worried about a young boy called Paul. I know something is wrong."

"Lorna," said Elijah, "all that is needed from you is to be with Paul."

"Elijah, I am afraid for him," I said. "Why do I feel fear? He is such a beautiful child."

"Lorna, in some cases angels are given the job of trying, if possible, to change the future of a particular individual or group. That's what we are trying to do for this child. We are whispering to many people, asking them to play a part; but only a few are listening and that might not be enough. You are a lifeline for Paul at the moment; you are one of the reasons that he is still here. You always listen, Lorna. Now go out to work on the gate and we will get Paul to call over to you and talk and laugh and have fun."

"Can you not tell me any more, Elijah?" I begged.

"No, Lorna. You alone can't change his future. Other people have to play their part too."

This was a time, and I see many of them, when a series of small events can build together into a big one. This is why when the angels prompt you to do something small, such as smile at someone or tell someone that they've done good work, however inconsequential it may seem to be at the time—you should do it! Apparently inconsequential things could turn out to be vital in the bigger scheme of things.

Every time I went out to do more work on the gate Paul would arrive. No matter what time of day it was—morning, late afternoon, or in the evening—he always appeared to help. He asked me would I invite Christopher to go fishing with him on his birthday. I told him that I was sure that Christopher would be happy to do that, but it would have to be Sunday—the day after Paul's birthday—as Christopher worked in a coal and horse yard on Saturdays. Paul said that the plan was that all his family would be going. He was very excited. He thanked me for letting Christopher go with them. I told him I was putting him in charge of Christopher, to mind him and make sure that he got back home safely, and to catch plenty of fish so that I could cook them for tea on Monday. Paul laughed and said he would do his best.

When Christopher got home from school that day I told him about the invitation to Paul's birthday. Christopher was delighted and got his fishing gear ready and left it in the hall in anticipation. The next time I was out painting the gate Paul arrived. It was only a few days to his birthday and he was so excited. We painted and Paul went home, happy. I watched him as he cycled down the road. I saw no change in his angels; they were so close to him, protecting him, ready to catch him.

I never saw Paul again. A day or two later Christopher turned the key in the hall door and came into the kitchen. He was extremely upset, and before he said a word I knew it was about Paul. "Mum, Paul died this morning. There was a tragic accident. I can't believe it. We were to go fishing for his birthday; let's call over to Paul's house, Mum."

I was devastated; it seemed so unfair. I comforted Christopher and gave him a big hug. I told him we needed to give his parents a little time before we could call over.

The following evening Christopher and I went over to Paul's

house; there were people coming and going. Paul's dad spoke with Christopher for a few minutes after we had a cup of tea. Then we said our good-byes and walked home. On the way Christopher said, "Mum, it felt so strange, Paul not being there; the house seemed so empty. I will always miss Paul."

I know those four beautiful angels of Paul's took him straight to Heaven with his fishing rod and fishing bag tied onto the back carrier of his bicycle. I know Paul is doing a lot of fishing in Heaven.

Perhaps six months after Paul's death, on one of those increasingly rare occasions when Joe was feeling well enough to get up, Christopher, now aged fifteen, and Joe went into Dublin to meet Matt, an old friend of Joe's in a pub in the city center. Christopher told me that the pub was dark and packed, with lots of noise. Christopher stood close to his dad, as people in the pub were getting very rowdy. His dad met Matt and the three of them started to walk back through the crowd to the door.

Someone pushed someone else and a fight started. Christopher said he was scared. Some men followed Christopher, Joe, and Matt out onto the street and started to look for a fight; one had a broken bottle in his hand. Joe told the men they were not looking for a fight, and they kept on walking. Suddenly the men started to push them. Christopher said he was really scared. All of a sudden he felt the strong presence of Paul. Christopher told me, "Mum, I'm sure he was there. It was as if Paul was there, really there, like you and me. He pushed those men back and pushed us forward. I could feel Paul protecting me and Dad. I was never so scared in my life as I was of those men from the pub, but when I felt Paul's presence I knew we would be safe."

I told Christopher to remember that Paul would always be there when he needed his protection. Many times I have thought of Paul over the years, and I thank him for protecting Christopher for me. I thank him for remembering that I asked him to keep Christopher safe.

Every day when I came back from doing the shopping I would take Joe a cup of tea and sit beside him to chat. One day Joe had a story to tell me. Joe's guardian angel sat right next to him and there were lots of angels sitting on the bed looking in Joe's direction and waiting to hear what he would say.

"Lorna, you won't believe it," he said, "Today when you were out a little child, a spirit, came skipping into the room. She was about three years old with long light brown tossed hair. She looked dirty, as if she had been playing in the mud and had mud cakes in her hands. She stood right there where you are sitting and she said, 'Dad, play with me.' Then she turned around and skipped out of the room."

I was delighted but very surprised! I knew what this meant. We were going to have another child. We'd always wanted another child, but Ruth was now about twelve, and given Joe's health it was the last thing I expected. It was a miracle. I thanked God and my angels.

Joe had never seen a spirit before. It was as if God and the angels were allowing him to see more, helping him to understand that he was more than just a body.

I didn't tell Joe straightaway that seeing this spirit meant we would have a new daughter; I just let him bask in the delight he felt about this beautiful little spirit. "Why did she call me daddy?" he asked in wonder.

I saw this little spirit before I was even pregnant. She was exactly as Joe had described. On one occasion I was in the kitchen making tea for Joe and as I was carrying the tray out the kitchen door this little thing, this little girl, skipped out the door of the dining room.

She looked so beautiful, and then she just disappeared. When I opened the door to the bedroom the first thing Joe said was that the little girl had been here again, calling him daddy and asking him to play with her.

This time I told Joe what this meant—that God was sending us another daughter. Joe found this very hard to believe. "God would have to pour an awful lot of essential life into me to let me father a child. That would need a real miracle!"

But shortly afterward I discovered I was pregnant.

One day I was standing in front of the mirror. Angels appeared around me as well as a golden light. Then I saw the energy of life spinning in my tummy—all colors, emerald blue, emerald green, emerald red, emerald purple. Then the swirl opened up and I could see the little baby, like a speck of dust. The sight filled me with emotion and love for my unborn child.

After the gap of twelve years since Ruth's birth the idea of being pregnant again took some getting used to. I had given away everything that a mother would need for a baby, so the angels had a lot of work to do to help—a lot of whispering in people's ears. But by the time my baby, Megan, was born, in 1996, I had everything that I needed for a new baby and I was very thankful to the angels and all who had listened to them.

Sometimes it is clear to me that the angels have been working very hard. That Christmas we had little money again. One evening just before Christmas we were sitting at the kitchen table having dinner when a knock came on the door. Christopher went to answer it then came back in helping a stranger to carry an enormous box.

Christopher introduced the man as Father Tom, one of the priests at his school.

Father Tom said, "I hope you don't think that I am intruding on your privacy. The home economics class agreed that I could give all their Christmas baking to a family in Maynooth and I heard you could do with it. On Christmas Eve I'll be back with a cooked turkey and ham. Don't worry. No one in the class knows where the food is going. That's why I came on my own, and I was hoping Christopher would be here to help me carry the box in."

I thanked him and invited him to have a cup of tea. As I made the tea Father Tom, Joe, and the children started to take the food out of the box. There was everything you could think of; there was so much food, all of it home baked. I couldn't believe it. I made the tea and thanked God and the angels. As I handed Father Tom a cup of tea and sliced up one of the delicious apple tarts I glanced at my children, seeing the light in their eyes. I turned to Father Tom and asked, "How did you know?"

Father Tom said he had just heard there were difficulties, but he knew no more than that. I looked across the table at Joe; he shook his head. I knew he didn't want to tell Father Tom the extent of his sickness. "Thank you for listening to your angels," I said. "And thank your home economics class on our behalf for bringing this abundance to our home."

On Christmas Eve Father Tom arrived at our home with the biggest turkey I have ever seen, as well as a wonderful ham. Sitting at the fire that Christmas Joe turned to me and said that he was ashamed because he could not provide properly for me and the children. I looked at him and said, "It's not your fault that you have been so sick over the years." I tried to comfort him. "You never intended to get sick. It makes no sense to talk that way."

Joe had said this many times before, and it's something I've heard frequently over the years from people who are ill. Although their poor health is through no fault of their own, they feel ashamed, a nuisance and a burden to their families. Sometimes I would say to Joe, "Why are you so cross today?" and he would say, "I'm not cross with you or the children; I am cross with myself for being ill, for not being able to look after you and the children properly. I can do nothing."

I smiled at Joe as we sat by the fire that Christmas and reassured him: "When you are feeling well, you work in the garden until you nearly collapse, and when you can you clean the kitchen, which is great to find when I come home from the shops. You do all you can do. Your children and I love you very much."

CHAPTER 25

Michael tells me who he really is

One evening I was feeling weighed down and burdened. I was constantly in prayer, asking God for miracles to help people who had asked me for help. It was late, the house was very quiet, the children were sleeping, and I was heading for bed, leaving Joe drinking a cup of tea by the fire. I turned on the lamp on the little dressing table by Joe's side of the bed and got into bed. I sat with pillows behind me, my knees up and my face in my hands, praying.

I don't know how much time had passed when I heard my name being called. As radiant as ever, Angel Michael stood beside the lamp, on the other side of the bed. But he looked different.

Angel Michael dresses in a way that fits with what he is communicating—this is how he helps me to understand his messages. This evening he looked like a prince. He wore a golden crown; at the waist he wore a gold and black belt, and his white and gold robe draped loosely over him and fell to above his knees. He was holding a scroll. He had shoulder-length hair that flowed as if there were a gentle wind. His thonged sandals crisscrossed up his legs, and on the top of each foot was a golden crucifix. His sapphire blue eyes were radiant and he had a smile of Heaven. He shone with an incredibly bright light.

"Lorna, God hears all your prayers," Michael said. "Get a pen and paper out of the drawer. I have a message for you, a prayer from God."

I did as Michael said, and as I sat up in bed with the pen and paper in my hand, Michael opened a scroll and read out these words:

Prayer of Thy Healing Angels,
That is carried from God by Michael, Thy Archangel.
Pour out, Thy Healing Angels,
Thy Heavenly Host upon me,
And upon those that I love,
Let me feel the beam of Thy
Healing Angels upon me,
The light of Your Healing Hands.
I will let Thy Healing begin,
Whatever way God grants it,
Amen.

When Michael had finished reading the scroll I asked him to read it again, but a little more slowly as I was having difficulty writing it all down. I found the language a little strange. It wasn't the sort of language I was used to, but this was how it was given to me. The Angel Michael smiled at me then reached out and touched my forehead with one of his fingers. "Write now, Lorna," he said.

As the Angel Michael read the prayer from the scroll again I found I had no problem writing down every word of the prayer. The words I have written here are the exact words I was given, even if they don't sound quite right to us.

Michael said, "Give this prayer to everyone who comes to see you. It has been given to you by God."

I thanked Michael and God on my own behalf, and on behalf of all who would benefit from this prayer.

Michael bowed his head and disappeared.

From the very first time I had seen Michael, in the bedroom in

Old Kilmainham all those years ago, I had known he was different; that he was a very powerful force, more powerful than most other angels. When I was about fourteen he had told me that he was an archangel, but that I wasn't to reveal it to anyone. It was only on this night, when he gave me the prayer from God to share and he told me to write: "That is carried from God by Michael, Thy Archangel," that I knew I could refer to him in this way.

Sometimes when Michael the Archangel appears he gleams, almost as if he were standing in the center of the sun. At these moments he can almost blind me with light and I have to ask him to dim it. His brightness shows that Michael is a powerful force beyond our comprehension and that like the sun he is giving our planet life itself.

Michael has told me that archangels are like generals among the angels; they have power over angels and souls, and all angels obey them. They send angels to all parts of the universe to do God's will and carry His messages.

There are many archangels, many more than are traditionally spoken of, and Michael is one of the most powerful. As Michael is the archangel of the sun, Gabriel is the archangel of the moon. All archangels are in union with each other: the angels surround God as He sits on His throne and are a very powerful force, defending the Heavens and keeping in line the ongoing process of creation.

The next day I told Joe that Michael the Archangel had given me a prayer from God. Joe started to write it out on sheets of paper so that I could give it to people who came looking for help. Later a friend offered to have printed copies made for me. To this day I still give that prayer to everyone who asks for my help, and many people have told me that the "healing angels" have helped in response to the prayer.

All angels do healing work, but there is a particular group of angels called "healing angels" who are called in by guardian angels when healing is required. There are literally millions of healing angels—in all shapes, sizes, and forms—and God is pouring healing angels on the world all the time. All we have to do is ask for their help.

We must always remember that the healing will happen in the way that God knows is best for us. Sometimes we may not recognize that healing has occurred as it may not have been the healing we asked for—it may be emotional or spiritual healing rather than physical. We need to watch out for healing and recognize when it has been granted. Often healing can seem small—perhaps somebody who has been depressed for a long time smiles or laughs; maybe someone who was in a lot of physical distress feels a lot better; or maybe a mother who has been stressed out and unable to cope suddenly feels happiness and joy.

Sometimes these healing angels communicate through children. A child may turn around and say something that is significant to its mother or another adult, something that helps them to understand why things are the way they are, and how to make them better.

One morning the following summer a mother and daughter came to see me. The daughter, Sophie, who was in her early twenties, had constant pain in her arm and through her body, arising from a car accident. The doctors had done all they could but were unable to do any more. She had been suffering from this pain for several years, and her mother was very worried. Sophie insisted on her mother seeing me first, and she sat reading a magazine in the little hall while I spoke with her mother.

I was about half an hour with her mother, and at the end I prayed over her, blessed her, and asked the healing angels for healing in every part of her life. I also gave her the Prayer of the Healing Angels. I walked out with the mother to join Sophie in the hall and straightaway I knew that angels had been there. The atmosphere was much brighter and warmer, and the air was whirling around with what I call the breeze of the healing angels. I smiled, knowing what had happened.

Sophie was fast asleep on the chair. Her mother gently woke her and she looked at us in a dazed way. Then Sophie suddenly smiled and said, "I haven't any pain anymore. It's gone. All the pain is gone!"

Sophie stood up while she was talking and was moving her body around more freely than before, bending her arms and legs, checking that all the pain was gone. She was like a child dancing up and down. She was laughing at the sheer delight of having a body that was pain-free.

"I feel fantastic, Lorna. I had a dream you put me to sleep and while I was asleep loads of angels surrounded me and touched me. They healed me."

I brought her into my little room for a blessing and to thank God and the angels for healing her. I hadn't even given her the prayer and already the healing angels had gone to work.

Sometimes people say to me that they believe I have a special connection to God and the angels, and that if they ask me to ask for something it will be granted. Sometimes it frightens me that people have so much faith in me. I am afraid that God won't always grant them the healing they are asking for if it's not meant to be. I know God always provides some healing, but sometimes people don't recognize it as what they get is not what they had envisaged.

I might get a call from a mother or father who had previously brought their child to see me and asked me to pray as they were having surgery that day. They tell me they bless the child every day in the hospital with the healing prayer, or that the child says the prayer. One child I know kept the prayer under his pillow all the time he was in the hospital. I also get calls thanking me and the angels, saying that healing was granted.

One Sunday morning I had just gotten back from Mass with the children when a knock came at the door. When I opened the door

I was surprised to see an elderly lady standing there. She said she was very sorry for calling to see me on a Sunday. She was in tears and my heart went out to her. I invited her in. She was quite elderly and un-well; she was dying and had a fear of dying in pain. She was asking for a miracle from God. I prayed over her, blessed her, and gave her the healing prayer. She left feeling much happier. About six weeks later she called unexpectedly again. She apologized and said she would keep me only a minute.

"God has worked a miracle," she said. "I was sitting on the sofa in my kitchen, feeling very unwell, when all of a sudden I felt a great stillness and peace within the room. I looked up and standing in the middle of the room was an angel. It was all dressed in white and seemed to be hovering; the angel shone like a brilliant light and smiled at me. The next minute the angel was gone."

That was enough for her; she had experienced her miracle. By letting her see that angel God had given her the gift of peace of mind and removed her fear of dying. The old lady said she knew she was going to die of her disease, but until that time came she was going to live her life to the full; she was going to enjoy life and let her family know how much she loved them. "I know now there is a place called Heaven, Lorna, because I have seen an angel," she said. "I am no longer afraid to die. I know that an angel will be there for me. When my time comes that angel will take my soul and just leave be-hind this wrinkly old body that's no good to anybody, not even me. So I'm not afraid to die—and that's a miracle!" I remember smiling a lot at the way she said this.

She had no fear and the wonderful thing was that she was, in a sense, looking forward to the day when the angel would come to take her soul, when her physical body would die.

"Wouldn't it be lovely," she said, "if, someday, when the time comes, I could come back as an angel myself to take the souls of my family that I love so much to Heaven."

The elderly lady was shining like a light herself and had a beautiful smile on her face. We said a prayer together and she left. I never saw her again.

One thing we must always remember is that the angels that God sends us from the heavens can really help us if we allow them to, if we open our hearts and allow the angels to come into our lives. We should not be afraid; there is no reason to be afraid. We feel fear because we don't understand angels; we feel fear because we don't understand God. Always remember that an angel will never harm you; no angel has ever harmed me, and I can assure you that no angel will ever harm you.

One Sunday when Megan was about two years old we were in the Dublin Mountains near the Sally Gap. We were away from the road in a deserted area that looked quite flat and grassy, with the odd small, scattered rock. As we started to descend the gentle slope more rocks appeared, and then further on the rocks got bigger and the slope became very steep—more like a cliff with some trees growing out of it. From the edge of the steep decline we could see a beautiful lake. The lake was in between the mountains, with a big house on the shore, and we could see deer grazing on the mountain on the far side.

After walking down the slope a little I sat on a rock and Joe and Ruth took Megan down a little further. I watched them walking hand in hand with Megan in the middle. I lay back on the rock and closed my eyes for a few minutes, soaking up the sun. Even though it was chilly I could feel the heat of the sun, and the rocks felt warm. After a little while I heard Joe, Ruth, and Megan coming back up and I opened my eyes and sat up. I looked toward the path but they were still out of sight. As they got closer I could see Megan in the middle with Joe on the right and Ruth on the left lifting her little sister and swinging her in the air. Megan was laughing her heart out, having great fun, skipping and jumping with the help of her dad and her big sister.

What happened next filled me with exuberance and delight: Megan's guardian angel appeared, skipping behind Megan. She appeared to skip right through her and danced along about three feet ahead of her. Megan's guardian angel looked like a young girl, with brown eyes as big as saucers. She was so bright and beautiful; her feet were bare and, of course, they did not touch the ground. She looked about eight, with long dark, plaited hair fastened with an orange, red, and green leather cord. There was a red feather in her hair and in the middle of her forehead she had a light in the shape of a star. For a brief moment I thought I saw wings. She wore a light gold-colored sleeveless tunic of no particular shape. Megan's guardian angel was radiant; her movements were graceful, like a feather.

Then this beautiful guardian angel skipped back into Megan's body and disappeared. No one else had noticed her presence, and the three of them continued walking up the path toward me.

Megan's guardian angel looks very different from my other children's guardian angels—they were not childlike, but this one was, and I believe this guardian angel will grow with Megan as she grows. Thinking back, I remember that Megan's first word had not been "Mum" or "Dad," but a word I had never heard before. I told Joe that the angels were telling me the name of her guardian angel, and I asked the angels to spell it for me so that I could write it down for Megan so she could have it when she was a little older.

When I'm working around the house, out in the garden, or even walking down to the shops, I always pray silently. One evening I was working hard at home as most mothers do; I had the house to myself, more or less, and Joe and Megan were fast asleep. Ruth was helping a friend babysit, Owen was playing sports, and Christopher was at a friend's house on the far side of town. It was dark outside, but through the window I could see the streetlight on the corner. I was enjoying the peace, being alone and yet not totally alone. I started to notice the stillness of the atmosphere, the change as time started to stand still; I couldn't hear a sound. I looked down at my hands and noticed the energy around them, flickering and full of sparkles. This energy is perpetually there, but sometimes it gets stronger and brighter just before an angel appears. It's not always like this; sometimes I don't notice anything and something just happens.

I walked out the kitchen door with a towel in my hand and bumped into a white angel in the hall. She told me to come to the front room then vanished. When I opened the front room door I saw another angel, a much more powerful and exceptionally beautiful angel standing by the window. She smiled at me. She was very, very different from any angel I have seen before or since. Her dress was stunning—fiery red and gold—I have never seen a dress like it. On top of her head was an exquisite crown and emerging from the center of the crown and flowing down over her whole body were millions and millions of fine, silklike threads, braided together. Each braid was entwined with diamonds and sapphires of all colors. This beautiful angel had dazzling wings, like fiery flames rippling constantly, with sparkling jewels within the feathers. I could see everything in exquisite detail and yet I find it very hard to describe this amazing angel. She was unique, perfect in every way; every part of her seemed to be alive. She was so dazzling, I had to look away for a moment because my eyes could not take in all the beauty.

Her face was radiant with life. She was perfect; her eyes were blue and shone like the sun, but a billion times more radiant. How can words describe that? All I can say is, when I looked into her eyes there was such gentleness, compassion, peace, and such love radiating from them. I knew this superb angel standing in front of me could see *everything*. It was as if she had knowledge of every particle within the universe—something completely beyond our human comprehension.

I was trembling; I was in the presence of such power. I was allowed to feel this power and to recognize it. There was another angel standing to my right behind me. I was only aware of its being there when it said, "Lorna, walk a little more into the room."

I took another few steps, not taking my eyes off the beautiful angel in front of me. I was conscious of the door closing behind me. The magnificent angel moved toward me saying, with a little smile, "Lorna, do not be afraid."

In that instant I felt such peace and joy within me. The angel continued, "Do you know who I am, Lorna?"

"No," I replied.

"I am the Queen of Angels."

"Do you mean you are the Mother of God?" I asked. I was shocked, but on another level I knew who I was with; my soul knew, but my human part was very shocked.

"Yes, Lorna," she answered, "I am the Queen of Heaven, the Queen of all the Angels, the Queen of all Souls. Lorna, don't be afraid. Ask me the question that is on your mind."

"Queen of Angels," I said, "I have seen you many times. You are the mother I have seen in the sky with a child." I remembered that when I was a child on the swing in Ballymun the angels had shown me her face.

"Yes, Lorna, you are right," she said.

"My real wish is that you, the Mother of God, would appear for the whole world to see." I was crying now. "For all hatred and wars to stop. For all the pain, all the hunger, all the destruction caused by wars—fought over material things, over religion, over power—to cease." I looked at her pleadingly, with tears running down my face. "The world needs a miracle."

"Lorna, I will reach into people's hearts. One day I will appear and the whole world will see me as you can now." The Queen of Angels gave me such a smile, her eyes radiating love, and the light that surrounded her like fiery flames reached out and touched me and took all my sadness away.

I asked her would I see her again, and she said yes. Then she was gone.

I believe that this will happen. The Queen of Angels has appeared to people in the past, and she continues to appear in different places today, but only to small groups. I believe that someday the Queen of Angels will appear for all to see, not just some, and that she will appear not just for a fleeting moment but that she will remain for some time, for the world to see and acknowledge her. She will come to provide the evidence that mankind in its weakness requires—and this will be the beginning of a major change for the human race.

CHAPTER 26

An evil spirit shows himself

Sometimes a person will let Satan enter their life. This can happen through deliberate, malicious intent or through feelings of jealousy, anger, or a perception that life hasn't been fair to them. For example, Satan frequently gains access to individuals when there is a dispute over property or a will. The extent to which Satan can darken a soul varies; his influence may give an individual what appears, externally, to be a great life, but the lives of those around them will be damaged; ultimately, if nothing is done the soul of the person involved will be destroyed.

Growing spiritually—reconnecting with God and the angels, and letting God's love and compassion back into the heart—is the only way of driving out Satan. The angels will help when you ask them. It doesn't even have to be the person who was affected who asks: a family member or friend can also pray for help, and I have seen many occasions where this has worked. It's worth remembering this when you come across evil in your own life: a prayer from anyone, of any belief or background, can and does make a significant difference.

People can grow spiritually unbeknownst to themselves; they may not notice it happening. Perhaps someone prayed for them. Perhaps as a child they asked and years later they will be spiritually awakened. I meet a lot of people to whom this has happened.

Over the years many people have come to visit me who are under Satan's influence, to some extent. I will always see it, because Satan can't resist showing off his presence.

One time a successful Irish businessman came to see me. He said he wasn't sure why he was there, but that a friend of his had convinced him to come—although he admitted it had taken his friend two years to persuade him to do so. He told me he had done some terrible things. He admitted that he never ever considered how his actions would affect others; as far as he was concerned there was only one person who mattered—himself—and one thing that mattered—money.

Something was happening to him, though. His old friends no longer liked him, and his family would have nothing to do with him. But I know that someone was praying for him and that was why he had come to me. He asked me why he felt no remorse. Somewhere, somehow, he knew he had done wrong; he knew he *should* feel remorse, but he didn't know *how* to feel it. He wanted to be able to feel remorse, and he wanted to get his friends and family back.

The man sat with crossed arms at my kitchen table and said he wanted to change; he didn't want to be like this anymore. His head was bowed but I could see there were tears in his eyes. Then I was shown the evil spirit of Satan coming forward.

The man was a little bent over the kitchen table, resting on his crossed arms with his head down, but I saw a distorted face rise, as if out of his chest, from the very depth of his being, and turn its head sideways. The man was sitting perfectly still, as if all this were unknown to him. The distorted face, the face of evil, looked at me and sniggered. This time, as on the other occasions when I have seen evil spirits within people, it seemed to be saying, "I almost fooled you this time. You nearly didn't catch me!"

For some strange reason I don't fully understand, evil spirits cannot resist showing themselves to me. And when this happens I know that Satan has lost again, and that God and the angels have won.

I prayed over the man, blessed him, then gave him the healing prayer, which he put into his wallet. Over the next few months I constantly prayed for him.

About a year later I got a phone call from him. He told me that his life had changed, that it had actually begun to change when he had left my house, but that he had been afraid to acknowledge it. He was trying to make restitution to at least some of the people he had hurt. He said his business was going well but he was now managing it in an honest way. He hoped he hadn't left it too late to thank me and God and the angels. I reminded him to keep asking the angels to help him, and never to forget to thank them for anything, no matter how small. To this day I pray for him.

One day as I was crossing the main road on my way to do the shopping in Maynooth I heard a voice say, "Slow down Lorna." I couldn't see anything other than a light beside me, but I knew it was Michael's voice. "Let's turn up this little lane so we can talk in peace." I turned right into a little lane and walked until I was sure I could not be seen from the road, and then, as I knew would happen, Michael appeared in human form—well, very human except I thought he looked a bit too new and too perfect. When I looked into his eyes I could see the angel in him.

"On your way to Maynooth we want you to walk slowly across the Canal Bridge," he said, "and take a look down along the canal as far as you can see."

"What's wrong?" I asked, "Tell me before I cross the bridge."

"Lorna," Michael said, "you are unaware at this moment of a little baby's soul, the soul of a baby that has been conceived but not yet born. At the moment you cross the bridge your two souls will become connected. You'll also become aware of the mother, but she will be like a ghost to you, very faint."

I felt as though he was talking to me as if I were a child, as if I wouldn't understand.

"Michael, I am a grown woman now with children of my own," I replied. "I don't understand what's going on, but I accept the connection between this little soul and myself. Will you walk over the bridge with me?"

"No, Lorna. You must walk over the bridge on your own. Walk slowly; there will be another angel on the bridge to help you understand, to help you to get to know this little baby soul as it grows in its mother's womb. Do whatever that angel asks. Every time you cross the bridge this angel will be there to meet you and accompany you for a part of the journey. Your connection to this baby's soul will grow stronger as the months pass."

We turned around to walk back up the lane and as we approached the main road Angel Michael disappeared. I looked in the direction of the canal bridge and sure enough I could see an angel waiting for me. He was tall, slender, elegant, and white as snow with a radiant light. I walked slowly, as Michael had told me to, and as I put my foot on the bridge I felt the connection with a little soul.

The angel was standing in the center of the bridge, and when I reached him we stood together. He looked at me with great gentleness and love saying, "My name is Angel Arabia." Angel Arabia touched my hand and I turned to look down along the canal. Everything was like glass; nothing seemed to move, as if it were a picture. I was allowed to feel the mother and the love she had for her unborn child, and I could feel her tears, lots of tears. As I stood there on the bridge someone walked past and said hello. I replied out of habit.

I walked the rest of the way across the bridge then down the hill toward the town. All the time the angel walked beside me. People and cars passed in both directions. I whispered, "See you soon, Angel Arabia." Then I went to do the shopping.

As time passed the baby grew in the mother's womb and I learned more about the little baby soul, the love the baby was sending to its mother and the mother's deep love for her unborn child. Even though I could never see the mother clearly—she always seemed like a ghost—I knew she was there and that she was struggling.

Every day I crossed that bridge at least once, sometimes much more frequently, and often I asked Angel Arabia, who was striding beside me as if in slow motion, "Why is the connection not as strong when I walk down the hill as it is on the bridge?"

Angel Arabia never answered me. One day I said to him, "Sometimes I feel as if the mother and child are in those two fields there, over that wall. At times I have wanted to climb over the wall and search for them, but I know they are not there, nor are they along the canal. Can't you tell me more?"

But Angel Arabia only replied, "When it is needed."

I have learned over the years with the angels that no matter how many times you ask a question they never deviate from the first answer they gave you, and sometimes they will not reply at all. I must have walked with Angel Arabia hundreds of times across the bridge, and I frequently asked for information but never got any answer other than "If and when it is needed."

One morning after the children had gone to school I told Joe I would head into town to get a few bits and pieces and his prescription from the chemist and that I would be as quick as I could. Walking from the cottage I noticed things were different. Angel Arabia was not waiting in his usual place but was standing at the end of my lane, on the main road, some distance from the bridge. I could see there a mist on the righthand side of the bridge, although not on the bridge itself.

I reached Arabia and we walked together. I could feel the silence, the unspoken words. I wanted to speak but knew I was not to. When I reached the bridge I saw that it was not any ordinary mist covering the canal water and the banks of the canal, it was angels! The whole area along the canal bank leading up to the bridge was laid with a milky white mist full of angels; snow white, beautiful angels, bright as a light.

I stood there overwhelmed by the beauty and strangeness of what I was seeing. Angel Arabia's hand touched mine. I heard the angels chanting as if in one voice. They were moving up and down along the canal bank all the time in slow motion within this mist. Some of them turned in my direction and acknowledged my presence; Angel Arabia told me they were getting ready. Tears came to my eyes, and at the same moment Angel Arabia withdrew his hand.

As we walked down the hill away from the bridge, I could hardly feel my feet touching the ground. The mist filled with angels pooled around my ankles. At the bottom of the hill Angel Arabia said, "It will not be long now."

I did the shopping quickly. I couldn't see any angels around me but I knew they were there. I said to them, "I have questions to ask." But I got no answer. I was thinking I shouldn't walk home by the canal, but when I reached the center of town I was pulled to the left, so I knew I was to walk back the way I came.

Angel Arabia was waiting for me, looking more radiant than before. We walked together back up the hill toward the bridge. I looked down along the canal and knew that if I fell into this mist I would not hit the ground but would be cushioned and protected.

In some way this cushioning was also a preparation for the arrival of the baby, but I couldn't fully understand at the time. I later realized that the misty path laid down by the angels was a path for the little baby's spirit. Angel Arabia was waiting for it. Every time I approached the bridge, I could see the mist, and in some way I was made conscious that this little baby's spirit was being ushered down by the angels.

A few days later Joe remarked that I had become very quiet, that it was as if I was somewhere else. I looked at Joe and said, "I don't think you would understand what is happening, even if I told you."

"Try me," he replied.

So I did. I told him a little about the angel at the bridge, about the spirit of a baby and its mother. He listened attentively and told me that he found it all hard to understand, but that he wouldn't ask any more questions. I thanked him and he gave me a big hug.

I don't know where the baby was born, if the mother was on her own or had someone with her, if it was full-term or born prematurely, but one day in March I just knew the baby had been born.

From that day on I lost all sense of time. I constantly felt the touch of Angel Arabia's hand, no matter where I was. The presence of Angel Arabia was so intense that I would not see someone walking toward me and I would bump into them. Angel Arabia still stood in the center of the canal bridge, hovering like a powerful force. Now when I approached the bridge he would descend to meet me, yet he would still be hovering above it at the same time.

One day as I was going down to collect Ruth from school I saw Angel Arabia standing at the end of the lane from the cottage. He indicated for me to cross the road. What I saw was breathtaking! A beautiful baby's spirit was crawling along the soft and smooth path that the angels had made. She looked as if she were crawling, her legs and arms moving, but in fact the angels were carrying her. I could see the angels' wings supporting her. Angels were all around, crawling along the path beside her, helping her, playing with her. The baby's spirit was very happy; I could hear her laughter. My heart was full of joy, and yet there were tears in my eyes. I had suddenly realized that the baby's spirit was coming to my house!

To this day I don't know why I was chosen by God and the angels to see this little miracle or why this little baby spirit was coming to my house. But she was. She was getting closer all the time. I don't know how long it took the angels to travel that distance with the baby's spirit, but one day I was told they were very near. That night I went to bed and woke the next morning as normal at six. I went into the kitchen and a brilliant light was shining in through the window. I got a glass of water and when I turned around Angel Arabia was standing at the kitchen door. I know I shouldn't have been startled, but I was—to this day the angels can take my breath away.

"Go back to bed," Angel Arabia said, "and move closer to Joe to make room for another."

I did as I was told. I could feel the little baby spirit coming into the house. Lying there in bed I could hear the sound of movement in the hall. I prayed and prayed and asked that everything would be okay for the little baby's spirit. The bedroom filled with mist as angels poured into the room. They had arrived. I could not see the baby's spirit but I knew she was down on the floor, surrounded by angels.

"Angels, can I sit up in bed?" I asked.

"No," I was told, "you're not allowed to look yet. Turn on your side and move closer to Joe so there will be more room."

Doing this I disturbed Joe and he asked sleepily if I was cold. I was nervous that Joe might wake at this crucial moment, although a bit of me knew the angels would not let him wake fully.

I felt the sheets being moved by the angels. I felt movement on the bed, and then I felt the baby spirit lying right next to me in the bed. I could still see nothing of the baby spirit, as I was facing Joe and the baby's spirit was now behind me. I was afraid to move in case I would lie on her or hurt her in some way. I felt a baby's hand touch my back.

"Can I turn around now?" I asked.

"Yes," the angels replied. "Turn around slowly and carefully; the little baby spirit is lying beside you."

I turned around, terrified of squashing her. "Oh my God," I exclaimed, forgetting Joe was beside me. I quickly put my hand to my mouth. Joe did not stir. There lying beside me was a gorgeous, naked, newborn baby girl. She was healthy and strong and moving her arms and legs. She was beautiful and perfect, flesh and blood, completely human in appearance, but more beautiful than any baby I have ever seen. She was radiant, the spirit within her lighting up the human body that I was being shown. Two angels stood by the side of the bed looking down on her. They were magnificent white angels, dressed in flowing white robes which draped over them perfectly. They had wonderful faces like porcelain, every feature was clear, and they shone like the sun. Their eyes glittered white as snow and their wings of feathers seemed to spiral and touch a light above them.

"Can I touch her?" I asked.

"No, you can't touch her, but you can put your hands above her," they told me.

I reached out and held my hands above her. As I did so she turned her head and looked at me. Her eyes were full of life and shone brighter than any of the stars in the heavens. She smiled, and at that moment I heard her say, "Tell Mummy I love her, and Dad, too."

Then the two angels bent over her and picked her up, their wings entwined around her. As they rose the heavens opened with gentleness and in a flash of light they were gone and the room was back to normal.

I knew it was over. I praised and thanked God.

Later that morning I went to Jim the butcher's and everyone was talking. I was asked had I heard the news? A newborn baby's body had been found along the canal bank near the bridge. No one knew who the mother was, or what had happened, but a man walking his dog had found the body early that morning. I realized then that the baby had been found at the moment the angels had disappeared from my bedroom. I was so happy. I cannot explain the happiness I felt, but it was a great joy and relief to know that the baby's spirit had gone to Heaven and my task was complete.

The local community was very upset; they were not aware of anything like this ever happening before. They were shocked to think that there might have been a young woman, perhaps a student from the college, who had felt it necessary to keep her pregnancy secret.

The police investigated, but as far as I know they never found the mother. Perhaps she will read this someday and realize that whatever the circumstances of her baby's death were, her little baby loved her and was never left alone—there were always angels with her, as there are with all babies, both those who live and those who die, whatever the situation.

The community was so moved by this baby's death that they took up a collection and bought a grave so the child could be buried properly. Before she was buried, the little baby was given a name. Bridget is buried now in the graveyard in Maynooth.

Joe was getting sicker and sicker and he started having a series of minor strokes. They were terrifying for him, and sometimes he would go blind for a few minutes, or his body would go completely limp. Walking became very difficult, and he frequently fell over. Despite my best efforts to watch him and catch him, he was black and blue all over. The doctors said they could do nothing.

The angels tried to cheer me up. One day I was walking around the housing estates nearby, enjoying the warm sun and watching everything around me, when I came to a green area. Children were out playing football and people were stretched out on the grass enjoying the good weather. I noticed a child in a wheelchair. She was curled up asleep. Her body seemed quite twisted and she was pitifully thin. It was hard to tell her age, but she was probably about seven. Her mother sat on the wall a short distance off, talking to neighbors.

As I got closer I could see the child was getting brighter, as was her wheelchair. Everything became still and silent; I couldn't believe what I was seeing. Her soul moved out of her body, leaving her sleeping form there in the wheelchair. It radiated light and looked just as that little girl will look when she goes to Heaven: perfect in every way.

Two angels appeared in front of her and took her hands—they were both girls who looked much the same age as she was. Then three more angels appeared, again all little girls, dressed completely in a white so radiant that a blue tint seemed to come from it. I was unable to move, overcome by what I was seeing. This little girl's soul had stepped out of her body to play with the angels. They played chase, but they never moved too far from the wheelchair. They held hands and played ring-around-the-rosy. I could hear their laughter; the little girl's soul was so free and happy. I tried to move forward, to put one foot in front of the other, but the angels would not let me move, no matter how hard I tried.

The little angels sat in a circle on the green grass near the wheelchair with the little girl's soul. I watched with fascination; I did not know what was going to happen next. All of a sudden an angel's hands touched a blade of grass and a daisy appeared. Then the other angels started moving their hands around, touching blades of grass with the tips of their fingers, and each blade they touched turned into a beautiful daisy. There in the middle of the grass was a circle of white, awash with daisies, and in the middle of it were laughing angels and a radiant little soul. The mother continued chatting nearby, oblivious to what was going on.

"Daisy chains," the little soul cried out, as they started to make daisy chains. They decorated her with them—around her neck, on her head like a princess's crown, around her arms and even around her ankles. They showed her how to make daisy chains with little slits in the stem, and she sat there making them on her own. There was such love and gentleness that I could feel tears running down my cheek from the joy and happiness of what I was seeing. I watched the little girl, admiring her daisy chains. Her face shone like the sun.

Then the angels put their arms around her, picked her up, and carried her to her wheelchair. She did not seem to mind. The soul lay down gently and snuggled back into her human body, which had remained sleeping all this time.

As suddenly as they came the angels left and the light was gone. The little girl moved in her wheelchair. I nearly fell over myself as I was released and able to move again. Everything around me came back to life. I heard the birds, felt the breeze, and saw the people. As I walked away from the little girl I looked over at her mother and thought to myself, how blessed she was to have such a pure soul in her family.

CHAPTER 27

Joe

Toward the end of his life Joe found it hard to remember where or who he was. He didn't always recognize me or the children. Fortunately the children never seemed to notice this. I used to sit and talk to him a lot, reminiscing, trying to help him to remember. I desperately wanted him to be with us fully for as long as was possible.

Almost every morning I would go down to the town—there was always something that was needed—and when I got home the first thing I did was peep in at Joe in bed to make sure he was all right. Then I would make tea for us both and sit on the little stool by the bed to chat.

One particular morning we were sitting like this, chatting, and Joe said, "You know, Lorna, I have been lying here in this bed since you left this morning, trying to remember things of the past; about our lives and the children. It scares me sometimes that I don't even recognize where I am."

As always there were a lot of angels around us. Suddenly all the angels that were sitting on the bed disappeared, except Joe's guardian angel, who remained. It was as if his guardian angel was supporting him, as if there was no bed there at all, even though Joe was lying down in it. Joe was a little confused.

"Hold my hand," I said, "and I will help you to remember."

Joe's guardian angel supported him from behind and lifted a hand above him, pouring the light of memory into him. This light, a white substance like whipped cream with silver sparks, appeared to come from his guardian angel's hand and entered the top of Joe's head. It continued to flow, never stopping until we had finished talking.

We reminisced and I was thrilled at the things Joe remembered as we sat there. He talked about our son Owen's First Communion Day, and how he had used his communion money to buy a new pair of football boots. Up until then Owen, who loved football, had always had hand-me-down boots; this was the first time he had had a new pair. Joe laughed about how Owen had tried on one pair after another, looking at the price and eventually making his decision. He was so proud of those boots.

Joe's eyes filled with tears of happiness at the memory.

Joe had always been nervous about my relationship with the angels; even though I had shared a lot with him, he was still afraid they would take me away. He felt more vulnerable because he was ill. Sometimes he would get anxious knowing that someone was coming to see me—especially when he was feeling particularly sick or weak. Sometimes he'd say things like "They are taking you away from me. I need you more than they do." My heart used to go out to him, but I knew I had to do what I had to do.

I remember one particular man and his wife who came to see me because she was dying and they were desperate. The man so needed his wife to live, but his wife was reconciled to the fact that she wouldn't, and instead she felt a need to grow spiritually. They used to come quite often, sometimes unexpectedly. Joe found this very hard and he would say to me, "I'm dying, too." Although he said it, I'm not entirely sure he believed it; Joe didn't really accept that he would die shortly.

As time went on conventional medicine could do no more for this woman than control her pain, and she, like many others, turned to alternative spiritual routes. With the support of her doctors she traveled to Brazil. I knew it would be her last journey, and that although it would take a lot out of her physically it was very important for her spirit. Sometimes people who know they are dying want to learn more about their soul's journey because it helps them to understand death better.

Her time in Brazil was brief, and when she came back, very weak from the physical effort, the first person she visited was me. She came to tell me about all that had happened over there and to get further help for her spiritual journey. Her husband sat beside me in the kitchen as she talked, telling me everything. At one stage she told him to shut up and not to interrupt. She was desperate to tell me everything herself, to be healed so that she could die in peace. When she left I hugged her, knowing I wouldn't see her again. As she went down the steps I saw a beam of light—her soul turned to look at me and I saw a perfect soul. She went home and went to bed, and never got out of it again.

The angels were telling me that time was really short for Joe, so I was constantly fighting with them for telling me things I really didn't want to hear. One day I was coming out of a shop carrying groceries when an angel appeared in front of me, surrounded by birds. "Go away!" I said.

The angel disappeared, but the birds did not. There were all kinds of birds—sparrows, robins, blackbirds, and bigger birds such as jackdaws and crows. They flew around me, their wings almost touching me. I reached out to push them away with my hands and eventually they flew away. Now I call that particular angel the "Bird Angel."

The Bird Angel was beautiful: extremely tall and elegant and dressed in white with long sleeves that were cut at angles with a golden sash around the waist. He wore a V-shaped necklace with a large green sapphire, about two inches thick, dangling from the point. His face was gold and his eyes white. He appeared only a handful of times, but each time before I saw him a lot of birds of all sizes would surround me and come up close to me.

When he could Joe loved to come and sit by the fire for a little while and he would sometimes struggle, with my help, to walk as far as the front gate. One evening as soon as we got outside the house birds came from everywhere and flew around his feet, picking at the stones, and some landed on the gate and started to clean their feathers.

"Where are all the birds coming from?" Joe asked. "I've never seen so many together."

I pointed. "They are here because the Bird Angel is standing a little distance from us," I told him.

Joe couldn't see him, of course, but his eyes lit up. He gave me a big smile and said, "I like the Bird Angel." Then we turned around and walked back into the house.

We talked about whether Joe should go into the hospital or stay at home. He said it would be easier on me and the children if he was in the hospital and died there, that he didn't want to be a burden. I would say to him, "No, Joe, you are not a burden. I love you and so do your children. We don't want you to die in the hospital. We want you to stay here at home with us."

A few days before Joe died the doctor called in around lunchtime and told Joe that maybe it was time he went into the hospital. I asked the doctor, "If Joe goes into the hospital now, what chance will he have of coming back home?"

"It's more than likely he'll never come back home," the doctor replied.

Joe and I looked at each other and we both said, "No." Joe told the doctor we had talked about his dying at home, and I added, "We have made our decision."

As I looked at the doctor standing at the end of the bed I could see his compassion and understanding. "Call me anytime day or night. The time doesn't matter," he said.

The next day Joe told me he would love a pork steak for dinner, so off I went down to Jim the butcher's and asked for a pork steak. He knew Joe was sick and said, "Sorry, I haven't any." He went out back and when he returned he said he would have pork steak the next day.

That evening Joe said he would like a little walk, so I helped him out as far as the gate. It was a bright night with lots of stars in the sky, but very cool. As we stood by the gate the Bird Angel appeared again, standing to the left of the lamppost on the lawn opposite the house. Joe rested, leaning on the gate for support.

"It's a beautiful evening," he said.

I turned to look at the lamppost again and the Bird Angel was gone. A flash of light in the night sky to my right caught my attention. "Joe, look!" I said.

Joe turned around to look in the direction of the house. A beautiful white bird flew out of the darkness toward us, growing brighter and becoming clearer as it got closer. The bird was flying low, growing bigger by the second. It was bright white and enormous and we could see all its feathers. It was magnificent.

"It's a white owl!" Joe exclaimed.

We thought it was going to hit us and ducked as the owl flew over our heads and straight into the light surrounding the streetlight. The light had grown extremely bright—when I think about it I realize it was unusually so. We could see the owl clearly as it flew through the light. Then it disappeared.

"That was a magnificent sight to see!" Joe said in astonishment. "That owl was so big and so white. Where did it go? It disappeared as it flew into the light. It was as if there was an explosion of light and then it vanished."

I smiled at Joe and told him that earlier when we were coming out I had seen the Bird Angel standing at the lamp and that it had turned itself into the white owl so that Joe could see it.

We had been out there longer than normal and Joe's legs were trembling. I helped him to the house and back to bed. I brought him a cup of tea and he told me to sit down beside him; he had something to tell me.

He opened the bedside dresser, took out an envelope, and handed it to me saying, "This is for your birthday. Tomorrow is a special day for you and Ruth. It's both of your birthdays."

I looked at the envelope in confusion.

"Open it!" he said.

I couldn't believe my eyes. Inside the envelope there was a hundred pounds!

"Joe, where did you get this from?"

Joe told me that he had been saving for a long time.

"I never told you, Lorna, but sometimes when visitors came they insisted on leaving me some money for cigarettes. I have been saving it up. I want you both to go into Dublin, have a meal out, and buy that ring I promised you so long ago."

Of course Joe meant the ring to replace my engagement ring, which had been stolen from the pawnbrokers. He had promised he would buy me another one and now he was doing so, but in what circumstances! For about six weeks Joe had been saying that he would try to stay alive for our birthdays; now I knew one of the reasons why.

I gave Joe a big hug and a kiss and I went up to Ruth's bedroom and told her that we would be going into Dublin in the morning for a treat to celebrate her sixteenth birthday, and that I was to buy a ring. Ruth ran into her dad's bedroom and gave him a big hug and a kiss, too.

Next morning Ruth and I caught the bus into Dublin. We walked the legs off ourselves but eventually found the sort of ring I was looking for at a little jeweler on O'Connell Street, and then we went for lunch. Sitting at the table, Ruth and I talked; she was planning to leave that evening to go away for the weekend with her friend's parents and family.

"Mum, do you think it's okay for me to go away for the weekend? I am really looking forward to it, but I'm worried about Dad."

"Go away and have a wonderful weekend," I said. "We won't say anything to your Dad about your going away, because it'll only worry and confuse him."

We had a great time that day, but I was very anxious about Joe and kept stopping to phone home and make sure he was okay. Fortunately the phone was beside his bed.

While we were out something wonderful happened that I was told of later. Megan, who was four, went in to talk to her dad, as she did frequently. She used to sit beside him on the bed and he would read to her, or she would draw pictures as she sat on the floor beside him. That day she told him, "Come and play with me"—the same words she had used when she had appeared to him before she was born. She was very insistent that he come and push her on the swing. From somewhere, it can only have been God and the angels, Joe was given the energy to get up and get dressed (something he hadn't done for weeks) and go out and push her on the swing. Christopher was there, keeping an eye on both of them, and he couldn't believe what he was seeing. Megan and Joe laughed and played on the swing for ten minutes and then Joe went back to bed.

When we got back to Maynooth I called into Jim the butcher's for the pork steak. When I offered to pay he said, "It's on the house! Tell Joe I was asking for him." I thanked him, and Ruth and I hurried home.

That evening the house was crowded with angels. The fire was lit in the front room and I moved from one room to another as I cooked the pork steak, potatoes, vegetables, and gravy. We sat around the coffee table by the fire having our dinner and celebrating our birthdays. Joe hardly ate anything. He said he had been looking forward to the taste of the pork steak, but all he could manage was a tiny bit. He noticed Ruth getting ready to go out and kept on asking Ruth where she was going. She told him she was going to visit a friend, but he was very confused.

While Ruth was in the kitchen getting ready to leave she said, "Mum, do you think Dad will be okay?"

"Your dad would want you to enjoy yourself on your birthday. Off you go and if anything happens I will call you straightaway," I replied.

Ruth ran back in to her dad, gave him a kiss, and said good-bye. Her brother Christopher came home, helped himself to dinner, and joined us in the front room by the fire. He sat and talked with his dad as he had dinner and then gave Joe a big hug and said he would be back later.

When I was alone in the room with Joe he said, "You know it has been very hard for me to stay alive for your birthday."

"I know," I said. "Thank you, it's the best birthday present I could have. And I love the ring. What more could I ask for?"

I gave him a hug. I could see all the angels around him and his guardian angel holding on to him. I smiled to myself. I had noticed how the angels were getting the children to say good-bye to their dad in such a gentle way. Christopher passed Owen in the hall as he went out, and Owen came and sat by the fire to talk to his dad. He too was going out. Megan went to bed, and Joe and I were left alone for the evening.

We sat by the fire talking a little and then Joe fell asleep. I watched the television, sitting beside him. Around midnight Joe opened his eyes. He was confused and didn't know where he was. I comforted him and told him it was okay, that he was at home. He looked at me and smiled. "You should go to bed now, Lorna," he said.

"I'll wait for you," I replied.

"No, you go ahead," Joe said. "I want to sit here for a little while on my own."

I kissed Joe, said good-night, and went to bed. Shortly afterward he came into the room. I don't know how he managed to walk; I believe his guardian angel carried him. As he got into bed beside me, Joe said, "Lorna, do you think I will be all right? Will I make it through the night?"

As I said, "Joe, don't worry. I will be looking after you. You will be okay," his guardian angel shook his head at me.

At some stage I must have fallen asleep cuddled up to Joe. I woke suddenly. Joe was having a bad turn. The room was full of light. It was crowded with angels and spirits; among them I saw the spirit of my da standing by the side of the bed. I looked into Joe's eyes and saw that the light was almost out. He didn't recognize me. There was no glow around him.

My da said, "Lorna, let him go. You know you cannot ask again."

I was holding Joe in my arms, my eyes full of tears. I knew I could not ask God to allow Joe to stay; I knew the answer would be no. I laid Joe back down on the bed. Christopher was staying out with friends, but I called out to Owen and he came running.

"Your dad is dying," I said. "His time is almost gone."

Immediately Owen jumped up onto the bed.

"Mum," he said looking at me, "I know Dad said we were to let him go, but I have to try. He's my dad and I love him."

I let him try. He sat on the bed calling his name and rubbing his face, trying to make him conscious. I didn't have the heart to tell him it wouldn't work this time. God had said no, and all the angels and souls were here to take Joe to Heaven.

I raced to the kitchen to phone for an ambulance. I did every-thing I usually did when Joe took a turn. I called a taxi driver we knew and asked him to call and collect Christopher on his way over.

Then Owen called out, "Mum! Dad's stopped breathing." I rushed into the bedroom and at the door I met Joe's soul, accompanied by his guardian angel. Joe looked so beautiful; he was radiant. He smiled at me, then he looked back into the room at Owen before disappearing.

The ambulance came and they took Joe's body away. Christopher and I followed the ambulance to the hospital in the taxi.

I don't remember much of the funeral. Joe's death was a big shock, even though I had known for so long that he was living on borrowed time. God had granted the miracle of life for Joe, and I knew God would not grant that miracle a second time. He had told me never to ask, because He would have to say no. It was extremely hard for me not to ask God, not to beg. I didn't want to let Joe go, but I knew I had to. I know he looks after me and the children every day, and I thank him for his love, kindness, and gentleness.

I wore that birthday ring for about two weeks after Joe's death. Then I took it off and never wore it again.

CHAPTER 28

A feather from Heaven

Shortly after Joe was buried I resumed seeing people and helping them with their problems. I always kept my private life separate from the work that God and the angels asked me to do. For the most part, people who came to see me were not aware of my loss. However, a few did find out and they were very kind. I received cards of sympathy from people who had come to see me—despite the many problems they had of their own.

It was a very difficult time for me, but long walks in the grounds of Maynooth College helped. I would walk around, visit the church, and walk along the long corridors of the college, looking at the pictures of young men who had become priests. I talked to Joe often and I asked him how he was faring. I told him how the children were doing and laughed with him, saying, "I know you know how they are doing anyway!" I could feel him walking beside me. One particular day, some months after Joe's death, I was finding it really hard to cope. I had seen several people that day and some of them had really tough problems—seriously ill children and very difficult situations. I was exhausted and distressed after they left, so I went out of the house and walked toward the college grounds. I would always wait until I went through the gates to talk to God about the things that people had come to me about, their hurt and pain and also their joy. I'd pray for all the problems of the world. I would ask God, "Can't you work a miracle?"

This day I was finding it hard to cope, and I shared a little with my guardian angel and with God. I told them I was feeling really down in myself.

Even now I can remember that day, walking through the college grounds, feeling the cold breeze, the rain hitting me in the face. I had no gloves and my hands were cold, I kept my hands in my pockets, and I could feel the little prayer book I had in one of them. I had to avoid the potholes on the circuit of paths at the back of the college, because they were full of rainwater and leaves that had fallen off the trees. A priest who I often saw walked by, saying his prayers. I smiled at him and kept going. On another of the paths I saw a mother out running with a stroller. She would run and then stop and then walk very fast and then run again.

I came around the bend of one of the pathways. There were big trees on my right and an open green and a graveyard with a big cross to the left. As I passed the graveyard I was talking to God about how I was feeling. I told him, "I don't think I can go on. I really need some help from you, my God, and from your angels. If you don't help me, I don't know how I'm going to keep going."

I took another right turn and directly in front of me, facing me, was the big old college building. I could see it clearly. Then the strangest thing happened. As I looked toward the college, directly above this beautiful old building, in the distance and far up, the sky filled with angels. They were very far away. At first I wasn't sure they were angels. I kept looking and saying to myself, "What else could they be?" When they got closer and closer, flying over the college, I was left in no doubt. They got bigger and bigger until they were enormous. They descended and got even closer. They were so beautiful—all gold and white. Their wings were magnificent, powerful, and beautiful; they took my breath away. I laughed and cried, my body was trembling.

"You have really given me something special!" I said. "You are lifting my soul and my heart. I realize now that no matter how bad things are there is a reason for this life—a reason to live, a reason for joy and happiness, and even our tears have meaning!"

All this time I kept walking, or I believed I was walking. My legs were moving, my feet were moving, and yet as I realized later the earth beneath me was not moving. Some of the angels turned to fly away from the college. They seemed to be going away from me, flying farther and farther away, growing smaller and then disappearing. I felt a bit sad.

Then I was told to look up, and there in the sky, way up, so far up it was unbelievable, I saw loads more angels. As these beautiful angels got closer I could see more angels above them. All of a sudden in between those angels, higher up again, I saw what I believed to be another angel. It was so high up it looked minuscule—it was a miracle that I was allowed to see something so tiny. I wondered how on earth I could see this little angel, which was so far away, and now it was falling down, down, down.

As it fell through all the other angels it didn't seem to get any bigger. I kept laughing, I was so full of excitement—I can still feel it now! I was trembling with delight. As it came closer I could see that it wasn't an angel; it was a tiny feather!

I watched in amazement as this tiny feather was guided downward by those enormous beautiful angels. It was spectacular to watch this feather descend like a snowflake. There was a strong breeze blowing that morning, but the feather kept falling, guided through the air to come directly to me. I was afraid that the breeze would blow it away, but I shouldn't have had any fear; I should have known better. The feather, with beautiful angels on each side, kept on floating down.

When it was nearly within my reach, but not quite close enough for me to grasp it, you know what I did? I jumped to catch it! I couldn't wait any longer for it to come closer. I jumped as high as I could. It felt as if I jumped five feet into the air, and reaching out I grasped the feather. I caught it and clutched it safely in my hand. I was exhilarated, clasping it close to my chest.

All of a sudden things changed. I became aware of raindrops on my cheeks, of the cold breeze. It was only then that I noticed an elderly couple walking toward me, and I realized, too, that time had stood still for me. Although I had thought I had been walking I hadn't actually moved from where I was when I first saw the angels. Now, recalling it, I see that from the moment I saw the angels over the college building I hadn't felt the broken stones under my feet or the unevenness of the path. This was because my feet were not actually touching the ground. I didn't feel the rain, the wind, or the cold. Then when I grasped the feather time started to move again. I remember the elderly couple smiling at me—they must have seen me jumping for something. I smiled back. Now, today, as I write this I wonder what those people thought that day. What did they see? Did they see what I jumped for?

I felt so happy and so exalted. It was one of the most wonderful mornings of my life, getting a gift like that from God and his angels. I praised God and gave him thanks for the feather. I thanked Joe, too, as I felt he also had something to do with it.

I cherish the feather that came to me through the gates of Heaven, guided by angels. It was a gift to help me feel better, to make me feel safe, to remind me that there is a reason to live, that there is hope in all circumstances. It also reminded me that we all have souls and they are perfect—no matter what we have done—that our bodies might die, but our souls don't, and that we all have wings of some kind or another, even if we fail to recognize them in ourselves or others. We are all, in fact, angels.

ABOUT THE AUTHOR

Lorna Byrne has been seeing and talking to angels since she was a baby. Now that her family is raised she talks openly for the first time about what she has seen and learned. She lives quietly in rural Ireland.

For more information visit www.lornabyrne.com.